PRIVATIZING PEACE

FROM CONFLICT TO SECURITY

ALLAN GERSON AND NAT J. COLLETTA

PREFACE BY RICHARD HOLBROOKE

 Transnational Publishers

Published and distributed by Transnational Publishers, Inc.
410 Saw Mill River Road
Ardsley, NY 10502, USA

Phone: 914-693-5100
Fax: 914-693-4430
E-mail: info@transnationalpubs.com
Web: www.transnationalpubs.com

Libary of Congress Catalog Card No. 2001053066

ISBN 1–57105–147–3 Hardcover
ISBN 1–57105–258–5 Paperback

Manufactured in the United States of America

Cover Image by Bruno Freschi O.C.
The Peace Bridge, a proposal for a single pylon curved cable suspension bridge over the Niagara River. The concept celebrates the "bridging" between two states or places, and the symbolic linking or bringing together in peace.

Table of Contents

ACKNOWLEDGMENTS

This book is the product of the experience and lessons drawn from many different individuals from diverse institutional backgrounds but connected by a common concern: peacebuilding and development. Its stimulus can be traced to an idea that Council on Foreign Relations President, Les Gelb, explored with Allan Gerson in the spring of 1998 as to whether, in light of the end of the Cold War, ways could be found for enabling the United Nations to play a more constructive role, especially in curbing the scourge of internal conflicts that had proliferated in the last decade. At about the same time, World Bank President James Wolfensohn, increasingly concerned about the Bank's growing portfolio of poor countries at war, called on Nat Colletta and others at the Bank to forge a more multi-disciplinary, multi-agency approach to the problem. At the United Nations, Secretary-General Kofi Annan had reached the same conclusion: that international organizations acting alone could not be expected to meet the challenge of the post-Cold War era to create conditions conducive to sustainable peace and development. "Partnering" became the operative word. The first order of business in this new vision was to strengthen partnering arrangements between the World Bank and the UN system. Toward this end, the Council of Foreign Relations established a Study Group on UN-World Bank Partnering with initial funding from the World Bank.

Soon after the Study Group convened, it became apparent that a wider net would have to be cast to include non-governmental and private sector representatives, insofar as these sectors would be critical to the success of any partnering efforts. A year and a half later, the conclusions reached by the Study Group were submitted to the World Bank and other interested parties. Key to the group's recommendations was the need for promotion of a more integrative approach centered around a new institutional structure for peacebuilding, a Peace Transitions Council. This thinking generated further dialogue among the authors and their colleagues, leading to the idea of a much broader study which would detail the elements of a radically new approach to peacebuilding. *Privatizing Peace* is the result. It is thus only fitting that our special thanks first go to the Council on Foreign Relations and the World Bank for their vision and support in launching this work.

Many individuals participated in various aspects these discussions. We are particularly grateful to Stephen J. Friedman and Louis Perlmutter (the Study Group co-chairs), Michael Reisman, Ted Sorensen, Senator Robert Kasten, John O'Reilly, William H. Luers, Herbert S. Okun, Mark Ellis, Catherine Gwin, Carol C. Adelman, Jane Cicala, Herbert J. Hansell, John J. Salinger, Charles A. Heimbold, Jr., Senator Richard Store, J. William Ichord, Andrew B. Kim, Ken Miller, John M. Scheib, Henry B. Schact, Carlos dos Santos, Zahi Khouri, Alan Batkin, David Birenbaum, Daniel Lubetzky, Martin Griffiths, Frank O'Donnell, Kofi Asomani, Mona Hamman, Reinhart Helmke, Nils Katsberg, Angela King, Bacre Ndiaye, Tapio Kanninen, Robert Piper, Teresa Whitfield, Nicholas Kraft, Andrew Mack, Ian Newport, Chukwuma Obidegwu, Barbara Balaj, Robert Chase, Robert Devecchi, Shepard Foreman, Arthur Helton, Paul Isenman, Lawrence Korb, Princeton Lyman, James Moody, Gustav Ranis, Barnett Rubin, Charles Rudnick, Mark Schnellbaecher, and Bruce Shearer. In addition, we want to thank our UK colleagues Kevin Clements, President, International Alert, and Jane Nelson, Executive Director, the Prince of Wales Business Forum, for sharing their institutional experience on the role of the business sector in conflict prevention and post-conflict reconstruction; and Ted Halstead, President, and Steve Clemons, Senior Vice President of the New America Foundation, for providing a home for completion of the last leg of the manuscript.

In addition to the assistance of the World Bank, generous funding was provided during the early phase of the project by the government of Morocco, whose Foreign Minister, Mohamed Benaissa, realized early on its implications for developing nations caught in conflict; the Smith-Richardson Foundation and the Ben and Esther Rosenbloom Foundation.

A multi-faceted work like this requires a great deal of data gathering and case material. We were fortunate to have the help of several excellent research assistants: Suzanne Spears and Irene Sang at the Council on Foreign Relations, Stephen Lu at the New America Foundation, Margharita Capellino at the World Bank's Post-Conflict Unit, and Pavlina Kostikova and Jillian Frumkin at American University's Program on International Peace and Conflict Resolution.

In the end, what emerged was the product of the thinking of many individuals as filtered and augmented by the authors, who necessarily take full responsibility for the ideas, analysis and conclusions herein presented. It is their fervent hope that this work provokes fresh thinking and new partnerships to ensure that peace and prosperity, not war, be the hallmarks of the new millennium.

PREFACE

Out of the misery that confronts the poverty-stricken world none is more devastating than the proclivity to be doubly victimized: first by lack of capital, and second by the scourge of war. Two-thirds of the world's poorest nations contain two-thirds of the world's ongoing armed conflicts. Today there is little room for arguing with a proposition long denied or overlooked: that war and poverty are inextricably linked. The statistics tell their own story.

If so, the antidote must lie, at least partially, in economic hope and opportunity. This is the message of this book by Allan Gerson, a leading international law scholar, and Nat Colletta, an internationally-recognized authority on peacebuilding and development. The authors affirm that to be poor does not mean to be without resources; it only means that limited resources are far from evenly distributed. Indeed, gross inequalities in distribution accompanied by poor governance, and not ideology or nationalism, are, they find, the primary sources of conflict in today's war-torn areas.

In this context, their work is the story of how economic opportunity and a sense of well-being can be created in less than stable conditions. They demonstrate that even in the despair and aftershock of war it is possible to balance the budget, to prevent fighting from re-erupting, and to inspire hope for a better future. Even as the post-Cold War era claims new victims as the price of multiplying internal wars, they suggest ways of attaching the future of countries struggling to consolidate fragile peace arrangements to the two great movements of the end of the twentieth century, globalization and privatization.

In the first place, war-torn countries must quickly acquire universally applicable skills in low-end technology, especially in information processing and telecommunications. The international community and the business community can help because, as Gerson and Colletta point out, it is in their self-interest to do so. Safeguarding existing investments and taking advantage of emerging markets require the establishment of a secure environment based on the rule of law. While governments may create jobs through public works projects or an expanded bureaucracy, over the long term only the development of a prospering private sector can ensure sustained livelihoods. And sustained employment, in an environment of security and the rule of law, is indispensable to consolidating peace and furthering development.

Operating on the proposition that whatever governments do not do best belongs elsewhere, in the non-governmental sector, they argue for radical reforms. What governments do best, they argue, is provide for the common defense from external and internal predators: the former through armed forces, the latter through maintenance of criminal justice systems. However, even in these realms, long considered the exclusive preserve of governments, the authors find room for the benefits of public-private partnerships through privatization.

Thus, if the answer (at least partially) to today's problems of war and poverty lie in enhanced economic opportunity alongside transparent governance, then two other caveats follow: (1) the approach must be based on a new integrative model establishing a new-found cooperation between the private sector, non-governmental organizations, international institutions, and governments; and (2) privatization of all but those services which are inherently governmental in nature (like defense and the criminal justice system) must follow. These are deliberately provocative ideas, as privatization would encompass a whole range of functions previously considered the exclusive preserve of governments and international institutions, ranging from humanitarian relief to construction of democratic institutions.

Both Gerson and Colletta have labored in the real world, giving their vision a practical grounding. Gerson has spent most of his career as an advocate on behalf of both government and human rights. Colletta has spent a good deal of his nearly 25-year career at the World Bank as a trained anthropologist and sociologist in a field dominated by economists. Together they bring a commitment to an integrated cross-disciplinary approach based on measurable results. *Privatizing Peace* represents the culmination of their efforts, and provides a challenging intellectual road map for addressing some of the world's most pressing problems.

Richard Holbrooke
New York, N.Y.
September 2001

INTRODUCTION

There may be another way out of the current scourge of recurrent armed civil conflict with its attendant toll of millions of wasted human lives and vast stretches of squandered economic opportunity. We have seen no evidence of it. The path herein proposed (which is, of course, only a partial solution) is an integrated unified field approach, centered around the privatization of many peace-related functions. The alternative—the retention of old methodologies—is fragmentation. It would continue what has been described as a pattern of international organizations acting as "stove pipes" (reaching upward or downward but without hands across to touch other actors), and NGOs as "food chains" (competing with one another for scarce resources and unable to integrate their efforts).

A unified field approach offers a new vision, one centered on partnering as a three-dimensional quest. It focuses immediately and directly on the intended beneficiaries, the people on the ground most in need of help. And it also looks to a new relationship among the "benefactors": NGOs, governments and multilateral institutions which have often been at loggerheads with each other, suspicious of one another's motives and unable to bridge the divide of insular institutional cultures. Here it seeks partnering and involvement of the private sector in keeping with the spirit of our times, the *zeitgeist* of globalization.

Globalization can be a force for peace, not merely for enhanced commerce. Success hinges on whether a new architecture can be developed for not allowing the new energy it unleashes to be harnessed rather than allowed to dissipate. Privatization of many peace-related functions carried out in union with civil society and the public sector, both national and supranational, can be its fundamental building block. With commitment to such an undertaking, the gnawing sense of futility that underlies so much of today's armed conflicts can give way to the promise of a better tomorrow.

The idea that governments and multilateral institutions are alone capable of peacemaking and peacebuilding is already recognized as an anachronism. In the age of globalization the open dissemination of knowledge, information and culture goes hand in hand with openness of markets and the enterprise of producers, rewarding whomever can deliver goods or services most efficiently.

Surely, peace is the supreme good which precedes all others. Economic growth and opportunity cannot be divorced from peacebuilding any more than it can be denied that the private sector is the engine of growth in our time. But there must be incentives of an economic and non-economic kind to induce adequate and responsible private sector engagement. There must also be adequate regulation—some self-imposed, some by treaties and conventions—to curb excesses and provide for transparency and accountability.

A proposed new institutional structure, a Peace Transitions Council (PTC), would allow for the evolution of a three-dimensional partnership—encompassing the United Nations and the World Bank, governments and civil society, and the private sector—cooperating on a global scale with regional nodes. It needs not be any more of a fantasy than the idea that the vacuum tube technology of the 1950s would one day be replaced by the integrated circuit boards of today.

Chapter 1

THE CHANGING FACE OF
ARMED CONFLICT

The twentieth century idea of curbing the scourge of war through supranational institutions—an initiative which led to the creation of the United Nations, and, to a lesser but no less important degree, the Bretton Woods Institutions (the World Bank and International Monetary Fund)—had run out of steam by the year 2000. The thinking which had preoccupied the statesmen and humanitarians who were the progenitors of this idea focused on interstate war, on aggression across recognized state frontiers. But as fighting between states ebbed toward the end of the century, intrastate war—conflict within sovereign or less-than-sovereign borders—picked up with a vengeance. The end of the Cold War precipitated this transformation. In the Cold War's wake, 101 civil wars erupted between 1989 and 1998. And according to the authoritative research of Peter Wallensteen and Margareta Sollenberg at the Department of Peace and Conflict Research of Sweden's Uppsala University, there were by contrast, only seven interstate wars during that period.[1] Although, as demonstrated by the University of Maryland's Center for International Development and Conflict Management, a downward trend occurred in the incidence of civil conflicts, from a high of 55 in 1992 to a low of 34 in 1997, by 1998 that trend reversed itself: there were 36 active civil-type conflicts in 1998, and no significant abatement since.[2]

---

[1]   Peter Wallensteen and Margareta Sollenberg, "The End of International War? Armed Conflict 1989–1995" in *The Journal of Peace Research*, Vol. 33, No. 3, 1996, pp. 353–370. Also see Margareta Sollenberg (Editor), *States in Armed Conflict 1998*, Department of Peace and Conflict Research, Uppsala University: Sweden, Report No. 54, pp. 1–28.

[2]   See Ted Robert Gurr's recent work with Monty Marshall and Deepa Khosla,

Many of these internal wars reflect deeply rooted ethnic and identity-related conflicts independent of Cold War factors. But their true nature has often been masked by the ideological overlay of the Cold War, where war by proxies became the rule. Other internal conflicts have had, and continue to have, less to do with ethnicity and identity than with greed and power. Here, conflict has often swirled over control of new systems of patronage centered around abundant natural resources and their potential for huge profits.[3] Lauri Nathan, of the Center for Conflict Resolution of the University of Cape Town, South Africa, has identified four basic structural conditions which spawn almost all of the ongoing civil conflicts in Africa: authoritarian rule; the exclusion of minorities from governance; socio-economic deprivation combined with inequity; and weak states that lack the institutional capacity to manage normal conflict associated with social and economic transformation.[4] Ruha Auvinen and Wayne Nafziger at the World Institute for Development Economics Research (WIDER) reached a similar conclusion in their study on the causes of complex humanitarian emergencies. On the basis of a comparative study covering 124 countries between 1980 to 1995, they found that that civil conflict is virtually always related to five factors: stagnation and decline in real GDP, a high ratio of military expenditure to national income, a tradition of violent conflict, high income inequality, and slow growth in average food production. More often than not, they concluded, "relative deprivation explains political conflict."[5]

Peace and Conflict 2001: A Global Survey of Armed Conflicts, Self-Determination Movements, and Democracy, Center for International Development and Conflict Management, University of Maryland, January 2001. Also see Gurr's earlier work, *Peoples Versus States: Minorities at Risk in the New Century*, United States Institute of Peace Press: Washington, D.C. Gurr surveys the behavior of some 275 politically active ethnic groups during the 1990s and pinpoints factors that encourage the assertion of ethnic identities. He identifies some ninety groups as being at significant risk of conflict and repression in the early 21st century.

[3]   See Paul Collier's work *On the Economic Causes of Civil War*, Oxford Economic Papers 50 (4), 1998; and Nat J. Colletta and Markus Kostner, "Reforming Development Cooperation: From Reconstruction to Prevention," in *Forum: Special Issue on War, Money and Survival*, ICRC, February 2000, pp. 96–99.

[4]   Laurie Nathan, "The Four Horsemen of Apocalypse: The Structural Causes of Crisis and Violence in Africa," p. 26. Originally presented at Consultation on the Nexus between Economic Management and the Restoration of Social Capital, World Bank and the Center for Conflict Resolution, Cape Town, October 11–13, 1999.

[5]   Auvinen, Ruha and Wayne Nafziger, "The Sources of Humanitarian Emergencies," *Journal of Conflict Resolution*, Vol. 43, No. 3, June 1999, pp. 267–290.

Regardless, however, of the causes of intrastate wars, humanitarian emergencies inevitably follow. Usually they are identifiable by the presence of "the four horseman of apocalypse": death, displacement, hunger, and disease. It is thus hardly surprising that civil wars tend to start in, and to especially scar, the world's poorest countries. In the last decade they have left a terrible legacy: more than five million dead, millions more driven from their homes, physical resources destroyed, and institutions and social cohesion weakened to the breaking point. Today, over 22 million displaced persons and refugees, compared to a fraction of that number prior to 1990, burden the responsibilities of the United Nations High Commission for Refugees. Its staff has risen from 33 with a budget of $300,000 and operations exclusively in Europe in 1951, to in 1999 a staff of around 5,000 and a budget of over $1 billion with operations in over 120 countries.[6]

Today, the scourge of civil wars challenges conventional wisdom about the nature of wars, the means for deterrence, and the handling of their aftermath. Traditionally, states have waged war against one another with professional armies. The majority of the casualties were combatants. A military victory signaled the end of hostilities. The subsequent peace, usually accompanied by a formal agreement, allowed each side to rebuild roads, bridges, houses, schools, and livelihoods. Over time, they would come to terms with the wounds of war. At the very least, there would be some form of peaceful coexistence. By contrast, the intrastate armed violent conflicts now plaguing the world are waged largely by youthful combatants with little formal military training. Civilians are increasingly targeted, and often left displaced, maimed, or dead. Stalemate rather than victory is the typical end. Resolved inconclusively, they stand ready to flare up again at the slightest provocation. Formal peace agreements have become rare; their full implementation even rarer. And "post-conflict" periods are rarely "post" at all, as small-scale violence often continues to torment war-torn areas, leaving them in a state of neither war nor peace.

In many instances, war continues by other means. Diplomatic means and economic tools gain currency as those of the battlefield are discredited. What persists is the will to weaken if not destroy one's adversary. With little trust and only fleeting reconciliation, former belligerents remain enemies; live ammunition may be foregone, but no reinvigo-

---

6   *The State of the World's Refugees: Fifty Years of Humanitarian Action.* Geneva: The UNHCR and Oxford University Press, 2000.

rated desire to live together peaceably replaces it. Billions of dollars in aid and thousands of peace-keepers (e.g., Bosnia and Kosovo) offer no guarantee of an end to this state of affairs. Nor can reintegration and reconciliation of ex-belligerents be legislated by any number of UN Security Council resolutions.[7]

Neither the United Nations nor the Bretton Woods Institutions, alone or in tandem, can control or prevent such wars. Indeed the institutional mandates and methodologies of these supranational organizations are often part of the problem. Any workable solution demands more comprehensive planning and a radical readjustment of insular institutional cultures. Others , the private sector, as well as non-governmental organizations and civil society generally must become engaged. A new partnership for sustainable peace must arise if efforts at political, economic and social peacebuilding are not to fail.[8]

---

[7]   See Nat J. Colletta and Taies Nezam, "From Reconstruction to Reconciliation: The Nature of War Determines the Nature of Peace," in *Development Outreach*, Vol. I, No. 2, Fall 1999.

[8]   *See* I. Elbadawi, "Civil Wars and Poverty: The Role of External Interventions, Political Rights and Economic Growth," presented at the World Bank's Development Economic Research Group Conference on Civil Conflicts, Crime and Violence, World Bank, Washington DC, Feb. 22–23, 1999, *obtainable from* <http://www.worldbank.org/ research/conflict/papers/war000.pdf> (study of 138 conflicts since World War II, linking civil wars and poverty and demonstrating that "poverty . . . influences the probability of a civil war."). *See also* Paul Collier, *Economic Causes of Civil Conflict and Their Implications for Policy* (World Bank, 2000), *obtainable from* <http://www.worldbank.org/ research/conflict/papers/civilconflict.pdf>.

Chapter 2

REDEFINING PARTNERSHIP: TOWARD A UNIFIED FIELD APPROACH

The Problem: Dual Fragmentation—Disorder and Response

The problem begins with fragmentation. Many state systems that bear responsibility for providing security for their populations have fallen apart. So too, to a lesser degree, have the systems intended to provide solace and relief. Compounding the problem is the fragmentation of the overarching political systems intended to serve as peace-makers and peace-builders. In this context, the idea of partnering has emerged, offering enhanced cooperation and coordination among all the relevant players and the promise of cohesiveness rather than fragmentation.

No adequate diagnosis of the problem, or prescription for a cure, can emerge without fully understanding the costs of intrastate wars. The experience of Guatemala is symptomatic. As presented to the UN Secretary-General in a report of February, 1998 by the Guatemala Historic Clarification Commission, the direct quantifiable costs of that internal conflict (1985–1992), without reference to lost lives and injuries, were found to come close to $10 billion. That amounts to 120% of Guatemala's 1990 Gross Domestic Product. The bulk of this amount is attributable to opportunity costs—that is, the costs resulting from lost production due to the death, disappearance, or forced displacement of individuals who had to abandon their daily activities as they were recruited into the militia, the army, or guerrilla movements. The destruction of physical assets included private and common property, and the waste of infrastructure: bridges, electrical towers, and the like. Other losses not easily quantifiable, like the loss of potential foreign investments, were not included in the $10 billion price tag of the damage wrought.

The costs of civil conflicts presently raging in Angola, Sierra Leone, the Congo and elsewhere, and those which have recently come to an uncertain end in the Balkans, East Timor, Rwanda and the Palestinian territories, have yet to be quantified. In all likelihood, they will mirror, if not surpass, the toll of Guatemala.

The Guatemalan experience is instructive for another reason: it shows a pattern of poverty abetting violence, and violence abetting poverty, creating a vicious cycle of economic injury and political grievance. The Historic Clarification Commission found that a primary factor for keeping the Guatemalan conflict going was the inability of the State to provide minimal social services in the neediest regions of the country. Armed confrontation had weakened the ability of the government to collect taxes. This resulted in the widening of its budgetary deficit, which further weakened the State's capacity to promote development, thus further fueling grievances and the readiness to take up arms. Ironically, governmental efforts to loosen repression only aggravated matters. In many cases, civil wars are sparked at the point where grievances and the opportunity to express them reach a point of confluence.

Yet, in Guatemala, as in most conflict countries trying to break the cycle of civil war, economic opportunities, or the lack thereof, can make a critical difference. If former combatants are offered few opportunities in civil life, they will be drawn to re-entry into military or guerrilla forces, or will be attracted to criminal economic activity. By contrast, disarmament, conversion from war to peace economies, reintegration and rehabilitation can lead to social, economic, and political recovery. But this cannot occur without an integrated, non-fragmented approach to peacebuilding.

Attempting to Overcome a Fragmented Response

Development of an integrated response to recovery has come slowly. Before 1994, it was largely non-existent. As demonstrated by Alvaro de Soto and Graciana del Castillo,[1] the United Nations and the World Bank had been given an ideal opportunity for a concerted approach to peacebuilding when called upon to implement the January 1992 El Salvador peace agreement. That agreement called for far-reaching political, social, and economic reforms. It included a rigorous economic stabilization and

---

[1]   Alvaro de Soto and Graciana del Castillo, "Obstacles to Peace in El Salvador," *Foreign Affairs*, No. 94, Spring 1994, pp. 69–83.

structural adjustment program which encompassed integration of economic and political goals. But the United Nations and the World Bank displayed little capacity, and small proclivity, for cooperation. The result, as de Soto and del Castillo characterized it, "was as if a patient lay on the operating table with the left and right sides of his body separated by a curtain and unrelated surgery being performed on each side." In El Salvador, the patient survived in spite of the doctors. De Soto and del Castillo, bringing to bear their enormous experience in the UN system, sounded a warning bell: the continuation of independent operations by the supranational institutions comes at the expense of the lives of the patients they are ostensibly trying to save. They pinpointed two key impediments to forging a more integrated response. First, the UN is severely over-stretched as states are increasingly turning to it for solutions to burgeoning peace and security problems. Second, the UN and the World Bank (as well as the International Monetary Fund) are, as the El Salvador experience epitomized, overseeing separate, simultaneous processes on a collision course. "El Salvador's dilemma offers a stark example," they concluded, of the need for the "integrated approach to human security". Under such an approach, military, economic, social and governance problems should be addressed jointly and coherently rather than separately.

In the intervening years since de Soto and del Castillo's warning bell, a number of international forces have converged, giving new cogency to their call. These include challenges and opportunities posed by: the end of the Cold War, the advent of globalization, and the rise of determined leadership at the United Nations and the World Bank.

Cold War's End

When the Cold War thawed, so did the paralysis of the United Nations security system that had gripped it since its inception. The automatic exercise of the veto by the superpowers any time their interests were threatened gave way to a readiness to explore collective options. Although the 1991 Gulf War demonstrated that superpower interests could coalesce, it seems still unclear whether that that event represented but a brief moment in history. Bosnia, Kosovo and Timor foreshadow the mix of new coalitions required in the wake of the Cold War. What is incontrovertible is that the Cold War's end also represents a decline in superpower interest in policing conflict and in budgeting for its prevention. Re-examining their priorities, both the United States and Russia have drastically reduced their foreign aid budgets. The slack has been taken up in part by the European Community in conjunction with other interested donor countries, especially Japan. This new combination of forces has sustained peacekeeping and peacebuilding operations. But the arrangement remains fragile without greater American and Russian support.

The Advent of Globalization

The rise of globalization has empowered new actors. For non-governmental organizations (NGOs) it has meant greater power to affect the international agenda. For the private sector it has meant a greater awareness that instability in one corner of the globe can easily affect business operations in another, and that they are not powerless to engage in a global preventive strategy. An ethos of social responsibility has begun to emerge, tied in part to globalization. Writing in the November 16, 1999 edition of the *International Herald Tribune*, the then president of the International Committee of the Red Cross, Cornelio Sommaruga, spoke of the implications of a graffiti sign: "First, Let's Globalize Responsibility." Although globalization is, essentially, a financial and economic phenomenon, he found that it can also have profound effects on conflicts and humanitarian crises. Globalization, Sommaruga concluded, is forcing us "to systematically develop contacts [between humanitarian NGOs and the business community] with the aim of simply getting to know each other better."

Historically, NGO and business community relations have suffered from mutual suspicion and differences of outlook. That divide is being slowly bridged. There is growing recognition of interdependence. The first Business-Humanitarian Forum was held in Geneva on January 27, 1999 under the co-chairmanship of Sadako Ogata, UN High Commissioner for Refugees; John C. Whitehead, Chairman of the Board of the International Rescue Committee; and John F. Imle, Jr., Vice Chairman of the Unocal Corporation. The conference brought together leaders of thirty major humanitarian organizations and multinational corporations. Its main contribution was mutual recognition of the shortcomings of channels of communication between the two communities, which were found to be nearly non-existent, and the need for more "dialogue."

In Washington, the US Chamber of Commerce organized in 1999 the first session of its kind aimed at business-NGO cooperation in addressing issues of social responsibility. In the United Kingdom, matters have progressed further. International Alert, an NGO which also serves as an umbrella organization for various international NGO groups, has worked closely with the Prince of Wales Business Leaders Forum to reach out to the business community, often working behind closed doors, to establish wide ranging contacts and trust in a manner that goes beyond the state of such relations in the United States. And in Paris, the International Chamber of Commerce has officially recommended to its membership that the ICC should establish a forum to deal with issues related to business and civil society from an overall perspective, and act as a rallying point for members.

If globalization has served as a force for empowerment, and is widely heralded as such, it has not done so with sufficient inclusivity. This is the message of UN Secretary-General Kofi Annan in his comprehensive "Millennium Report—The Role of the United Nations in the 21st Century," issued on April 3, 2000. "Inclusive globalization" is deemed "the central challenge we face today . . . to ensure that globalization becomes a positive force for all the world's people, instead of leaving billions of them behind in squalor."[2]

The Rise of Determined Leadership

Neither the transformations brought by the end of the Cold War nor the empowerment wrought by globalization would, however, have had significant impact on peacebuilding were it not for the fact that the United Nations and the World Bank gave rise to a new visionary leadership. UN Secretary-General Kofi Annan and his counterpart, World Bank President James Wolfensohn, worked together only loosely in advocating the benefits of "partnering." Each came to his position through a common conviction: unless their organizations developed new and better ways of checking the spread of civil wars and building on the gains made by peace-makers, their institutions' credibility would be undermined.

Largely independently of each other, they advocated a "holistic" approach anchored in "partnering" arrangements. Each has advocated reaching out to the private sector and NGOs. Each has recognized that

---

[2]   Annan, Kofi A., "We The Peoples: The Role of the UN in the 21st Century," UN Department of Public Information, New York, 2000.

the challenge to their institutions lies in successfully moving them into the still-uncharted territory of peacebuilding through establishing relationships which overcome their disparate operations and insular cultures.

But turning around institutional cultures that show little proclivity for integrative efforts even within their own systems is no easy task. Organizational boundaries can be rigid. Organizational cultures tend to be complex and deeply embedded, especially as the size of institutions grows and little changeover of staff occurs. Systems theory, the study of systems change within large organizations, teaches that integration between systems cannot be achieved by simply creating a network of separate parts. Rather, changing an existing institutional environment demands an understanding of interconnectedness. Organizational routines, standard operating procedures, structures, governing rules and distinctive sets of beliefs must all be addressed and reformed if a new mission is to take root. The challenge for UN Secretary-General Kofi Annan and World Bank President James Wolfensohn was to build partnering arrangements on the solid basis of cultural change within their own organizations. To do so, they would have overcome inherent institutional resistance to such change.

For Annan, this meant overcoming a mind-set wary of a more activist approach. Many would prefer that the institution retain a posture based on a reading of the UN Charter which would continue to place emphasis on sovereign equality (Article 2–1) and non-"interference in matters which are essentially within the domestic jurisdiction of any state" (Article 2–7, UN Charter). In this view, peacebuilding and the creation of "good governance" was never intended to be part of the UN agenda, in recognition of the fact that the UN was never well suited for this purpose. For Wolfensohn this meant overcoming a mindset that insists that the World Bank's Articles of Agreement require it to stay on the sidelines of political conflict, and that only after armed conflicts have ceased—through victory, a durable cease-fire or armistice—is it appropriate for the World Bank to enter. But by then the damage will have been done, and whatever capacity for conflict prevention that the World Bank possesses will have been dissipated.

Today, Annan and Wolfensohn have largely steered their respective institutions away from these narrow perspectives. Although this movement may seem radical, in historical perspective it represents a return to initial principles as applied to present exigencies.

The Solution: Toward a Unified Field Approach

Partnering across institutional lines is not a new idea, but one deeply rooted in the blueprints for the post-World War II era. Those understandings envisioned joint efforts by the United Nations and the Bretton Woods Institutions. In many respects, they foresee a unified field approach to peace. The elements for ordering the chaos of the new political universe were seen as parts of a whole. Peace was seen as a problem of law, and law as a question of the right code of conduct and institutional controls.

These blueprints emerged during the dark days of World War II as statesmen and diplomats in Washington, London and Moscow searched for a post-war unified approach to peace. They believed that ordering the political universe around the rule of law, as applied by the Allied powers, was essential to prevent a recurrence of the scourge of war which engulfed the world shortly after the conclusion of the First World War. Quite independently of these political efforts at Princeton University's Institute of Advanced Studies, Albert Einstein was laboring on a unified theory of the physical universe. These unrelated efforts shared certain assumptions and were equally grounded in a belief in an inherent order to the universe, if one could but discover or devise the right formula. Einstein sought to develop a unified field theory to reconcile the seemingly random and unpredictable behavior of atomic particles during nuclear fission. The predictability and order he had so unerringly charted in the macro-universe of cosmos and planets seemed applicable to all aspects of the physical universe. Neither Einstein's nor the post World War II planners' efforts at achieving an ultimate order fully achieved their objective. Yet each left its mark for decades to come.

Albert Einstein's belief in inherent order in the universe sought to address the observation that in nuclear fission seemingly random behavior occurred. While other scientists sought to apply the unleashing of that energy toward construction of the atomic bomb, Einstein sought to develop a unified field theory to reconcile the ostensibly random behavior of atoms with that of the predictable movement of planets that he had earlier charted with absolute accuracy.

Like Einstein's Unified Field Theory, today's international system remains a work in progress, a constellation of entities created by the architects of the post-World War II order to thwart aggression. The United Nations was established to contain war and to consolidate peace through a system of collective security. The World Bank and the

International Monetary Fund were created to reconstruct societies after the ravages of war and to establish a stable monetary system. The overarching objective was always the same: in the inimitable words of the preamble of the UN Charter, "to save succeeding generations from the scourge of war which twice in our lifetime has inflicted untold sorrow on mankind." Still, a product of its times, the post-World War II plan was centered on giving exclusive reign to institutions and governments. Although its charters were clothed in the language of "We, the Peoples," the "micro" aspects of peace-making and peacebuilding—humanitarian organizations, civil society institutions, and the private sector—were hardly considered part of the equation. To the extent they mattered at all, they were considered independent particles fated to act randomly.

Today the impetus is for union and the integration of these components into a unified whole. As formulated by Secretary-General Kofi Annan in his Millennium Report: "Greater consistency must be achieved among macroeconomic, trade, aid, financial and environmental policies, so that all support our common aim of expanding the benefits of globalization. Conflict prevention, post conflict peacebuilding, humanitarian assistance and development policies need to become more effectively integrated. In short, it is exceedingly difficult to navigate the transition to a more global world with incomplete and incomparable policy fragments."[3]

Moreover, as Annan also recognized in the Millennium Report, "the rapid pace of change today frequently exceeds the capacity of national and international institutions to adapt. Part of the solution may lie in the emergence of 'global policy networks'. These networks—or coalitions for change—bring together international institutions, civil society and private sector organizations, and national governments in pursuit of common goals. Our involvement with global policy networks has been extensive but largely unplanned. We need a more focused and systematic approach."[4]

In this undertaking, interaction builds on interdependence, linking the macro and micro aspects of peace-management and peacebuilding. Like the integration of global markets by multinational organizations where market forces drive a restructuring of entire industries, forcing new strategic alliances and broader integrative strategies, so too the multilateral institutions gain from greater efficiencies, global optimiza-

---

[3]   *Ibid.*
[4]   *Ibid.*

tion of resources, reduction of duplications and economies of both scope and scale. Optimizing the global structure of peacebuilding thus requires a strategy to restructure the peace "industry" to stretch and adapt itself beyond existing boundaries.

In adapting themselves to this challenge, neither Annan or Wolfensohn were acting without precedent. Although the UN Charter provides little or no role for the United Nations in peacemaking or the negotiation of peace, but confines it largely to deterrence and enforcement functions, in practice (beginning with UN Under-Secretary Ralph Bunche's successful mediation of the 1948–1949 Arab-Israeli war) UN negotiators have proven their mettle at peacemaking. Similarly, although the World Bank's Articles of Agreement provides no role for it in issues of governance—as for example, in combating corruption—the World Bank has in fact adapted itself, sometimes circuitously, to meet this objective.[5]

The Need for Multiple Perspectives

Radical institutional change requires, however, recognition that new ways of thinking almost invariably come up against institutional resistance when they would alter routinely accepted and often hidden organizational rules and practices. This is especially true where change requires allowance of multiple perspectives—those of contending institutions and organizations—in altering processes of decision-making.

Crossing institutional boundaries can provoke culture shock. Many of the seemingly self-evident propositions that have previously guided members of a particular organization need to be re-examined. That which is intuitively obvious to one institutional culture may be unacceptable to another. This is particularly true if professional disciplines are crossed, so that neither institution finds itself sharing the same perception, or able to collect mutually meaningful data on important problems. To accommodate the discomfort, models for a new integrative order are best drawn not from any single discipline but from a range of them. The differences between the economist who favors econometric models and econometric variables, and the political advisor or businessman who prefers a more pragmatic approach, cannot be resolved by imposing one discipline over another. Each position predisposes its particular models of

---

5   Ciorciari, John P. "A Prospective Enlargement of the Roles of the Bretton Woods Financial Institutions in International Peace Operations," *Fordham International Law Journal*, Vol. 22, No. 2, December 1998.

analysis, sets of assumptions, organizing concepts, propositions and infer-ence patterns that drive the examination of particular sets of forces and factors that bear on a set of problems. In this context, if the prospect of a new integrated model is to be realized, there must be a synthesis reflect-ing the full range of concerns. The payoff is that multiple perspective models reveal insights about a problem not obtainable otherwise, and build on the realization that intractable problems can neither be formu-lated nor resolved independently.

Based on the literature and experience of systems change, one inevitably comes to the realization that the more focused and systemic approach to peacebuilding which Kofi Annan and James Wolfensohn sought for their organizations could be achieved without a synthesis of competing institutional values in which neither institution's key disci-pline prevails yet, this is inherently difficult to accomplish from the inside out. A catalyst is needed to provide an independent approach. It is here that the private sector, in conjunction with non-governmental organizations, can play an essential role.

Peacebuilding requires the structuring of intelligent alliances to engage multiple perspectives. It provides global partners with a systemic way of managing interactions. But where diverse organizations with dif-ferent cultures and charters are involved, collaboration becomes exceed-ingly difficult. A unified field approach applied to peacebuilding, with the introduction of the private sector and non-governmental organiza-tions, provides the potential for unfreeing institutional log-jams.

NGOs have traditionally been involved in emergency humanitar-ian relief and have increasingly expanded operations into development and reconstruction. The private sector has traditionally remained aloof, hesitant to commit beyond the stage of philanthropy and investment to the exercise of leadership in global peace issues. Yet, as Rosabeth Moss Kanter has observed in the May-June 1999 issue of *The Harvard Business Review*, there is within this private community genuine movement from "spare change" to "real change"—real change in affecting global as well as domestic problems of poverty and conflict. Thus, Kanter concludes: "Indeed, a new paradigm for innovation is emerging: a partnership between enterprise and public interest that produces profitable and sus-tainable change for both sides."[6] Driven by a younger generation in the business community, originally largely in the telecommunications and

---

[6]   Kanter, Rosabeth Moss. "From Spare Change to Real Change," *Harvard Business Review*, May/June 1999.

computer sectors, and widened to include most prominently the oil, natural resources and apparel industries, there is a well-spring of new energy that can be tapped in the service of peacebuilding.

The challenge is not only to tap this well-spring of energy but to harness it. Here experimentation with new modalities is called for. Speaking before a meeting of the Business Humanitarian Forum in Washington, DC on November 1, 1999, Mrs. Sadako Ogata, UN High Commissioner for Refugees, proclaimed: "At all levels, in the financial, political and even personal sphere, we live in an era of experimentation and partnerships. . . . We should not be frightened by new association, even if the expertise, prior experiences, and even respective languages are so different. Being new, these associations are most exciting. But as with any new terrain, exploration must be bold and careful at the same time."[7]

Inching Toward Partnering

For the World Bank, as an institution that prided itself on being apolitical, the break with the past has been particularly difficult. The Wolfensohn-inspired Framework for World Bank Involvement in Post-Crisis Situations of 1998 enjoined the Bank staff to respond to post conflict situations with greater "ingenuity, creativity, and initiative appropriate to individual country situations."[8] As guides to how that "ingenuity" and "creativity" might evolve, several innovations were proposed: increased field presence and "watching briefs" (intelligence) in situations where Bank involvement is still precluded; inter-agency cooperation; and increased risk exposure. Development of better political skills to address the special needs of war-torn societies was also deemed essential. Here, partnership with the United Nations was cited as the cornerstone. Yet the Framework stopped short of any reference to the seminal ideas about peacebuilding articulated by former UN Secretary-General Boutros Boutros-Ghali in his 1992 UN Agenda for Peace, and in the subsequent UN Agenda for Development (1994). Indeed, no World Bank Framework document makes reference to those texts. World Bank President James Wolfensohn and UN Secretary-General Kofi Annan both advocated integrative peacebuilding efforts, but each on the basis of distinct different approaches.

---

[7]   The Business Humanitarian Forum. "Building Mutual Support Between Humanitarian Organizations and the Business Community," Washington DC, 1999.

[8]   *Post-Conflict Reconstruction: The Role of the World Bank*. Washington DC: The World Bank, 1998, p. 69.

Only relatively recently has the World Bank issued a new Operational Policy on Development Cooperation and Conflict in which cross-institutional coordination and allegiance to the goal of partnering is pronounced. Annan, who tended to distance himself from Boutros Boutros-Ghali's embrace of "nation-building"—an embrace which caused US opposition to Boutros-Ghali's reappointment in 1995—has subsequently endorsed the concept of "nation-building" in Kosovo and East Timor, two territories in which the United Nations has been given stewardship. In that undertaking, the World Bank is its putative partner, although not officially in Kosovo and still at arm's length in East Timor.

This represents a significant advance over the more cautious approach employed by Annan when he first assumed the Secretary-General position in 1996. At first he gave priority to UN reforms to stave off the threat of further cutbacks in US funding. But, as he was aware, a larger challenge loomed: saving the United Nations from irrelevance. At the 1996 Dayton peace talks on the future of Bosnia, the United States had no qualms about excluding the United Nations, notwithstanding its interest in participation, convinced that it was likely to do more harm than good. By contrast, the World Bank had a representative in attendance at Dayton ready to contribute the World Bank's expertise, resources, and skills to bridging differences.

Thus, despite outward appearances which suggested that the United Nations had sprung back to life after fifty years of Cold War-induced irrelevance, it was in fact faring badly. During the Cold War, it had relevance, if only as "a dangerous place," the phrase used by former US Ambassador to the UN Daniel Patrick Moynihan to describe the situation that then prevailed. After the Cold War, it appeared to be losing not only relevance, but also the capacity to cope with the growing list of problems laid at its doorstep. Former Secretary-General Boutros Boutros-Ghali's attempt at converting the UN from a peacekeeping to a nation-building organization had failed in Somalia and Cambodia. UN peacekeeping operations had grown dramatically in strength since 1989 with the creation of twenty-five peacekeeping operations, but the number of emerging armed conflicts outpaced them. Conflicts which seemed to have exhausted themselves re-ignited like embers in a wind-stoked fire. The United Nations seemed helpless, although it was spending unheard-of sums of money.

This was the dilemma that confronted Kofi Annan, who came into office at a time when more than half of Africa had become the site of internecine conflict. The Cold War had paralyzed the institution, but now that it had regained its strength it still seemed powerless to confront the epidemic of civil wars that gripped the African continent and other parts of the globe. The choice was stark: the UN had either to reassert itself or risk irrelevancy. The opportunity came as the United States began to adopt an increasingly interventionist posture toward Bosnia and Kosovo in the name of basic human rights. Picking up the refrain, Annan declared before the Fall 1999 UN General Assembly's opening session that the world could no longer allow the sovereignty of member states to shield them from the consequences of outrageous misconduct: "Massive violations of human rights will not stand." If massive human rights abuses could no longer be protected by the shield of sovereign equality and sovereign immunity, it meant that UN protectorates like those established in Bosnia, Kosovo and East Timor might become the rule. The once-discredited notions of Boutros Boutros-Ghali about "nation-building" were being rehabilitated with a vengeance.

With nation-building re-legitimized, and with the World Bank poised to be a big part of the picture, Kofi Annan made his first visit to World Bank headquarters in Washington for the purpose of addressing the World Bank staff. In the October 25, 1999 open meeting at the World Bank, the first ever attended by any UN Secretary-General, Annan announced that the two institutions would seek to mesh their efforts to jump-start war-torn economies and establish "good governance." Along these lines, he announced that the UN and the World Bank would soon send a Joint Assessment Mission (JAM) to East Timor to assess the steps necessary to administer that territory and steer it toward independence.[9]

Some mechanisms for UN-World Bank cooperation had already been put in place over the previous three years. Mid-level representatives of the World Bank and the United Nations had met in New York and elsewhere as part of the Conflict Prevention and Post-Conflict Reconstruction (CPR) Network. At their last meetings in Ottawa in June, 1999 and in New York on November 4–5, 1999, further practical steps were taken to foster cooperation. The various players were identified and common objectives defined. Key among them was the proclaimed need to develop not only closer cooperation between the various UN bodies and the World Bank, but to also enhance the capacity of NGOs to develop and implement peacebuilding projects.

---

[9]   Kofi Annan, "Peace and Development—One Struggle, Two Fronts," Address to the World Bank Staff, Washington, D.C., October 19, 1999, pp. 1–10.

Among the issues on which consensus was reached were the following: that it is important to develop a culture of prevention; that peacebuilding practitioners need to look at the root causes of conflict rather than become engaged only when conflict is imminent; and that good programming cannot be implemented and sustained without a blending of political and development tools. It was also recognized that donors must take a regional approach, that relief and peacebuilding is a response too heavily weighted in favor of external actors and should be readdressed in favor of local actors, and that premature elections do not solve conflicts. Attention was also drawn to the advantages in communication opened by websites and electronic discussion forums, particularly by that of the World Bank located at http://www.worldbank.org/peacebuilding.

One indirectly related but no less crucial front, the Joint United Nations Program on AIDS (UNAIDS), had begun in December 1995 to attempt to slow the growth of the epidemic and to combat its effects on individuals and societies. With the participants, the World Bank and five UN agencies (UNDP, UNICEF, WHO, UNESCO and UNFPA), it moved to establish joint operating groups at the country level to promote an integrated approach to prevention of HIV and mitigation of its impact.

These fledgling efforts at cross-institutional ties had the implicit blessings of the two supranational institutions. The Annan-Wolfensohn joint declarations of October 1999 at World Bank headquarters gave them explicit endorsement, including the idea of reaching out to the private sector and NGOs. Both leaders had come to the realization that they had no other choice. To fail to reach out toward new partnering arrangements would be to ignore the challenge posed by civil wars and strife, primarily in poverty-stricken countries. It would have signaled incapacity if not indifference in the face of crying need and thus endangered the viability of their own organizations, raising questions about their capacity to fulfill their own declared mission. At a time when the benefits of "partnering" in the form of strategic alliances were being increasingly recognized as a critical instrument, not merely a tool of convenience by the business world, the supranational institutions would have appeared oblivious to its benefits. Globalization was mandating alliances as an essential aspect for survival in the new age, a lesson that could hardly afford to be ignored.

For its part, the United Nations had already begun an extensive outreach to the private sector through UNOPS, the UN Office of Project Services. Since its establishment in 1995, UNOPS had grown into a $1 billion a year business, with a total portfolio of projects worth $4 billion, an annual turnaround of around $800 million, and an income of $50 million, which covered all costs. UNOPS is totally self-financed. It is also a business that respects "social responsibility." The values that underlie the conduct of the business are exactly the values enshrined in the Charter of the United Nations. This business arm of the United Nations is not small business anymore, said its Executive Director, Reinhart Helmke, at Headquarters, as he briefed correspondents on "The UN and Business: A Partnership for the New Millennium," a conference held at the Jacob Javits Convention Center in New York on 31 May and 1 June, 2000. There had been ups and downs in the relationship between the United Nations and the private sector, but over the past few years, more and more private sector companies had made agreements with the United Nations to make some monetary contributions. The new partnerships, however, are moving in a different direction. It is no longer a matter of making a financial contribution to some United Nations project; now private sector companies agree with the United Nations on a joint objective and work side by side with the organization in order to achieve that objective.

New partnerships are not about obtaining funds from the private sector, or about Member States not paying in contributions. It is more a recognition that the magnitude of moving into a conflict situation and revitalizing a shattered economy is of such proportions that, even with double or triple contributions from governments, the job cannot be done by the United Nations alone.

The new type of partnership must evolve, and trust must be built. Levels of trust between private sector companies and agencies of the United Nations have not been very high. "As confidence and trust in each other evolves," Annan said, "it is reasonable to assume that certain decisions of the kind that private sector companies take, could be taken in the framework of a larger set of international values."

At the World Bank, a similar outreach to the private sector was spearheaded by its Business Partners for Development Program. For more than a decade this program has been developing practical partnership-building training tools, which are currently being tested in relatively difficult working situations with oil, gas and mining companies. Recently it has begun to think of bringing the full weight of private sector expertise to bear on post-conflict situations through partnership arrangements, in coordination with the Bank's Post-Conflict Unit.

BP Amoco and Business Partners for Development in Colombia

As Colombia's civil war nears the end of its fourth decade, President Andres Pastrana seeks enhanced foreign direct investment to take his country out of a recession that began in 1999 and has been marked by an estimated 19.8% unemployment rate in 2000.[10] Pastrana's government would like to double its coal production over the next five years, and continue earning $3.7 billion per annum (as of 1999) for its oil exports, though it may be a net oil importer by 2004. It also hopes to export electricity and natural gas in the near future. This is likely to be enormously difficult in light of the skyrocketing number of attacks by the two largest guerrilla groups (the Revolutionary Armed Forces of Colombia—FARC, and the National Liberation Army—ELN) that target foreign and domestic energy companies.[11] As Mr. Alvaro Reyes Posada of the Colombian economic research group, Econometria, said: "What [the attacks] show is that the government cannot provide these companies the protection they need."[12] As a consequence, BP Amoco's oil exploration and production is not maximized and the government is increasingly unable to reach sought natural resource export levels.

Despite these problems, BP Amoco remains in Casanare, where it seeks to reduce bombings and other security risks by addressing many of their causes: rapid urbanization,[13] poor infrastructure, lack of government authority, and limited regional capacity for management of project revenues. It also seeks to address charges that BP Amoco itself has been engaged in a variety of human rights violations ranging from treatment of workers to turning a blind eye—when it could make a difference—to government abuses.

BP Amoco established a community affairs team in 1992, marking significant change in social programming and project implementation in Casanare,

---

10   "Colombia," April 2001 Report, Energy Information Administration, US Department of Energy. http://www.eia.doe.gov/emeu/cabs/colombia.html.

11   The Cano Limon oil and gas pipelines were bombed 87 times in 2000, and 739 times since 1986, spilling more than 2.3 million barrels of oil. Dudley, Steven. "Rebels Pull the Plug on Colombian Exports: Guerrilla Attacks Raise Cost of Doing Business for Key Energy Sector Companies," *Washington Post*, November 23, 2000, p. A48. In 1999, 76 bombings were committed against foreign corporations, as well as 20 against locally owned operations. Wade, John. "Violence, Crime Continue to Cast Shadow Over Future Oil Investment in Colombia," *Oil and Gas Journal*, January 17, 2000, Vol. 98. In October 1998, for instance, in clear breach of international humanitarian law, the ELN blew up the OCENSA pipeline, killing over 70, injuring another 20 and leaving 10 more missing. *Ibid.* The guerrilla groups have also attacked and destroyed more than 500 electricity pylons since the beginning of 1999.

12   Dudley, Steven, *supra* n. 11.

the department in Colombia where it operates.[14] It conducted workshops and public meetings with communities to diagnose their development needs and submitted proposals on such issues to municipal authorities. It then undertook a tri-sector partnership approach with the World Bank's Business Partners for Development (BPD) program, which aims to promote long-term business interests while meeting the needs of civil society and the state. Since the early 1990s BP Amoco and BPD have collaborated on the "Working for Casanare" project to stabilize the local social and financial environment.[15]

The partnership between BP Amoco and BPD demonstrates support, or a "buy-in," from municipal authorities, NGOs (local and international), and local community members. Kathryn McPhail, principal specialist in the World Bank affiliate, the International Finance Corporation's (IFC's) Technical and Environment Department and author of *How Oil, Gas, and Mining Projects Can Contribute to Development*, explains that the requirement is based on the idea that partnerships between project developers, NGOs, local communities and governments are essential to raising living standards and reducing poverty by generating sizable revenues, creating business and job opportunities, and bringing new roads and access to water and power.[16]

BP Amoco and BPD's collaborative efforts aim to strengthen health care, security, and education services; identify cultural sensitivities to project planning; negotiate equitable concession agreements with private sector companies; strengthen policies for public consultation and promotion of transparency in project planning and implementation; and build capacity at local levels to absorb incremental revenues for development purposes. The resulting plan has offered new avenues for reconciling disputes between BP Amoco, the community, and the government, while establishing BP Amoco as a responsible corporate actor.

[13] *Colombia Location Report*, http://www.bp.com. Casanare's 44% population growth and conversion from 68% rural to 62% urban between 1985–1997 is largely a factor of immigration to work with BP Amoco.

[14] Davy, Aidan, "Tri-sector Partnerships for Social Investment: Ownership and Control of Outcomes," Business Partners for Development Natural Resources Cluster Working Paper No. 5, June 2000.

[15] BP Amoco operates as British Petroleum Exploration Colombia (BPXC) in the Casanare Department where the Cusiana and Cupiagua oil fields exist as the largest in the western hemisphere with combined reserves of 1.6 billion barrels. Discovery of its potential 434,000 barrels of daily crude oil production (in 1999), which represents over half of Colombia's total, was made in the early 1980s. *Colombia Location Report*, March 2000, http://www.bp.com.

[16] McPhail, Kathryn, "How Oil, Gas, and Mining Projects Can Contribute to Development," *Finance & Development*, December 2000, Vol. 37, No 4.

Yet if the potential of "partnering" has been heralded by the World Bank and UN leadership, and expanded to encompass the private sector and NGOs, and East Timor has been declared the new proving ground, successful implementation of partnering has only just begun. The effort is clouded in part by problems of definition, in part by the absence of structures through which partnering can manifest itself, and in part by legal and institutional barriers created by decades of non-communication. Each party has its set of expectations about the benefits of collaboration. But asymmetry of effort can result in failure. Making these expectations redound to the benefit of all concerned requires mutual trust and confidence which must be built from the ground up. Partners need to be willing to stick together long enough to learn how to make the partnership work.

Defining the Field

The first task is to define the field. Just how widely does the World Bank wish to cast its net? Is its interest limited to "post conflict" situations, or does it extend to conflict prevention? How far does the increased interest by the United Nations in poverty eradication—a subject declared as a priority for the new millennium—extend? In this regard, several definitional markers are in order.

The realm of peacebuilding is functionally distinct from other strata of a peace process. Although there is some overlap, peacebuilding begins where traditional approaches end. The United Nations Charter vests the UN with responsibility for deterrence of war through diplomatic measures and the threat of economic, political and military sanctions. As a last resort, it may authorize collective security measures against aggressors. Newer modalities like peacekeeping and peacemaking augment the organization's tools. The former entails monitoring newly established but fragile cease-fire arrangements and the like; the latter refers to direct involvement in peace talks. Peacebuilding goes one step further. It assumes that the belligerents have made a genuine commitment, and that the cessation of fighting is not a temporary or tactical expedient. In this context, the peacemakers are often at risk, their experiment uncertain, and under pressure to show results or tangible gains to skeptical constituencies. Here the multilateral institutions and others can provide assistance in showing immediate tangible gains, and in laying the social and juridical infrastructure for attracting foreign investment in order to stabilize the emergent state's economic and political institutions.

UN-World Bank partnering is thus not primarily about the provision of more effective emergency humanitarian relief. Humanitarian relief only marginally engages the World Bank. It is rather a development agency that wants to resurrect its role in reconstruction. To be sure, there is interest in better coordination of humanitarian relief. This has been the subject of much study within the UN community aimed at better inter-agency coordination and full use of new fledgling UN machinery through the UN Office of Humanitarian Affairs established in 1992 and its successor, OCHA, the Office for the Coordination of Humanitarian Affairs, established in 1997. But the primary interest in UN-World Bank partnering arrangements lies in bridging the gap between relief and development. The World Bank surely shares the concern articulated in a recent report by the UN Inter-Agency Standing Committee (IASC) over the inability to transfer the momentum of crisis response to recovery, rehabilitation and development activities. It too recognizes the need to move from relief to recovery and rehabilitation in a manner that will no longer be characterized as "notoriously slow . . . as opportunities to undertake relief, recovery and development in a coherent and simultaneous manner have all too often been ignored or abandoned."

Partnering strategies for peacemaking build on the conviction that peace cannot be compelled, but is a problem of will rather than law or economics. Economic inducements and its opposite, enforcement measures such as economic sanctions, can act as a prod. However, achieving durable peace requires a more comprehensive approach. A collaborative alliance offers leverage, allowing each organization to use its capacity to respond to post conflict situations to maximum advantage in creating environments conducive to peace.

In this context, the prospect of meaningful UN-World Bank partnering must confront the following questions. Given their histories as institutionally distinct and at times rival organizations operating from different disciplinary premises, how realistic are the hopes for overcoming their differences and merging their resources in the interests of jump-starting war-ravaged economies and introducing patterns of "good governance" realizable? What are the risks inherent in undertaking a unified field approach? Does momentum for change at the leadership level of these institutions have the full support of other levels of the organization, as well as donor governments, in undertaking major systemic change?

Realizing the gravity of the problem, leaders of the United Nations and the World Bank have reached out to each other and to the private

sector, NGOs and Civil Society. Both supranational institutions now seek
to bridge their longstanding separation and disparate institutional cultures. The United Nations has traditionally been preoccupied with the
politics of peace, tending to dismiss the role of economics in conflict resolution. The World Bank, preoccupied with macroeconomics, long
ignored the political realm as beyond its mandate of poverty eradication.[17] But today there is new agreement about one basic point: the
scourge of intrastate war will not be contained unless the vicious cycles
of poverty and relative deprivation, economic greed and political grievance, are broken. Armed civil conflicts weaken the ability of a state to
provide minimal social services and development in the neediest regions,
further fueling grievances and readiness to take up arms.[18] Creation of
employment and other economic opportunities can nurture and sustain
fragile peace arrangements. But this requires close United Nations-World
Bank partnering,[19] and engagement with the private sector and civil
society as well. Over the long term, only the growth of new enterprises
and investment coupled with the empowerment of people are capable

---

[17]   Disregard of the politics of target countries was said to be required by the
Articles of Agreement of the International Bank for Reconstruction and Development
(IBRD), July 22, 1944, 60 Stat. 1440, 2 UNTS 134, *as amended*, 16 UST 1942, 606 UNTS
294. Article IV, Section 10 states that "[o]nly economic considerations shall be relevant" in the Bank's dealings—and a narrow interpretation has taken this to pre-
clude the Bank's consideration in lending decisions of a State's political conduct,
including repression at home or aggression abroad. In the early 1990s, this view
began to change, especially with regard to World Bank activity in the West Bank
and Gaza, and Section 10 was construed more liberally to conclude that "[v]iola-
tion of political rights may . . . reach such proportions [as] to become a Bank concern due to significant direct economic effects or if it results in international
obligations. . . ." *See* John Stremlau and Francisco Sagasti, *Preventing Deadly Conflict:
Does the World Bank Have a Role? A Report to the Carnegie Commission on Preventing
Deadly Conflict*, Carnegie Corporation of New York, June 1988, p. 104, *obtainable from*
<http://www.ccpdc.org/pubs/world/world.htm> (quoting Ibrahim Shihata, "Issues
of 'Governance' in Borrowing Members," The World Bank, Nov. 30, 1990, pp. 35–36).
See also J. Ciorciari, *supra* n. 13 (discussing evolution of legal interpretations of the
IRBD Articles of Agreement and the resulting limitation on the Bank's activity in
post conflict situations—still crucial in debates about expansion of the Bank's role).
[18]   *See* Guatemala Historic Clarification Commission, *Guatemala: Memory of
Silence*, Annex to Letter from the Secretary-General addressed to the President of
the General Assembly, UN Doc. A/53/928 (April 27,1999), citing the neglect of rural
areas as a factor responsible for the continuation of Guatemala's civil war.
[19]   The case for World Bank engagement in the prevention and resolution of
civil wars is also argued in John Stremlau & Francisco Sagasti, *supra* note 25.

of providing the economic and social security and community resilience[20] that may salve the sources of conflict.

The United Nations Millennium Declaration—approved by the largest gathering of heads of state since the UN's founding—endorses the central role of "conflict prevention and post conflict peace building and reconstruction" in the UN's work agenda. Economic recovery is essential in fulfilling the UN's mandate of preventing and resolving conflicts.[21] The Millennium Declaration pledges to work toward "greater policy coherence and better cooperation between the United Nations, its agencies, the Bretton Woods Institutions and the World Trade Organization, as well as other multilateral bodies"—with a view "toward achieving a fully coordinated approach to the problems of peace and development."[22] Drawing upon the groundbreaking recommendations of the Brahimi Report on United Nations Peacekeeping Operations in its entirety,[23] the Millennium Summit cautioned that "peacekeeping operations should not be used as a substitute for addressing the root causes of conflict—those causes should be addressed in a coherent, well planned, coordinated and comprehensive manner with political, social, and developmental instruments."

Yet close and effective UN-World Bank cooperation continues to be hampered by differences over mandates and the appropriate roles they confer. Within the World Bank, controversy smolders over expanded engagement in conflict prevention and peace consolidation. Within the UN system, the lines between long-term development and post conflict reconstruction, and where agencies such as the UN Development Program may fit, remain blurred.

---

[20] Nat J. Colletta and Michelle L. Cullen, "Resilient Communities: Building the Social Foundations of Human Security," in *New Paths to Social Development: Community and Global Networks in Action*, Washington, D.C.: World Bank, June 2000, pp. 35–46.

[21] See United Nations Millennium Declaration, para. 9, adopted as UN General Assembly Resolution 55/2, UN Doc. A/RES/55/2 (Sept. 18, 2000) (issued on behalf of the Heads of State and Government gathered at the United Nations Millennium General Assembly).

[22] United Nations Millennium Declaration, *supra* note 29, para. 30.

[23] U.N. Special Envoy Lakhdar Brahimi was commissioned by Secretary-General Kofi Annan to recommend ways to improve U.N. peacekeeping, after the shocks of Rwanda and Bosnia. *See* Report of the Panel on United Nations Peace Operations, Annex to Identical Letters dated 21 August 2000 from the Secretary-General, U.N. Doc. A/55/305 & S/2000/809 (Aug. 21, 2000).

Compounding the difficulty in establishing new patterns of cooperation is the gnawing realization that breaking the cycle of poverty and war may exceed the capability of both the United Nations or the World Bank, operating separately or in tandem. Conflict settlement requires the injection of optimism and hope born of employment and economic opportunity. Otherwise, fragile peace arrangements can rarely be sustained. And, over the long term, only the private sector is capable of growing new enterprises, opening investment opportunities, and providing employment and economic security that endures. Moreover, the private sector can do more than serve as a source of foreign investment and economic growth. It can also be the catalyst for integrative approaches by the United Nations and the World Bank. Thus, not only closer UN-World Bank cooperation is at issue, but also the question of how to achieve active and comprehensive engagement by the private sector, alongside non-governmental organizations (NGOs) dedicated to relief, rehabilitation and reconciliation.[24]

The timeliness of such an effort is underscored by the fact that, as government representatives debated at the UN Millennium session, a few blocks east on the Avenue of the Americas, the State of the World Forum organized an alternative forum which encompassed the restless new global civil society movement. Invigorated by the coming together in Seattle, Washington, and Quebec City around the presumed evils of globalization, this movement's aim coalesced around confronting the failed global architecture embodied in the IMF, World Bank and WTO and calling for structural reform, greater transparency and citizen accountability. The State of the World Forum brought together activists that ranged from George Soros' Open Society Fund, to the Environmental Defense Fund, the International Labor Movement, and Human Rights Watch, among many others. Ironically, for all its distrust of international institutions, consensus emerged for strengthening the United Nations as the only body capable of sustaining peace.

None of this has gone unnoticed by global corporations, particularly those with business in war-torn countries, and especially companies in the extractive industries from petroleum to gold, diamonds to precious forest woods. Global companies ranging from BP Amoco to De

---

24   The United Nations Millennium Declaration, *supra* note 29, para. 30, resolves "[t]o give greater opportunities to the private sector, non-governmental organizations and civil society, in general, to contribute to the realization of the Organization's goals and programmes."

Beers and Rio Tinto are now shaping and being shaped by globalization. On the one hand, the processes of merger, acquisition and integration in the pursuit of emerging markets and profits leads to a homogenization of products and consumers, providing further fuel for critics from Seattle to Prague to Quebec City. On the other hand, new corporate structures are emerging to promote ecological and human rights campaigns in consort with organizations like Greenpeace and the World Wildlife Fund. The information revolution, spearheaded by CNN's coverage of the far reaches of the world, have strengthened the call for global integrity and accountability. Thus, increasingly, globalization means that stakeholder participation and responsibility will have to be managed as an integral part of doing business anywhere in the world.

Yet this same corporate global reach has also rendered states weaker in the face of increasing cross border flows of money, ideas, people, goods and services. The unfettered free market, while an effective economic instrument for the generation of wealth, can, it has been recognized, lead to widening disparities between rich and poor. And, it has been argued, the globalization of culture, or its commodification, can lead to the promotion of insecurity and civil war. One need only look to West Africa to see the emergence of a new kind of warlord state, where arms flow, along with diamonds, money and combatants cross seamless borders of once "successful" post-colonial States.[25] In short, the private sector can be both a cause and a remedy to problems of war and peace. The central question is whether and how it can be transformed, in partnership with the United Nations, the international financial institutions, and the NGOs and civil society to contribute to peace rather than serve as its nemesis.

Assuming, however, that attracting private sector investment in troubled areas is, on balance, a positive development, achieving such development is not easy. It requires innovation. A mix of non-economic as well as economic incentives will have to be devised. Similarly, involvement of the private sector in the larger work of formulating strategy for

---

[25] William Reno, "Sierra Leone: Warfare in a Post-State Society," pp. 1–33, and Christopher Clapham, "Putting State Collapse in Context: History, Politics and the Genealogy of a Concept," pp. 1–10, papers presented at Conference on State Collapse and Reconstruction: Lessons and Strategies, Graduate School of International Studies and ICRC, Geneva, December 7–9, 2000. Also see I. William Zartman, Editor, *Collapsed States: The Disintegration and Restoration of Legitimate Authority*. Boulder, Colorado: Lynne Rienner, 1995.

post-war recovery will require innovative thinking. To accomplish these twin goals, a new structure is needed which would enable the private sector to have a seat at the table with representatives of the United Nations and its various constituent bodies, the World Bank, and the NGO community as part of a post-conflict strategy aimed at successful war-to-peace transitions through an integrated approach. With this in mind, we now turn now to an examination of the potential role of the private sector in conflict prevention and post-conflict peacebuilding.

Chapter 3

THE PRIVATE SECTOR: PROBLEM OR PANACEA?

Privatization, simply put, is the transfer of assets, or service delivery, from the government or a public service agent, such as the United Nations, to private hands. It is a broad concept. It can often leave public entities with limited involvement beyond policy guidance. Or it can entail significant regulation and supervision. At its best, it creates meaningful partnerships between public entities and private service providers, leaving governments and other public entities as the lead agent on matters of strategy and direction but leaving day-to-day operations in the hands of the private sector.

Privatization can take many different forms from "outsourcing," or sub-contracting services to a private agent for profit or not for profit, to management contracting, franchising, asset sales or long term leases, volunteerism, and the "commercialization" of public services or facilities. Subsidy schemes utilizing vouchers are a typical means of privatization, whereby individuals are given redeemable certificates to purchase services on the open market. In addition to providing greater choice, vouchers introduce consumer demand into the equation, bringing pressure on service providers to offer high-quality, low-cost services. Food stamps, education vouchers, and low-income rent subsidies are examples of voucher systems in practice. The private sector may build, finance and operate public infrastructure, such as toll roads and airports, recovering costs through user charges.

While there are of course numerous advantages and disadvantages and cons to privatization, depending on the particular context, the primary benefit that makes it worthwhile will invariably be the prospect of increased efficiency and quality through the promotion of managed

or regulated competition. The potential downside of privatization—
which is usually accompanied by the liberalization of prices, installa-
tion of a trade regime, and fluctuating interest and wage rates—
encompasses a wide range of problems, often including the collapse of
the industrial base, skyrocketing unemployment, inequities in the distribution of property and assets, and political and social upheaval.

Privatization:
"Gradualism Versus Shock Therapy" Lessons for Peacebuilding

There are two opposing strategies for the transition process from centrally
planned economies to market economies. Janos Kornai, Professor of Economics
at Harvard University and Permanent Fellow of Collegium Budapest, identifies
them as the strategy of organic development (Strategy A) and the strategy of
accelerated privatization (Strategy B).

Strategy A:

1) Envisions the private sector's share of output growing as new private firms
   appear and the state sector shrinks with the sale or liquidation of state-
   owned companies;
2) emphasizes the creation of favorable conditions for bottom-up development of the private sector;
3) calls for the privatization of state-owned companies through the sale of
   state assets, preferably to outsiders;
4) stresses the importance of hard budget constraints and consistent enforcement of bankruptcy and accounting laws; and
5) emphasizes sociological considerations: the development of a solid, prop-
   erty-owning middle class is seen as essential to the consolidation of capitalism.

Strategy B:

1) Emphasizes the rapid elimination of state ownership;
2) calls for privatization primarily through some form of giveaway;
3) foresees dispersed ownership;
4) develops "people's capitalism"; and
5) emphasizes ethical considerations: every citizen must be given an equal share
   of the former property of the state for reasons of fairness.

Ten years after the transition process in Central and Eastern Europe has
started, it shows that strategy A has been superior to strategy B. Hungary as well
as Poland followed the A Strategy and show more successful macro-stabilization

than the Czech Republic (then Czechoslovakia) and Russia, that followed Strategy B. However, the key aspect was not the "speed" of transformation, as many economists and politicians might have thought. Mr. Kornai says: "The transition from socialism to capitalism has to be an organic process ... the emphasis has to be on consolidation, stability, and sustainability, not on breaking speed records." There are important lessons from this experience for "Privatizing Peace." First, it is not an all or nothing affair; rather balance and "organically" build processes with a focus on cohesion and stability are primary. Second, there are bound to be important trade-offs in the early days between economic efficiency and political stability.

Source: Kornai, Janos. "Making the Transition to Private Ownership." *Finance & Development*, pp. 12–13, September, 2000

The keys to managing the potential negative fallout of privatization are regulation, information, transparency, and accountability of transactions. Providing a stake in the process for shareholders through increased participation in decision-making and the provision of social safety nets and unemployment insurance for those most affected can help enormously to cushion its negative impact.

Rethinking Privatization

The fear of privatization of peace-related functions arises out of a series of misconceptions about the meaning of privatization that tends to cloud thinking on the subject. Perhaps the biggest misconception can be cleared up with a single statement: *Privatization is not replacement.* Even the most ardent supporters of privatizing peace functions do not expect the private sector to supersede the public sector. The private sector is surely no substitute for the United Nations and other international organizations, but it can proceed on parallel tracks, with adequate supervision, toward a common objective.

In fact, privatization requires the public sector's cooperation. The private sector can more effectively manage the use of scarce resources, but it is weak when it comes to formulating broad policy objectives and gaining political legitimacy. Although the public sector has proven woefully inept in running day-to-day operations, it is experienced in what the private sector lacks.

The capabilities of the public and private sector clearly complement one another. Fundamentally, privatization and partnership go hand in hand. But privatization of peace involves—indeed, *requires*—a partnership that extends into an area that international institutions have so far ignored.

The Benefits of Partnering

How can the private sector aid the public sector in the area of peace? Four advantages are worth noting. First, the private sector already has many of the same interests as the public sector, e.g., a secure and predictable environment in which to work, cost-effective means of achieving results, and satisfied clients. Thus they share a common interest in eliminating key obstacles to peace.

Second, the private sector can be a trusted intermediary. For example, in discussions with the head of a new business foundation in Colombia, the Foundation for Ideas for Peace, it was noted that the business community was in direct contact with the Forces Armades Revolutionaire Colombia (FARC), the insurgency command. When asked how this was possible, the business leader responded that the leader of the FARC had said: "We do not trust the government because they are corrupt and ineffective. We do not trust the army because they believe that they can militarily defeat us. But we do trust the business community because we know they have self-enlightened interests and can deliver on their promises."[1] As a trusted party, the private sector is capable of mediating conflict between antagonistic parties. The private sector's intermediary skills are also useful as a middleman between international organizations and their beneficiaries. The people whom these organizations attempt to assist are typically clients of the business community. Goods and services need to be provided. In the face of weak and failing states such as the Sudan, Afghanistan, and Somalia, donors are becoming increasingly convinced that private and non-profit organizations are the only credible way to assist people in need while isolating those in power.

Third, the private sector thinks and functions pragmatically and instrumentally. As a result, politics and ideology are not burdens. Thus,

---

[1]   The source for this and other related material in the next few pages is a conversation with a leading Colombian businessman and member of the Ideas for Peace Foundation, a businessmen's' forum exploring alternative initiatives to building peace in Colombia, June 2000, Cartagena, Colombia.

one Colombian business leader, when asked what the private sector's contribution to the peace process might be, recounted an interesting proposition. He said: "When I asked Marulunda, the FARC leader, what his expectations were from the private sector, he quickly responded, 'I have a payroll to meet . . . we are paying our people on average about $300 per month. There are about 25,000 people.'" Quickly doing the numbers on the back of an envelope, the businessman came up with around $90 million dollars per annum. Seemingly a small price to pay for peace, considering what the war has and could cost the business community, not to mention the government and civil society.

The problem of an alternative sustainable livelihood still remained. To facilitate a solution, the business leader suggested investments which would lead to jobs—more importantly, investments that would be owned by the FARC guerrillas themselves, such as large-scale plantation agriculture in which the guerrillas became "shareholders" and not simply estate labor. The Federal Land Development Authority (FELDA) palm oil plantation scheme in Malaysia is an excellent example of a shareholder approach to plantation agriculture. In Malaysia, after the racial riots of economically marginalized rural Malays against prosperous Chinese businessmen, the Government instituted a new economic policy to give Malays a leg up in the economy. A large part of this was the privatization of large plantations into a laborer-owned arrangement called the Federal Land Development Authority or FELDA scheme. Malays were given subsidized shares in the socially-owned new palm oil estates, as well as land for a house and the cultivation of garden crops. This form of affirmative action proved to be a successful means of redressing grievances of rural Malays through the State's provision of a stake in the economy. As the palm oil state economy grew, the entire economy grew and the situation resulted in a win-win situation for both Chinese and Malays, and led to a peaceful state of relations. This approach recognized that indigenous ownership, rather than sweat labor for low wages, was a key to sustainable peace.

In closing, the Colombian business leader summed it up by saying: "We have made a pragmatic assessment of the situation. We either follow our children and families already safely abroad and have a fire sale on our remaining assets, or we decide to sacrifice 40% percent of our profits to preserve the remaining 60%." Indeed, today, with the prospect of the FARC providing security and the international financial institutions providing infrastructure investments, from roads to electricity and schools, the privatization of peace efforts through integration of public and private efforts is perhaps the only hope for sustainable peace in Colombia.

Finally, the private sector operates on the principle that less is more, or, equivalently, that efficiency is king. Unlike the public sector, where the level of expenditure is often taken as a sign of one's commitment, the private sector seeks to maximize results from a minimal use of resources. These advantages have only grown stronger with the advent of globalization. An increasingly interconnected world enhances the private sector's interest in peace, since a disturbance in one part of the world can lead to ripple effects that influence events thousands of miles away.

The private sector has a role in peace processes in myriad ways. The process of peace is complex and multi-staged, from peacemaking to peace-keeping and enforcement to peacebuilding. To varying degrees of effectiveness, the private sector has an important part to play at almost every stage. Moreover, at each step, the rise of globalization and the shift in the nature of war only serves to increase the private sector's influence.

In speaking of privatizing peace, we suggest injecting the private sector in all UN and other multilateral peacemaking, peacekeeping, peace-enforcement, and peacebuilding efforts. The anticipated result is greater clarity of mission, better articulation of performance objectives, and the delineation of measures for judging results in an open, transparent and accountable framework.[2]

Before further investigating the relative advantages of privatizing many of the functions in war-to-peace transitions traditionally left to the exclusive province of governments or international organizations, it is useful to first examine the impact of war on the business of doing business in war-torn societies: on investment, risk management, and corporate strategic decision-making.

---

[2]   *Privatization: Lessons Learned by State and Local Governments*, United States General Accounting Office, Washington, D.C., March 1997; *Privatization: Principles and Practice*, Lessons of Experience Series, International Finance Corporation, World Bank Group, Washington, D.C., September 1995.

Chapter 4

INVESTING IN WAR-TORN SOCIETIES: NOT BUSINESS AS USUAL

The Impact of War on Foreign Direct Investment

It is axiomatic that war impacts a country's economy by creating a drop in private investment, both domestic and foreign.[1] To stop the downhill spiral, once a cease-fire or its equivalent has been obtained, and reverse the trend requires the active participation of a number of actors concerned with the economic and social redevelopment. Among these, the local and foreign private sector is increasingly recognized as pivotal. A December 2000 report from the Washington-based Institute for Policy Studies, "Top 200: The Rise of Corporate Global Power," reports that of the world's 100 largest economic entities, 51 are corporations and only 49 are countries, and that the combined total sales of the world's 200 largest corporations constitutes more than a quarter of the world's total economic activity. As official development assistance (ODA) continues to decline, especially in war-torn countries, foreign direct investment becomes an increasingly important source of external funding for development.

The level of official development assistance and official aid has been declining in absolute terms since the beginning of the 1990s. Between 1991 and 1998 ODA decreased by 23%. Conversely, between 1990 and 1998, the world foreign direct investment flows grew by 220% in mon-

---

[1]   F. Stewart, F. Humphreys and N. Lea, "Civil Conflict in Developing Countries Over the Last Quarter of a Century: An Empirical Overview of Economic and Social Consequences," *Oxford Development Studies*, Vol. 25, No. 1, 1997, p. 20.

FDI/ODA to developing countries

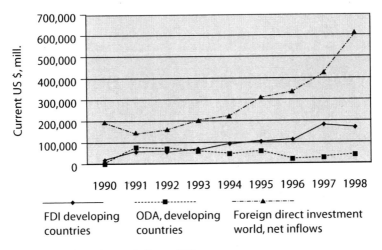

Source: World Bank, World Development Indicators, 1999

etary value.[2] In developing countries, this growth was more dramatic: in a decade FDI inflows increased in absolute terms by 532%, reaching a level of approximately $155 billion in 1998. As a percentage of world FDI inflows, the developing countries' share grew from 12% in 1990 to a peak of 37% in 1997. In 1998 and 1999, this percentage decreased to about 25% of worldwide FDI.

The bulk of FDI are still concentrated in developed countries. Not only are FDI unevenly distributed between developed and developing countries, they also are distributed unevenly among developing countries. For instance, the five largest host countries over the past decade—China, Brazil, Mexico, Singapore and Indonesia—accounted for 55% of FDI inflows to all developing countries in 1998.[3]

While these figures for developing countries as a percentage of total global FDI portray a gloomy downward trend, in the aggregate foreign investment in the world's poorest countries has actually steadily risen

---

[2]   This and subsequent statistics—unless otherwise indicated—come from the World Bank, *World Development Indicators*, Washington DC: World Bank, 1999. The data on FDI in 1999 are based on the UNCTAD World Investment Report 2000. World Bank and UNCTAD data in some cases differ. For example, FDI world inflows in 1998 are $619 million for the World Bank and $680 million for UNCTAD; in the same year, the World Bank estimates an inflow of $154 million to developing countries, and UNCTAD of $179 million. UNCTAD estimates for 1999 are: $865 million world inflows and $207 million inflows to developing countries.

[3]   United Nations, *World Investment Report 1999*, New York: UNCTAD, p. 19.

over the past decade, from an annual average of under $1 billion in 1987–92 to nearly $3 billion in 1998, according to UNCTAD. Although the bulk of this investment is in countries seeking the wealth under the soil, so to speak, from oil to diamonds, gold and copper, a new trend in the "soft side" shows electronics and communications on the rise. Microsoft's business in Africa is growing by about 30% per annum, and Ericsson and Nokia mobile phones are hugely popular where one cannot hope to get a phone line for years.

Regional FDI Trends in Select War-torn Areas

Africa

Twenty of the forty-four countries in Sub-Saharan Africa are either in war or recently emerging from war. Not surprisingly, it is the region that receives the lowest FDI inflows, accounting in 1998 for less than 2% of global FDI inflows. In the 60s and 70s, investments in resource extraction made Africa the second largest host region for FDI to developing countries. Since the 80s, the presence of conflict and political instability in a number of countries contributed to shape investors' perceptions of Africa as a particularly risky region. In the past decade, it has never accounted for more than 5% of inflows to developing countries. In 1997, the region's record inflow of $7.7 billion represented only 17% of the inflows to China alone in the same year.

Regional distribution of FDI inflows to developing countries (1998)

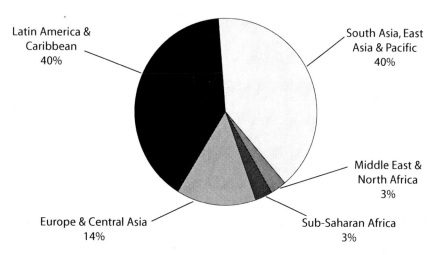

Latin America & Caribbean 40%

South Asia, East Asia & Pacific 40%

Middle East & North Africa 3%

Europe & Central Asia 14%

Sub-Saharan Africa 3%

Source: World Bank, World Development Indicators, 1999

Sub-Saharan Africa is also the region with the highest incidence of major armed conflicts in recent years. In 1998 and 1999, 11 conflicts took place in Africa, 10 of which were in Sub-Saharan Africa. Following a decline in conflicts between 1992 and 1996, this represents a negative development which brings the continent back to the 1990 and 1991 levels—the previous peak years for the decade—and reverses the trend that culminated in 1997, when a decrease in the number of conflicts was matched by a record FDI inflow.

Conflicts and FDI in Africa

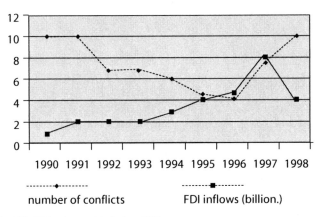

Source: World Bank, World Development Indicators, 1999

Some African countries that experienced conflict in the past seem to have recovered from it and now represent attractive locations for investors, Mozambique and South Africa in particular. Angola is noteworthy, as it was the main FDI recipient in the region in 1999, although it must be noted that the FDI almost exclusively concern off-shore oil extraction. The renewed FDI inflows experienced in the 90s is concentrated in a handful of countries, partly due to the fact that foreign investment in Sub-Saharan Africa continues to be mostly resource-based. Most African countries that have experienced a major armed conflict in the past five years receive low FDI inflows. Of the 20 bottom FDI recipients in the region in 1998, 10 are countries that suffered a major armed conflict in the last 5 years.[4]

---

[4]   UNCTAD data differ from the World Bank's—in particular, Gabon is one of the top 10 countries. Yet they show a similar pattern: of the bottom 20 countries, 9 underwent a major armed conflict in the past 5 years.

FDI inflows, bottom 20 recipients, 1998

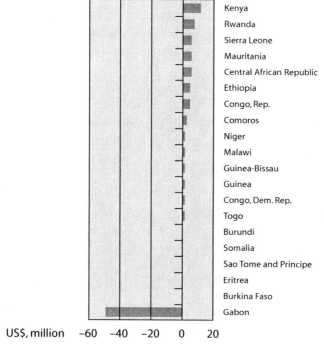

| US$, million | −60 | −40 | −20 | 0 | 20 |

Source: World Bank, World Development Indicators, 1999

Overall FDI in absolute terms has actually risen over the last decade from $834 million in 1990 to $4.39 billion in 1998. However, as an aggregate, the war-torn countries of Burundi, the Republic of Congo, the Congo Democratic Republic, Guinea-Bissau, Rwanda, Sierra Leone, Somalia, Sudan, Liberia, Eritrea, and Ethiopia never represented more than 2% of total inflows to Sub-Saharan Africa between 1991 and 1997. Their share rose to 9% in 1998, mainly due to a marked rise in inflows to Sudan (371 million in that year).

Europe and Central Asia

The European and Central Asian region experienced an upward trend in the incidence of conflict at the beginning of the 90s, from two major conflicts in 1989 to 5 in 1993 (Azerbaijan, Bosnia and Herzegovina, Georgia, Tajikistan and Croatia). Data for those countries are not available before 1993; later available data show that the FDI flows to the conflict-affected countries are below the regional average, with the exception of oil-rich Azerbaijan. As a percentage of aggregate FDI flows to Europe and Central Asia, inflows to those countries represent never more than 9 percent between 1994 and 1998, and never more than 5 percent if Azerbaijan is excluded.

Although the conflicts in Tajikistan and Georgia reached a settlement in 1994 and the one in Bosnia and Herzegovina in 1995, they remain among the bottom five countries in Europe and Central Asia with regard to FDI inflows. Bosnia and Herzegovina in particular is the country that receives the lowest inflows in the region.[5] Among the bottom ten countries are also Albania and Macedonia, which have been directly affected by the regional conflict in South East Europe.[6] Croatia and Azerbaijan are among the top ten recipients of FDI. However, in the case of Azerbaijan, its consistent inflows target the oil sector, and mainly through a single consortium;[7] the country has the third-lowest GDP per capita in the region.

Bosnia and Herzegovina is a particularly illustrative example of the failures and obstacles to peacebuilding and foreign investment. With

FDI inflows, bottom ten recipients, 1998

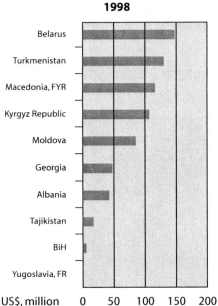

Source: World Bank, World Development Indicators, 1999

---

[5]   UNCTAD, *World Investment Report 2000.*

[6]   Data is not available for Former Yugoslavia.

[7]   Azerbaijan International Operating Company, see *EIU Country Report,* July 2000, p. 22.

over $5.1 billion in post-war reconstruction assistance, BiH was still unable (and perhaps unwilling politically) to make the necessary structural changes to transition from the State-controlled economic policies of the former Communist system to privatization of state assets, liberal markets, and a generally more open economy. Interviews with businessmen in a survey conducted by the World Bank showed major concerns over the inadequacy of the banking system, the onerous transaction costs of state payment bureaus and business licensing and registration regulations in each of the three entities, high tax rates, corruption, porous borders and a non-functioning judiciary. The Dayton Peace Accord was premised on the return of some 1.2 million refugees to reasonable job opportunities generated by private investment, and a stable tax base to run government services, all under the umbrella of a NATO-supported environment of military and political security. Such a stable environment was intended to set the conditions to attract both domestic and foreign private investment. Unfortunately none of this happened, with private investment in the early years of peace being about $160 million or the equivalent of less than 5% of total donor aid. With business licenses taking anywhere from 6–9 months to obtain, a multi-layered set of inspections making bribes a necessity to get anything done, illegal taxes at every turn, a separate payments bureau that virtually held a monopoly on capital flows for each entity, and lack of protection of property rights and other necessary commercial laws, it is no wonder that the business environment for investors was perceived as being especially inhospitable.[8]

An important lesson to draw in the BiH experience is that wars can be opportune situations to rethink and reform the role of the State by getting it out of productivity per se, and releasing physical, financial, social and human capital to better perform public functions of education, health, infrastructure and security; and to manage rather than control the economy by efficiently and effectively regulating emerging private markets, investing in human and institutional resources required for improved productivity and competitiveness in the increasingly global economy, and putting in place the governance institutions of law and justice.

---

[8] See "Why No One Will Invest in Bosnia and Herzegovina: An Overview of Impediments to Investments and Self-Sustaining Economic Growth in the Post Dayton Era," International Crisis Group, April 21, 1999, pp. 1–25. Also see *Report on New Foundations: Private Sector Development in Post-War Bosnia and Herzegovina*, Washington, D.C.: The World Bank, February 1997, pp. 1–45.

South, East and South East Asia

Out of 24 countries in this region, four countries that suffered from conflict in the last decade figure among the bottom ten recipients of FDI in 1998: Cambodia, Sri Lanka, Myanmar, and Indonesia (data for Afghanistan is not available). For example, in Indonesia in 1999 the mining industry contributed nearly $1.5 billion to Indonesia's economy. Export revenues worth $3.3 billion represented more than 11% of total exports that year. But the advent of violent ethnic conflict in far-flung mineral-rich areas from Aceh to the northern Moluccas and Irian Jaya, coupled with the uncertain transaction costs of a new layer of potential rent seekers accompanying the governments new decentralization plans (under the new law about 90% of mining royalties is supposed to go to the provinces and the local districts), does not bode well for future investment. According to PriceWaterhouse Coopers, more than 150 exploration projects in Indonesia have been suspended or withdrawn or are inactive. Meanwhile, exploration investment has fallen from a high of $345 million in 1997 to $165 million in 1999. Downstream companies which provide services for drilling and laboratory testing are already feeling the effects.[9]

FDI inflows, bottom 10 recipients, 1998

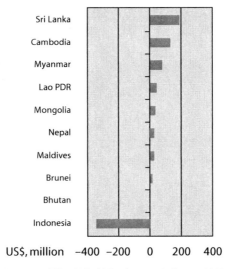

US$, million   −400   −200   0   200   400

Source: World Bank, World Development Indicators, 1999

---

[9]   Sadanand Shume, "Indonesia: Poor Prospects for Digging," *The Far Eastern Economic Review*, February 8, 2001, pp. 24–25.

While foreign direct investment is not a traditional tool of peace-making, it could serve that purpose. It could thus reverse the negative perception that still prevails in many quarters that most multinationals stand to profit more from war than peace. Today, profitability and security remain, of course, the key determinants of corporate entry into trouble spots; but accomplishing positive social and economic change while making a profit has become a factor in foreign direct investment decision-making.

The Determinants of FDI

It is not easy to discern to what degree low FDI inflows are directly related to present or past conflicts. A host country's attractiveness to FDI is determined by several factors, economic and political. According to one theory, the motivation for firms to undertake direct investment is that the host country offers a location advantage[10] that makes it profitable to invest there rather than simply produce at home (or somewhere else). Location advantages include not only resource endowments but also economic and social factors such as market size and structure; prospects for market growth and degree of development; the cultural, legal, political and institutional environment; and government legislation and policies. Three characteristics of the allocation of FDI are particularly noteworthy:

1)   Attractiveness to FDI is competitive, and developing countries are now more and more participating in the "location tournaments"—policy adjustments, promotional campaigns and incentive programs designed to attract investment by multinational corporations.[11]
2)   A country's comparative advantage is dynamic; it changes over time in the process of economic development, depending on its performance in physical and human capital accumulation.
3)   Finally, FDI has a self-reinforcing impact (catalytic effect) that can operate through a variety of channels, including promotion

---

[10]   Dunning J., *Multinational Enterprises and the Global Economy*. Workingham, England: Addison Wesley, 1993.

[11]   D. Wheeler and A. Mody, "International Investment Location Decision: The Case of US Firms," *Journal of International Economics* 33, 1992, p. 57.

of specialized inputs (trained labor, marketing and distribution services), reputational effects, etc.[12]

Although the countries mentioned above do not represent an exhaustive list of countries that have suffered from conflict, they have all undergone a "major armed conflict" as defined in the SIPRI Yearbook: "The use of armed force between the military forces of 2 or more governments, or of one government and at least one organized armed group, resulting in the battle-related deaths of at least 1000 people in any single year and in which the incompatibility concerns control of government and/or territory."[13] Such classification allows us to consider only conflicts that reach a high level of violence.

The impact of war differs depending upon the nature, intensity and duration of conflict. Nevertheless it can be assumed that the impact of conflict is more severe when it is protracted and geographically pervasive, and where the government loses its capacity to collect taxes and provide basic services. Where "quasi-government" structures are able to maintain core functions, the costs may be limited to a certain extent. International wars tend to have less harmful effects than internal conflict (in the former case, states often strive to maintain social services as a part of the war effort).[14] With regards to the latter point, all but two of the violent conflicts in 1999 were internal.

From the above figures, it emerges that conflict-affected countries—to a different degree depending on the characteristics of the conflict and generally with the exception of countries that possess significant natural resources—receive a smaller share of world investment inflows. For most investors, doing business in a country with an ongoing conflict or undergoing a transition from war to peace can represent a daunting challenge regarding the structure of investment and the management of risk. Conflict has two types of effects on FDI: *indirect impacts*, inasmuch as conflict-affected countries are prevented from developing the characteristics to be competitive in the emerging global economy; and *direct impacts*, as conflict and political instability discourage investors by signaling that there is a higher risk of experiencing direct losses.

---

[12]   *Ibid.*, p. 64.
[13]   Stewart, Francis, "War and Underdevelopment: Can Economic Analysis Help Reduce the Costs?" *Journal of International Development*, Vol. 5, No. 4, 1993, pp. 357–380.
[14]   F. Stewart, F. Humphreys and N. Lea, *supra* note 36, p. 20.

However, some "brave firms" seek profits where other fear to tread. In the 1960s and 70s nationalization and expropriation were the biggest fears as emerging nations acted to finance their new-found independence. Anglo-American lost copper mines in Zambia; BP and Exxon lost oil fields in Iran and Venezuela; and in Uganda, the entire Asian Indian population saw their years of economic sweat swept away by Idi Amin.

Meanwhile, the absence of the rule of law, combined with iron-fisted authoritarian regimes, also served to entice investors to partner with dictators from Indonesia to Zaire to Nigeria, largely in the mineral extraction sector. Corruption, crime and bad policies, as well as war exacted their toll on foreign investors. A survey of 121 European and American firms last year by Control Risks Group (CRG), a security consultant firm, found that two-fifths of investors had held back from an otherwise attractive foreign investment because of perceived corruption.[15]

Corruption and War Scare Off Foreign Investment in Philippines

The government of the newly elected President, Mrs. Gloria Macapagal-Arroyo, has come under increasing pressure from business associations, lawmakers and government watchdog groups to bring the former President, Mr. Joseph Estrada, and his associates to justice. Analysts say that fears of more bomb blasts and other forms of protest have created uncertainty and further dampened hopes of luring back foreign investors. The executive secretary to Mr. Estrada, Mr. Edgardo Angara, said that the year 2000 was one of the worst in the Philippines' history due to a series of manmade and natural disasters. The Philippines' total national debt, including foreign and domestic borrowing, grew by nearly 40 billion pesos to 2,009 trillion pesos in August 2000. Businesses are also suffering. The insecurity in the Philippines has scared away foreign investors. Local companies had to cancel expansion plans and many wealthy Filipinos have transferred their money to different countries. The governor of the Philippine Central Bank, Mr. Rafael Buenaventura, believes that as soon as the peso bounces back to 47 pesos to the dollar and is stabilized, the country will win back the confidence of portfolio investors. Mr. Buenaventura added: "Maybe they'll start coming back now that the Nasdaq has cooled off in the United States."

References: Landler, Mark. "Officials Call Market Down But Not Out In the Philippines." *The New York Times*, Friday, January 19, 2001, p. A10; Sims, Calvin. "Ousted President Is Barred From Leaving Philippines." *The New York Times*, Wednesday, January 24, 2001.

---

[15]   "Risky Returns," *The Economist*, May 20, 2000, pp. 1–6.

The US government lists 74 countries in which physical security is a problem, of which 34 are in civil war. In such places a high cost of doing business is the provision of security. Oil firms in Algeria are reputed to spend as much as 8–9% of their budgets on security. In Colombia the figure is roughly 4–6%.[16]

With the arrival of NGO watchdogs from Global Witness to the Environmental Defense Fund, reputational risks have begun to be taken more seriously by large multinationals, be they Shell in the Nigeria Delta area, or De Beers in Sierra Leone, Angola and the Congo.

Shell in the Niger Delta: Mitigating a "Paradox of Securities"

The Nigerian government sees oil production—which averaged 2.14 million barrels per day in 2000—as essential to Nigerian security.[17] Nigeria's resources make Nigeria the sixth-largest crude oil producer in OPEC (Organization of the Petroleum Exporting Countries) and the fifth-largest supplier of crude oil to the US, and account for 80% of Nigeria's federal revenue, 90–95% of export revenues, and over 90% of foreign exchange earnings.[18] However, the majority of Nigerians rely on pastoral and agricultural economies. According to Dr. Okechukwu Ibeanu, Professor of Political Science at the University of Nigeria, this "paradox of securities" has come into direct conflict with providing communal security for its citizens.[19]

In the 1990s, the Royal Dutch Shell Group received much media attention when it was implicated in supporting the repressive Abuja government regime and causing environmental damage in the fragile ecosystem of the Delta. The Ogoni people of the Delta organized the Movement for the Survival of the Ogoni People (MOSOP), founded and led by Ken Saro-Wiwa. MOSOP sought self-determination, control of the oil resources beneath their land, and compensation for Shell's alleged resource-degrading operations. Following the government arrest of MOSOP supporters during nonviolent protests and the controversial death of Saro-Wiwa November 10, 1995, Shell's activities in the region were highlighted worldwide. Shell's subsequent activity shows how the private sector can insure itself against such security threats and still operate in alliance with both the state and civil society.

---

16   *Ibid.*
17   "Nigeria," April 2001 Report, Energy Information Administration, US Department of Energy. http://www.eia.doe.gov/emeu/cabs/nigeria.html.
18   *Ibid.*
19   Ibeanu, Okechukwu, "Oiling the Friction: Environmental Conflict Management in the Niger Delta, Nigeria," *PECS News*, The Woodrow Wilson Center, Vol. 2, Issue 1, Spring 2000.

Shell responded by offering forums for dialogue, environmental protection, transparency via the Internet and published public reports, and sustainable development projects alongside oil excavation. The *Shell Report 2000* carries a pledge from its chairman, Mark Moody-Stuart, that Shell will continue to pursue a business strategy that "generates profits while contributing to the well-being of the planet and its people." In that spirit, Shell has worked with KPMG and PriceWaterhouseCoopers to verify health and safety of workers, to monitor environmental attention, and to develop an ethical code of conduct for its workers. Still, Shell continues to face the task of mitigating such a security paradox, and balancing the interests of local civil society and the NGO community with government and shareholder demands for increased productivity.

In a letter to London-based advocacy group Global Witness, BP Amoco has promised to publish details of its annual net production and payments to Sanagol, the Angolan State oil company, as well as its levies and taxes paid to the Angolan government. Drawing the implicit connection between profits from natural resource, arms expenditures and the perpetuation of conflict, NGOs have been bringing increased pressure on such large oil companies as Exxon, Mobil, BP Amoco, Shell and Chevron to publish their various payments. Arms and corruption scandals have also recently emerged in France surrounding the state oil company ELF Aquitaine and its linkages to arms purchases in Angola.

In January KPMG, an international consulting firm, carried out a diagnostic study of Angola's secretive oil sector under auspices of the IMF-monitored economic reform program. This is viewed as the best channel to create transparency and help resolve the long-running conflict between Jonas Savimbi's UNITA resistance and the Government.[20]

Transnational corporations are seeking numerous ways to survive in uncertain investment environments, ranging from better risk insurance and subcontracting arrangements to working more closely with surrounding communities to generate employment and the spread of profits locally, to donating goods and services to meet the needs of medicine and food. Managing political risk, through innovative and comprehensive measures, along with management of traditional economic and financial risks, thus, is increasingly becoming a normal part of the corporate business cycle for businesses engaged abroad.

---

[20]   Nicholas Shaxson, "BP to Give Details of Angola Oil Operations," *Financial Times*, February 12, 2001, p. 29.

Chapter 5

THE MANAGEMENT OF POLITICAL RISK

In 1992 a World Bank survey of foreign investors identified the following obstacles to investment: (i) market access; (ii) levels of technology and skills to make productivity cost effective; (iii) degree over control, particularly owner rights and foreign exchange; (iv) clarity and transparency of laws and regulations; (v) attitudes toward foreign investment in terms of institutions; and finally (vi) degree of political stability.[1] Political risk is a particular concern in war-ravaged environments. Political risk analysis is directed at locating the sources and projecting the probability of politically determined losses for an investment in the future. Once political risk has been identified and assessed, risk management strategies can be enacted to avoid or mitigate the losses for a specific project in a specific context. Such strategies normally take the form of differential structuring of investments and availing of some form of risk insurance guarantees.

The field of political risk assessment and management has over the past decades. The analytical and organizational tools to deal with political risks, in fact, are driven by the evolving nature of the risks faced by foreign investors on the ground. In the 60s and 70s, the most common risks were confiscation, expropriation and nationalization; yet, while in 1975 there were 83 cases of expropriation, from 1981 to 1992 there were no more than 11 such cases.[2] By the end of the 70s, inconvertibility became the main risk, as newly independent states emerged and struggled with their lack of capital and with their own efforts at nation-build-

---

[1]   Also see Report on New Foundations: Private Sector Development in Post-War Bosnia and Herzegovina. Washington, D.C.: The World Bank, February 1997, pp. 1–45.

[2]   *Ibid*, p. 8.

ing. The end of the Cold War order brought to the fore the traditional risk of war and civil disturbance. Since 1991 the majority of claims paid by political insurers have been for damage due to civil strife; in most cases, strife derived from ethnic divisions.[3]

Every foreign direct investment project faces a variety of risks, some specific to its sector, others to its country and policy environment and others that are of a more general nature. A typical project faces both commercial and political risks. *Commercial risks* consist of (a) project specific risks connected with developing and constructing the project, operating and maintaining the assets, and finding a market for the output; (b) broader economic environment risks related to the interest rate changes, inflation, currency risk, international price movements of raw materials, and energy inputs, all of which have a direct impact on the project but are beyond the control of the investors.[4]

Along with financial and economic factors, domestic politics of the host country play an important role in the decision-making process of foreign investors. The critical interface between the world of politics and that of economics is represented by political risk. *Political risk* can be defined, very simply, as the possibility that political decisions, events or conditions in a country, including those that might be referred to as social, will affect the business climate in such a way that investors will lose money or they will not make as much money as they expected when the investment was made.

While commercial risk is clear, there is still no unanimity as to what constitutes political risk and how to measure it. Examples of political risk range from the risk that a government will impose a quota of national employees on the investor, to the risk that it will fail in paying for a shipment of goods, to the risk of damage to the investment facilities as a consequence of war. The distinction between political and other types of risk is often ambiguous in practice. The best way to differentiate types of risk is by analyzing the cause. A risk is political when it relates to a potential government act (law, decree, regulation, administrative decision, etc., either in the host or home country of the investors) or to general instability in the political/social system (war, strife, frequent changes in government, etc.).[5]

---

3   L.D. Howell, ed., *The Handbook of Country and Political Risk Analysis*. The PRS Group, 1998, p. 8.

4   IFC, *Project Finance in Developing Countries*, 1999.

5   G.T. West, "Managing Project Political Risk: The Role of Investment Insurance," *The Journal of Project Finance*, Winter 1996.

What these risk assessment scenarios in war-torn societies have in common is that political actions are the root of the problem. A classification of which losses count as political (or social) can be based on the categories of political risk covered by the main public insurance agencies:[6] a) *inconvertibility*; b) *expropriation*; c) *war damage*; d) *civil strife damage*; and e) *breach of contract*.

A number of commercial and academic political risk forecasting models are available today. Their underlying assumption is that every type of loss has one or more predictor (or indicators) in the social, political or international field that can brief the investors on the likelihood of its occurrence. Once such indicators are defined, it can be determined which variable or which combination of variables are likely to result in a loss. For example, if ethnic tension in a country is high and rising, the occurrence of civil strife—and consequently the potential damage to facilities or production—can be projected. Therefore, according to a simple model, the variable ethnic fractionalization—alone or in combination with other variables, e.g., authoritarian government—is likely to bring about civil strife, which in turn is likely to cause a loss for the investor.

Indonesia's Angry Farmers Scare Off Mining Investors

In 1998, following the Asian financial crisis and the fall of the former authoritarian president Soeharto, a chain of protests and demonstrations were staged by local residents, mostly farmers, against the oil and gas multinational companies operating in Indonesia. Mining firms have had numerous conflicts with local communities and administrations over tax, land, environmental and human rights issues. This has led to a drop in the mining exploration activities in Indonesia. Even the largest oil producer, PT Caltex Pacific Indonesia, has had a decline in its output due to fire of its four oil wells set by protesting farmers.

The protesters were demanding higher compensation payments for their farm land that had been acquired at low cost by Caltex during the Soeharto era. According to Caltex spokesman Poedio Oetomo, Caltex denied better compensation because the farmers "had failed to forward authentic documents of their claims." Caltex, a joint venture between U.S. oil companies Chevron Corp. and Texaco Inc., with 750,000 barrels per day makes up 80% of Indonesia's total oil production. However, because of the possible decline in its oil output due to violent conflicts with the local communities, "Caltex might not be able to help Indonesia meet its OPEC quota."

---

6   See L.D. Howell, ed., *supra* note 58, p. 4.

Indonesia's Minister of Energy and Mineral Resources, Purnomo Yusgiantoro, put all contracts for gas and oil extraction and mining on hold until January 1, 2001. After this date the country's regions were officially given autonomy and foreign and local mining companies were invited to sign new mining contracts with regional governments. Presumably relations will improve between oil producers and local farmers when the farmers' concerns are taken into account.

Reference: *The Jakarta Post*, December 2000

On the other hand, recent research by Paul Collier at the World Bank indicates, that contrary to conventional wisdom, ethnic fractionalization is not the leading correlate of violent conflict, but ranks below the availability of readily tradeable primary commodities and levels of unemployed youth. Like any business endeavor, a ready stock of cheap labor combined with the consistent ability to meet a payroll, mixed with a modicum of effective leadership and management, can readily constitute the means for financing a rebellion or civil war. He notes: "Civil wars are far more likely to be caused by economic opportunities than by grievance, and therefore certain rebel groups benefit from the conflict and have a very strong interest in initiating and sustaining it . . . such wars from Sierra Leone to Colombia create profitable opportunities for a minority of people at the same time as they destroy them for the majority.[7] Indeed, rebel groups such as the RUF in Sierra Leone, UNITA in Angola, and the FARC and ELN in Colombia stand to benefit greatly from tactics which aggravate corporate risk. Scaring away competition provides rebel forces with *de facto* monopoly power over various industries, especially those concerned with mining and extraction of natural resources.

There is little need here to further examine the construction of country risk indicators, since this has been done extensively in the recent professional literature.[8] It is important to emphasize, however, that "country risk ratings" offered by various publications and consulting

---

[7]   Paul Collier, *Economic Causes of Civil Conflict and Their Implication for Policy.* Washington, D.C.: The World Bank, June 2000. Also see *Conflict Diamonds*, a Report by Louis Gorux, World Bank, November 2000; and "Congo—In the Heart of Darkness," *The Economist*, December 2000.

[8]   See in particular L.D. Howell and B. Chaddick, "An Assessment of Three Approaches," *The Columbia Journal of World Business*, Vol. 19, No. 3, 1994.

companies have a limited practical value in investment decisions relative to project risk. Risk, in fact, is not a quality inherent to a country, a government or an environment; it is "a property associated with an individual investor and a prospective investment."[9]

Different industries have different susceptibilities to political risk, and will be affected in different ways by certain actions or conditions. For example, nationalization/ expropriation is more likely to concern the extractive, utility or financial service sector of an economy than the manufacturing sector. A company relying on imports will suffer more from trade restrictions than an import-competing firm. The investment location is another important factor, particularly in relation to the trend towards decentralization as the new model for developing countries, and the consequent increasing authority of regional and municipal governments. The investor attributes (like nationality, religion, ethnicity, culture) and the time frame of the investment are also important factors that influence the intensity of risk.

Business Strategies for Managing Risk

Political risk is an important factor in business decisions. Yet many companies still seem to adopt a loose definition of political risk, and often they equate political risk with "political instability." As a result, investors tend not to get involved in countries, or entire regions, where they perceive a high degree of political instability. In avoiding countries considered to be politically unstable, one overlooks, however, the potentially high returns available and the extent to which a firm can control and reduce risks where it is an inherently large enterprise relative to the scale of the country in which it is operating.

In the pre-investment planning phase, a company can enact several strategies to mitigate forecasted risks. The structure of the investment, in fact, is not independent from risk but it will in large measure determine its susceptibility to changing government policies and other political events.[10] Once the company has analyzed the political environment of a country and assessed the consequences of a projected investment, it can structure the investment so as to minimize the consequence of risk on its profitability. Risk mitigation strategies at this stage include:

---

[9]   G.T. West, *op. cit.*, 1996, p. 6.
[10]   A.C. Shapiro, "Managing Political Risk: An Approach," *The Columbia Journal of World Business*, Vol. 16, No. 3, Fall 1981.

a) *Avoidance,* when the degree of risk that firms are willing to bear is not matched by the expected returns on investment.

b) *Negotiating* with the host governments, generally in the form of seeking special rights or *concession agreements.*

c) *Transfer of risk* by sharing of equity ownership of a prospective investment with other foreign investors, project financiers, and local interests in the country, for example through joint ventures or by bringing nationals into management. In this respect, purely financial considerations might sometimes become secondary to political considerations, as partners—in particular local partners—will be chosen on the basis of their political "clout."[11]

d) *Risk minimization* through a range of techniques, to either reduce the amount of assets at risk or to minimize the incidence of a loss. Techniques to minimize losses include 1) keeping local affiliates dependent on sister companies for markets and/or supplies (vertical integration), 2) concentrating research and development facilities in the home country, 3) establishing a single global trademark, 4) controlling transportation, and 5) sourcing production in multiple plants.

e) *Loss prevention* through the enactment of various public and community relations programs.[12] Developing local stakeholders (consumers, suppliers, local employees, local bankers, etc.) provides protection from adverse government actions.

f) *Insurance* to transfer risk to a third party, the insurance agency. Political risk insurance (PRI) is perhaps the most common form of risk management, although its role is often underestimated due to its character of secrecy, whereby private insurers and most national ones have a legal basis for denying payment of a claim if the existence of a policy is made public.

Coca-Cola Returns to Angola:
The Cycle of Investment, Divestment and Reinvestment

Another option for reducing business risk is divestment, as for example Coca-Cola's decision to pull out of Angola in 1975 when the country faced the beginning of today's ongoing civil war. When does, or should, a company retract investment and/or return to invest?

---

11   G.T. West , *op. cit.,* 1996, p. 7.
12   *Ibid.,* p. 8.

> The ramifications of in-and-out investment can be similar to development projects of recent decades that resulted in short-term assistance and minimal capacity-building. Divestment from a region leaves a hole in the economy, perpetuates instability, and depletes resources that might lead to a conflict's resolution. On the other hand, in the case of several corporations in Myanmar (formerly Burma), their divestment has been condemned in many quarters for its impact on strengthening the nation's repressive military regime. American foreign investment in Myanmar was banned by the US in 1997, and the European Union and International Labor Organization have imposed sanctions against multinationals investing in the region.
>
> Coca-Cola re-entered Angola 26 years after having pulled out in 1975. It has undertaken the construction of a $33 million plant along the banks of the Cuanza River. Despite poor infrastructure, a curfew that mandates employee schedules, rebel ambushes and the presence of land mines, Coca-cola aims to prove—along with operating oil and mining companies—that investment can be profitable in this war-torn region. It employs an anti-corruption code of conduct, refusing to pay bribes, and calls upon government guards for security. The company has also determined to work with the IMF on economic reform in Angola, and has begun extensive worker training programs to empower populations at risk.
>
> As Coca-Cola has demonstrated in Angola, risk management entails not only determining when and how to enter into risky environments, but also knowing when to exit and how to re-enter.
>
> Cauvin, Henri E. "Braving War and Graft, Coke Goes Back to Angola," *The New York Times*, April 22, 2001

Political Risk Insurance—How Does it Work?

Insuring business against political risk is not a new endeavor for investors engaged in unfamiliar environments. Yet the dramatic rise of foreign direct investment into development countries has led to a "renaissance"[13] in the field in the past few years. PRI offers several benefits to the investors. Besides the traditional rationale of providing compensation for a possible loss, purchasing insurance is an active way to deter and prevent losses. Insurers, in particular those linked to one or more governments, play an important (though not much publicized) role in the settlement of investment disputes and claims, so that potential claims are often resolved before any loss occurs. The presence of insurance can

---

[13] *Ibid.*

also allow a project developer to assemble financing for a project that appears to face insurmountable political problems.[14] This is particularly the case for large projects in the infrastructure sector, where obtaining long-term debt financing in the presence of a high level of risk is often very difficult. However, political risk insurance can be prohibitively expensive, especially for smaller businesses. Yet, properly supplied at affordable rates, political risk insurance carries the promise of involving the private sector in responsible humanitarian relief and peace consolidation efforts.

The political risk insurance market is rapidly evolving, and investors can choose among a variety of players and services. Today, the three types of insurers available for foreign direct investment are multilateral entities, national agencies, and private sector underwriters. The services that the different insurers offer are becoming increasingly homogeneous, as the market is becoming more competitive. In particular, private insurers are dramatically improving the nature of their offers.[15] Traditionally, long-term coverage of investments has been the exclusive domain of public sector underwriters, whose coverage was provided for up to 20 years. However, the rapid evolution of the field in recent years, and above all the emergence of a stronger reinsurance market, has led many private insurers to extend their traditionally limited coverage period—before 1995, more than 3 years was an exception, now it is common to obtain up to 10 years coverage—thus significantly eroding one of the comparative advantages of public versus private programs.

An important specific advantage of government-owned and multilateral agencies is that their guarantees are backed by their implied or explicit power of retaliation against host governments taking actions against foreign investors (although private insurers, in particular the American Insurance Group, the biggest private political risk insurer in the US, try to enhance their deterrent power by employing prominent personalities that can use their political connections in the event of a claim). Public sector underwriters, though, are not universally available, as they have eligibility restrictions as to national ownership or project attributes. They usually insure only national investors—in the case of MIGA, the World Bank's Multilateral Insurance Guarantee Agency, member states' nationals. Also, they insure only projects that conform

---

14   *Ibid.*, p. 5.
15   *Ibid.*

to their specific developmental mandate and environmental and social criteria (MIGA and OPIC, the Overseas Private Investment Corporation). In addition, unlike private insurers, they require the approval of the host country.

Differences between the private and public schemes are being eroded by the trend towards increased cooperation. In the words of G.T. West, senior advisor at MIGA: "If both groups were property insurers, it could be said that [private insurers] install lightning rods (i.e., provide services to mitigate the extend of a loss) and [public insurers] both install lightning rods and seek to influence the weather (i.e., to reduce the frequency of lightning strikes on the building)."[16] Furthermore, additional resources for extending coverage can be raised through reinsurance programs and, under MIGA's Cooperative Underwriting Program (CUP), private resources can now be backed by a public insurer's leverage. The result of such new developments is the increased availability and use of PRI, which represents a powerful instrument for promoting private-sector investment in countries at risk and therefore, potentially, an important tool of peacebuilding.

Political Risk Insurance as an Incentive for Peace

Aside from military and technological aid, the private sector also plays an important role in providing economic incentives for a peace agreement. A good excellent example of a public and private sector interface which can provide an incentive for peace involves political risk insurance. As discussed earlier, political risk has increased throughout emerging markets globally with negative effects on investments, both domestic and foreign. Public risk insurance mechanisms like MIGA at the World Bank and OPIC, the US government risk insurance agency, can partner with private investors to spread risk and encourage investment in areas which otherwise would not have the injections of foreign capital required to break a vicious cycle of conflict and to move on to a development track. The following overview of the activities of MIGA and OPIC indicate the myriad opportunities available to the private sector concerned with mitigating the risk of engagement in problematic areas.

---

[16]   *Ibid.*

The Multilateral Insurance Guarantee Association (MIGA)

The debt crises of the 1980s spurred the awareness in the development community (and in developing countries) that sustainable growth required the involvement of the private sector. Foreign private investment, in particular, represented an expandable resource that would not aggravate debt problems. The Multilateral Insurance Guarantee Association (MIGA) was created in 1988 to supplement the activities of the International Bank for Reconstruction and Development (IBRD), the International Finance Corporation (IFC), and other international financial institutions in promoting private sector development, specifically by supporting the role of foreign investors in economic development.

MIGA offers investment insurance against political risks such as transfer restriction, expropriation, breach of contract, and war and civil disturbance to investors (including state-owned corporations operating on a commercial basis) who are nationals of a member country[17] other than the country in which the investment is to be made. MIGA insurance is intended to complement the national and regional investment insurance agencies by filling the gaps in the policies that they offer: reinsuring or coinsuring other suppliers, insuring investment in countries restricted or excluded by the policies of other insurers, or providing types of coverage not offered by other insurers or on terms more favorable for the investors, so as to encourage them.[18]

As for eligible investments, MIGA can insure new investments, expansion, modernization, financial restructuring of existing projects, and acquisitions that involve the privatization of state enterprises. The forms of investment that can be insured include equity, shareholder loans, loan guarantees issued by equity investors, loans to unrelated borrowers in certain circumstances, and technical assistance, management and franchising and licensing agreements provided that they have terms of at least three years and that the investor's remuneration is tied to the project's operating results.

The peculiarity of MIGA with respect to the thriving market of political risk insurance is its developmental mandate: "To encourage the flow of investments for productive purposes among member countries, and in particular to developing countries" (art. 2 of the Convention). In the fiscal

---

[17]   Presently, MIGA's membership amounts to 149 countries, of which 127 are developing countries. Sixteen countries are in the process of fulfilling membership requirements.

[18]   MIGA, *The First Five Years and Future Challenges*, p. 4.

year 2000, it is estimated that MIGA facilitated FDI inflows amounting to $5.45 billion, approximately 2% of total flows to developing countries in that year. Since its creation, cumulative amount of FDI facilitated by MIGA through its political risk insurance has been estimated at $35.95 billion.

In order to be eligible for MIGA's guarantees, the prospective investment must contribute to the sustainable development of the host country. For this purpose, the Underwriting Authority must verify (i) the economic soundness of the project, (ii) the contribution to the development of the host country,[19] (iii) compliance with the host country's laws and regulations, and (iv) consistency with the declared development objectives and priorities of the host country.[20] Being an investment insurer and not an institution providing financing to a project, unlike the IFC or IBRD, MIGA has a limited leverage in changing the design or implementation of a project, although it can request modifications of the project in cases where environmental problems are involved. Therefore, it tends to either approve or deny coverage to the project as it is presented.

In fiscal year 2000, MIGA issued 53 new guarantees contracts in 26 developing countries, bringing the cumulative number of guarantees contracts issued to 473 in 75 developing countries, for a total issued coverage of $7.1 billion. Approximately 28% of the gross guarantees portfolio is in International Development Association (IDA) countries. The agency's capacity has rapidly expanded in its 10 years of operation. Helped by reinsurance treaties with the private market, it is now able to provide political risk insurance for up to $200 million per project and $620 million per host country.

It is important to note that MIGA is required to obtain host government consent to the issuance of a guarantee of investment. Accordingly, MIGA insurance is particularly suited to projects traditionally sensitive to changes in host government policies or commitments, by encouraging the fair treatment of the investors.[21] The original expectation was

---

[19]   The developmental impact of a project is assessed by looking at such factors as its potential to generate revenues for the host country; its contribution to maximizing the host country's productive potential and in particular producing exports or import substitutes and reducing the vulnerability to external economic changes; the extent to which the project will diversify economic activities, expand employment opportunities, and improve income distribution; the degree to which it will transfer knowledge and skills to the host country; and the effects of the investment project on the social infrastructure and environment of the host country.

[20]   MIGA Operational Regulations.

[21]   *Ibid.*

Distribution of the portfolio by sector (2000)

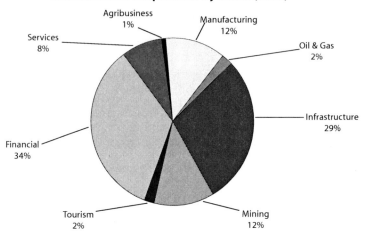

Source: MIGA, *Annual Report*, 2000

that MIGA would be particularly useful to foreign investors in electric power and other energy supply projects and in projects to privatize telecommunications. Now its portfolio includes several industrial sectors. Among them, infrastructure is the fastest growing sector.

The geographical diversification is not as developed as the sectoral. The largest portion of MIGA's guarantees is concentrated in Latin

Distribution of the portfolio by host region (1999)

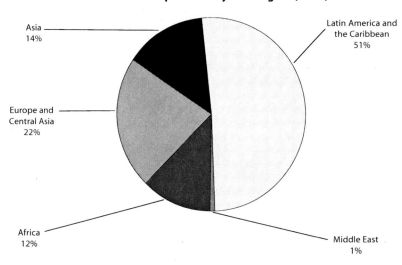

Source: MIGA, *Annual Report*, 2000

America and the Caribbean region, and three Latin American countries are the top three host countries in MIGA's portfolio: Brazil, Argentina and Peru, followed by Russia and Turkey.

Although MIGA has insured some projects in conflict-affected countries, only 11% of the contracts of guarantees issued (305 as of October 31, 2000) concern projects in 23 countries that have recently suffered from conflict or where a conflict is currently under way. MIGA's role in targeting conflict-affected countries is still limited, as it is demand-driven and thus only indirectly facilitates decisions to invest in conflict-affected countries.

A survey among MIGA clients show that for a majority of them (73% of the 57 firms surveyed in 1998) securing MIGA coverage was "absolutely critical" in the decision to proceed with a project. Another survey, among investors who applied for insurance in Bosnia and Herzegovina, shows that all nine respondents would not invest in the country without insurance. An important feature of MIGA's political insurance allows projects in risky locations to find sources of finance.

An indicator of the investment interest in conflict-affected countries is the number of Preliminary Applications (PAs) and Definitive Applications (DAs) that MIGA receives. Preliminary applications are filled before the investment is made or irrevocably committed, and they are the basis for MIGA's determination whether a project is eligible for coverage. If it is, the next stage requires the investors to fill a definitive application, which is the basis for the preparation of a Contract of Guarantees. Unlike the PA, the DA is subject to an application fee. A closer observation of PAs for Bosnia and Herzegovina shows that a majority of them are dropped, sometimes because of problems related to the situation in the country and sometimes because the investor simply does not pursue a project.

Below is a list of the PAs and DAs active as of October 2000 in some selected conflict-affected countries.

The Overseas Private Investment Corporation (OPIC)

OPIC's mission is "to mobilize and facilitate the participation of United States private capital and skills in the economic and social development of less developed countries and areas, and countries in transition from nonmarket to market economies, thereby complementing the development assistance objectives of the United States . . ." OPIC accomplishes its mission of promoting overseas investment and risk mitiga-

MIGA Application Status		
	Das	Pas
EUROPE/CENTRAL ASIA	45	412
Albania		11
Bosnia Herzegovina	4	19
Croatia		13
Macedonia	1	4
Yugoslavia		4
Azerbaijan		33
Georgia	4	20
Tajikistan		1
TOTAL	9	104
AFRICA	37	304
Algeria		8
Angola	1	13
Burundi	1	2
Congo, D.R.		10
Congo, Rep.		4
Liberia		2
Mozambique	5	29
Rwanda		
Sierra Leone	1	5
South Africa		8
TOTAL	8	81
MIDDLE EAST	2	67
Lebanon	1	2
West Bank/Gaza	1	10
TOTAL	2	12
ASIA	26	387
Cambodia		5
Sri Lanka	2	7
TOTAL	2	12
LATIN AMERICA	46	387
Colombia	1	18
Conflict affected Countries	22	238
World	**154**	**1582**

tion by (1) assisting US investors through loans and loan guarantees, (2) providing equity to businesses overseas, and (3) advocating the interests of the American business community overseas.

Private sector investment overseas contributes substantially to both the national and foreign policy interests of U.S. citizens. It strengthens and expands the U.S. economy by improving U.S. competitiveness in the international marketplace. It also helps less developed nations expand their economies and become valuable markets for U.S. goods and services, thereby increasing U.S. exports and creating U.S. jobs.

As part of its overall mission, OPIC serves as an advocate on behalf of U.S. business clients that have made long-term investments in emerging markets and developing nations. OPIC also works with host country governments to help create economic climates that attract U.S. investment, facilitating the entry of hundreds of U.S. businesses into new markets abroad.

OPIC sponsors and participates in numerous seminars and conferences throughout the U.S. and overseas to increase awareness among U.S. companies, especially small and medium-sized firms, of real opportunities for business expansion through overseas investment, as well as the OPIC services available to assist them. To enhance its outreach, OPIC often works closely with other federal government agencies, state and local governments, private organizations and multilateral institutions.

OPIC is a self-sustaining agency, operates at no net cost to the U.S. taxpayer, and has accumulated reserves of more than $3 billion. OPIC has supported investments worth nearly $121 billion, generated $58 billion in U.S. exports, and helped to create 237,000 American jobs. Currently, OPIC programs are available for new and expanding business enterprises in approximately 140 countries and areas worldwide. OPIC has recorded a positive net income for every year of operation. All of OPIC's guaranty and insurance obligations are backed by the full faith and credit of the United States of America. Risk insurance makes investment possible for a private sector energy company like Enron to invest in such areas as Gaza and the West Bank.

Former projects between OPIC and Enron include:

1993   OPIC insured $100,000,000 for a petroleum project in Trinidad and Tobago

1995 $200,000,000 insurance for gas-fired power generation in Turkey

1996	OPIC insured $200,000,000 for an offshore oil and gas development project by Enron in India
1996	$10,000,000 finance for gas-fired power generation in Turkey, working with Trakya Elektrik Uretim ve Ticaret A.S.
1998	$13,000,000 insurance for natural gas pipeline in Brazil; $250,000,000 insurance for power generation in Brazil
1998	$200,000,000 in finance, $200,000,000 insurance for natural gas processing and storage facility in Venezuela (with Accroven SRL)
1998	$16,323,000 insurance for power generation in the Philippines
1999	Work in Bolivia re: conservation; $85,817,000 finance for gas pipeline in Bolivia with Gas Oriente Boliviano, Ltda.
1999	Continued work in India; $60,000,000 finance, $31,700,000 insurance to work with Dabhol Power Company in India
1999	"Reliable energy and economic development are critical to achieving peace in the Middle East. A $22.5 million OPIC insurance commitment to Enron Corp. for its investment in the Gaza Power Generating Private Limited Company will help meet energy needs throughout the Gaza Strip and generate new opportunity and economic development."
1999	$51,873,000 Finance for power generation in Brazil with EPE (Empresa Produtora de Energia, Ltda.); also $62,310,000 finance for energy pipeline in Brazil with Gasocidente Do Mato Grosso LTDA)
2000	OPIC financed electric power generation facilities in Guatemala

Source: http://www.opic.gov/subdocs/public/publications/99ar%2Dprojects.htm.

Private Political Risk Insurance

The availability of political risk insurance at affordable rates represents a powerful instrument for promoting private sector investment in countries at risk and is therefore an important tool for promoting sustainable peace. Such risk insurance is available through companies like the American International Group, Inc. (AIG), a private US-based insurance and financial group that directs individuals, small and large businesses, and business professionals on how to manage their investments. AIG provides industry risk analyses of over 20 industries in more than 130 countries worldwide, and has a subsidiary devoted to political risk insurance.

Business and Conflict: Corporate Analysis and Decision-Making

The last decade has seen the increasing size, power, and influence of multinational corporations (MNCs). The growing importance of

MNCs has led to calls for them to take on greater responsibility in global events, especially conflict situations. Unfortunately, few of those calling for such engagement adequately understand how corporate managers, as distinct from politicians and policymakers, approach engagement during armed conflict and in its immediate aftermath.

In an attempt to fill this gap, the New York-based firm Political and Economic Link Consulting conducted an extensive study to explore the relationship between MNCs and armed conflict.[22] The study concluded that "certain factors predominate in the operational decisions of MNCs":

Geographic Impact of Conflict: Contrary to the beliefs of many analysts, MNCs often have little concern for the presence or geographical range of conflict. Instead, MNCs care more about whether conflict is likely to spread. Conflicts that are restricted to one part of a country often pose few problems to MNCs whose facilities are located in other areas. For example, a conflict that rages in the countryside but is unlikely to spread to urban areas is not much of a risk to MNCs. Furthermore, geographical barriers (such as mountain ranges or deserts) that physically contain conflicts reduces an MNC's estimation of a country's risk factor. Finally, in situations where the geographic stability of conflict is assured only by governmental military forces, MNCs look seriously at the capability of the military to maintain a cordon around conflict areas.

Severity of Conflict: An MNC's estimation of risk varies with the type of conflict that is occurring. MNCs often categorize conflict into three categories:

1) *Terroristic conflict* occurs when opposition movements conduct only occasional acts of violence. This type of conflict is widely tolerated by MNCs.

2) *Incursional conflict* occurs when the government still maintains control over the country, but the opposition frequently and effectively breaks through government lines. Usually only natural resources or infrastructure investment can encourage MNCs to invest in areas troubled by this type of conflict.

3) *Territorial conflict* occurs either when the government no longer has clear control or when the opposition has *de facto* control over

---

[22] Detailed results of this study can be found in an article by Jonathan Berman, President of Political and Economic Link Consulting, in the Fall 2000 issue of the *Harvard International Review* entitled "Corporations and Conflict: How Managers Think About War," pp. 1–8.

the country. Very few MNCs that do not provide for their own security are willing to tolerate the risk involved in countries undergoing such territorial conflict.

Nature of the Government: To the extent that the business environment can be separated from the conflict environment, MNCs are willing to overlook the risks involved with armed conflict. MNCs will tolerate conflict if the business environment—including commercial rules and regulations, free flow of information, lack of impediments from anti-conflict measures such as curfews, and basic utilities—remains stable. In this case, stability refers both to the ability of the government to protect the business environment from the opposition and to an agreement by the government not to interfere with the business environment for the purpose of bolstering their own forces.

Nature of the Opposition: The greatest threat to MNCs is posed by opposition groups that are hostile to foreigners or to private property. In such cases, the opposition is likely to attack the property and facilities of MNCs, and in the case that the opposition overruns the government the MNCs are almost guaranteed to lose their investment. Much less threatening are groups that merely want sovereign control of territory. Lacking any direct hostility to MNCs, these groups are unlikely to attack them, and no matter which way the conflict is resolved the MNCs are likely to be able to continue their operations. Past actions also matter: groups that consistently attack MNC facilities—such travel terminals or actual plants—are considered more threatening than groups that rarely attack MNCs directly.

Character of the MNC's industry: Four factors regarding the type of business an MNC is engaged in can influence its willingness to tolerate armed conflict in a country:

1) *Essential vs. Discretionary Product*. An MNC that produces goods or services vital to the economy considers conflict inherently less risky because both the government and the opposition rely on its continued business.

2) *Stability of Technology*. For an MNC whose industry relies on technology, the less stable the technology the better. Stable technology causes governments to consider an MNC less valuable in and of itself. The value of an MNC is far more pronounced when it plays a key role in implementing new and constantly advancing technology.

3) *Supply or Market Potential.* A country that has the resources to be a substantial supplier (for example, Angola with its oil supplies) can attract MNCs despite the presence of conflict. Similarly attractive are countries that have large markets or that serve as gateways to other markets.

4) *Duration of Payback Period.* MNCs will function in a conflict or post conflict nation if the projected time period of stability would allow them to have a return equal to or greater than their initial investment.

Investment Structure: The mechanisms surrounding how MNCs will invest capital in conflict situations are vital. Political risk insurance can greatly increase MNC activity in risky areas; similarly, activities that will shorten the payback period—for example, an MNC can establish low-infrastructure industries that have quick production times—will also be favored. MNCs also reduce their risk by keeping as many assets as possible outside of the conflict country. Such a strategy could involve such actions as using offshore banks or putting heavy industrial plants in neighboring countries instead. Finally, risk can be greatly reduced if a multilateral development organization decides to participate with the MNC in investment through loans or guarantees.

However, while traditional actors in post conflict contexts—the World Bank, the United Nations and its affiliates—are held accountable to international norms and institutional mandates, the private sector remains largely unregulated.

Chapter 6

THE UNITED NATIONS: GLOBAL LEADERSHIP AND THE AGENDA FOR PEACE

As of mid-2000 there were 14 UN peacekeeping operations around the world involving some 28,900 troops from 38 different countries. While the number is down from the highs of over 70,000 in the early 1990s, it is also three times the 1999 number of around 9,000 troops. Although complaints abound from the developing countries that they are carrying an uneven burden of troop provision, implicitly subjected to a subtle form of exploitation, the developed countries continue to bear the bulk of the financial burden with the US alone accounting for some 30% of the costs. In the first 45 years of its existence, the UN spent only 23% of its budget, or about US$ 3.6 billion, on peacekeeping. In the past 10 years this figure has increased dramatically to about 77% of the UN budget, or roughly US$ 12.1 billion.[1]

The UN was not envisaged to deal with problems of conflict within states. States have rejected calls for legitimating humanitarian intervention in sovereign states, even during times of genocide. Despite the efforts of scholars to reinterpret the UN Charter to permit intervention in intrastate conflict on humanitarian grounds, this idea has never been fully accepted. In any event, it remains questionable that the UN has the capacity to provide security in such environments in a timely and cost-effective fashion. In the first instance, the UN is in point of fact not capable of mobilizing a peacekeeping force until the UN Security Council provides the mandate. Then problems arise of matching up a diverse

---

[1]   Martin, Keith, "New Measures in Conflict Prevention," *Canadian Foreign Policy*, Vol. 4, No. 1, pp. 139–43.

quality of trained soldiers, non-standardized weaponry and systems of command and control, and poor communications, not to mention the logistical nightmare of supplying such a force once it is in the field. Recent experience in Sierra Leone brings into sharp focus the challenges of a peacekeeping versus a peace enforcement mission. With Guineans and Kenyans handing over their weapons to the rebels, and some 500 UN troops embarrassingly taken hostage early on, complicated by a not-so-subtle feud over the mission leadership itself between India and Nigeria, it is no wonder that only the professionalism of a Gurkha unit, reinforced by a British battalion flown into Freetown overnight, kept the country and UN mission from collapsing into total chaos.[2] The UN itself is painfully aware of such shortcomings. The recent Brahimi Report, reviewing peacekeeping in its entirety, concluded that while strengthening the peacekeeping capacity of the UN is necessary, a more honest assessment of the UN capacity to bring peace in a given situation also needs to be made on a case-by-case basis, as to whether the UN should become engaged.

A Formal Look at the UN Charter

Chapters VI and VII of the UN Charter refer respectively to the "Pacific Settlement of Disputes" and to "Action with Respect to Threats of the Peace, Breaches of the Peace, and Acts of Aggression."

Chapter VI becomes relevant when antagonistic parties are involved in "any dispute, the continuance of which is likely to endanger the maintenance of international peace and security."[3] To resolve these situations Chapter VI calls for peaceful means: specifically, "negotiation, enquiry, mediation, conciliation, arbitration, judicial settlement, resort to regional agencies or arrangements, or other peaceful means of [the opposing parties'] own choice."[4] When the parties are unable to reconcile, the Security Council is given the right to recommend or propose a potentially peaceful solution to the conflict. At no point does Chapter VI mention military force; the Security Council's actions are limited to recommendations or proposals only.

---

2   "Peacekeeping: The UN's Missions Impossible," *The Economist*, August 5, 2000, pp. 22–24.
3   UN Charter, Article 33.
4   UN Charter, Article 33.

Chapter VII is far harsher than Chapter VI. Like Chapter VI, Chapter VII calls for action by the Security Council to counter threats to international peace or security, including acts of aggression.[5] Moreover, Chapter VII gives the UN the right to engage not only in recommendations but also in more severe measures. Chapter VII provides three steps in which the UN may respond:

1) Provisional measures undertaken "to prevent an aggravation of the situation."[6] These are meant to be implemented without taking into account the particular claims of any parties involved in the dispute.
2) Non-military measures to restore peace, including "complete or partial interruption of economic relations and of rail, sea, air, postal, telegraphic, radio, and other means of communication, and the severance of diplomatic relations."[7]
3) If non-military measures fail, then military measures by "air, sea, or land forces"[8] by members of the UN.

Of note is the fact that both Chapters VI and VII only come into effect when there occur threats to *international* peace. The Charter explicitly states elsewhere that the UN is not able to intervene "in matters which are essentially within the domestic jurisdiction of any state,"[9] although this phraseology has been given wide berth to deal with apartheid in South Africa and its progeny. Moreover, the Charter also states that "this principle (Article 2:7) shall not prejudice the application of enforcement measures under Chapter VII."[10]

Complications of the UN Charter

As many commentators have observed, there is a wide gap between the original intent of the Charter and its subsequent implementation. "The Charter originally assumed that Chapter VII would be invoked when states failed to settle their disputes peacefully under Chapter VI and the Security Council determined that their continued conflict was

---

5   UN Charter, Article 39.
6   UN Charter, Article 40.
7   UN Charter, Article 41.
8   UN Charter, Article 42.
9   UN Charter, Article 2.7.
10   UN Charter, Article 2.7.

a threat to international peace and security."[11] However, two problems quickly impeded the strict observance of the Charter.

First, there was a lack of Security Council unanimity during the Cold War. "The deployment of troops as foreseen by Chapter VII required full co-operation and agreement among the permanent members of the Security Council."[12] Unfortunately, "the Security Council was paralyzed by the split between the communist countries, the People's Republic of China and Russia, and the free-market capitalist countries, France, the United Kingdom and the United States."[13] Rather than follow through with full Chapter VII deployment, the UN General Assembly essentially invented the process known as peacekeeping, later sanctioned by the International Court of Justice. Peacekeeping operations do not quite fit under the mandates of Chapters VI or VII. "They fall somewhere between Chapter VI and Chapter VII in the sense that they go beyond what is mandated under Chapter VI, yet do not reach the 'military enforcement' stage mandated under Chapter VII. Former UN Secretary-General Dag Hammarskjold is reported as having said: 'UN peace-keeping might be put in a new Chapter six and a half.'"[14]

Second, humanitarian outrage steadily built on a global scale, reinforced by the "CNN effect" in exposing state brutality of their own citizenry, seemingly in the face of the impotence of the international community to do anything about it. The UN Charter clearly calls for action only in the event of a threat to international peace or security. However, several events caused the UN to rethink the narrow focus of Chapters VI and VII. The genocidal rampage by the Khmer Rouge in Cambodia was one of the first such humanitarian crises to do so. As a result of its inability to halt the slaughter of the 'killing fields,' in 1988 the UN General Assembly passed a resolution accepting the principle of intervention within a sovereign state by non-governmental organizations (NGOs) on humanitarian grounds.[15]

On April 5, 1991, in response to Iraq's crackdown on its Kurdish population, the UN Security Council passed Resolution 688, which

---

[11]   Gene M. Lyons, "A New Collective Security: The United Nations and International Peace," *The Washington Quarterly*, Spring 1994, p. 171.

[12]   Colonel John S. Bremmar, "The Changing Nature of Peacekeeping—A Canadian Perspective," *International Defense Review*, 31 December 1994, p. 113.

[13]   "Time To Re-Think Security Structures For The New World (Dis)Order," *Defense and Foreign Affairs Strategic Policy*, 31 January 1994, p. 8.

[14]   *Ibid.*

[15]   *Ibid.*

demanded that Iraq allow the UN to intervene. Significantly, the resolution claimed that a threat to international peace and security existed in the flood of Kurdish refugees; it also claimed that the Security Council was "deeply disturbed by the magnitude of the human suffering involved."[16] The import of this resolution was that "the Security Council for the first time linked humanitarian concerns to international peace and security and gave humanitarianism greater weight than nonintervention."[17]

On December 3, 1992, in the wake of the conflict in Somalia, the Security Council issued Resolution 794, which established the next step in its response to humanitarian crises. The Security Council determined that "the magnitude of the human tragedy caused by the conflict in Somalia, further exacerbated by the obstacles being created to the distribution of humanitarian assistance, constitutes a threat to international peace and security."[18] Unlike the case of Resolution 688, Resolution 794 made no attempt to link humanitarian suffering to something like refugee movement; instead, "this was the first time the Council recognized that an internal humanitarian crisis was in and of itself a threat to international peace, despite the absence of any transboundary effects."[19]

While the new interpretations broadening legitimate responses to internal conflict pursuant to the UN Charter proved a boon for those seeking intervention in humanitarian crises, it also significantly complicated the process of peacekeeping. First of all, UN troops brought in under the auspices of Chapter VII (ignoring the consent of the parties) often exacerbated humanitarian situations. Second, UN troops brought in solely to safeguard humanitarian operations (for example, protecting United Nations High Commission for Refugees and the International Committee of the Red Cross) were often called to task for either providing humanitarian support to the "bad" side or failing to adopt military operations. At times, the sudden decision by the Security Council to give military objectives to humanitarian troops proved disastrous when undermanned and under-equipped troops had to advance against

---

16   S/RES/688.
17   Thomas G. Weiss, "New Challenges for UN Military Operations: Implementing an Agenda for Peace," *The Washington Quarterly*, Winter 1993, p. 51.
18   S/RES/794.
19   Guenther Auth, "Protecting Minorities: Lessons of International Peacekeeping," American Society of International Law, Proceedings of the Annual Meeting, 1997. pp. 429–459.

an unpredictable opposition, as in Somalia and Sierra Leone. Furthermore, even in the strict realm of humanitarian operations, the use of military force often became necessary—and hotly debated.

The result was confusion over the overlap of UN peacemaking, peacekeeping, and peace enforcement functions. The situation has been further complicated by the broad range of purposes for which UN troops have been deployed. Yet a series of working definitions of the distinctions among appropriate UN operations in response to contemporary crises can be drawn.

Peacemaking: Of all three terms, peacemaking is the only one that does not refer to the use of military force. Instead, peacemaking is a process that emerges almost solely out of the directives of Chapter VI, which calls for peaceful means to bring combatants to the table. In other words, peacemaking is a non-military process that occurs before a cease fire has been reached for the purpose of having the combating parties reach a settlement. By its very non-military measure, peacemaking tends to have the consent of all parties involved; the UN is essentially called in as a mediator.

Peacekeeping: This peace operation only occurs after a ceasefire has *already been reached* by the combating parties. The UN conducts peacekeeping when all the combating parties consent to have the UN bring in a military force to monitor or enforce the conditions of the cease fire. Finally, as former UN Secretary-General Boutros Boutros-Ghali put it: "Three particularly important principles [of peacekeeping] are the consent of the parties, impartiality [of the UN troops], and the non-use of force except in self-defense."[20]

Peace enforcement: By far the most difficult of the three types of peace operations, peace enforcement is also the most ill-defined. Like peacekeeping, peace enforcement is characterized by military intervention. However, peace enforcement does not follow the three principles of peacekeeping that Boutros-Ghali described. Peace enforcement does not require the consent of the parties involved; in fact, even if the parties wish to continue fighting amongst themselves, the UN may deem it of sufficiently high importance to send in troops. Peace enforcement does not necessarily have to be impartial. If one side is clearly violating the peace or aggravating the situation, UN troops can act solely against that side. Alternatively, UN troops could favor one side over another. Peace enforcement is also not purely defensive. UN troops are allowed to go

---

[20]   Boutros Boutros-Ghali, "Supplement to *An Agenda for Peace*," 3 January 1995, A/50/60—S/1995/1.

on the offensive and actively pursue military objectives against those who threaten peace. Finally, unlike peacekeeping, peace enforcement seems to occur both before and after the attainment of a cease fire by the groups. In other words, if a cease fire is unlikely to materialize, or if a cease fire has been agreed and then violated by one or more of the conflicting parties, peace enforcement comes into play.

The table below attempts to summarize the key features of the three terms; hopefully a comparison will help to distinguish the three.

	Peacemaking	Peacekeeping	Peace Enforcement
Relevant Chapters	Chapter VI	Chapter VI/VII	Chapter VII
Use of Force	No	Self-defense only	Yes
Consent from Parties	Yes	Yes	No
Cease fire Reached	No	Yes	No
Impartiality	Yes	Yes	No
Goal	Create cease fire	Enforce cease fire	Impose peace

A Review of Select UN Peacekeeping Experiences

To illustrate the above definitions, a review a number of select UN peace operations underscores how the changing nature of war in the post-Cold War era has impacted upon the changing nature of peace. The earlier days of positioning forces in a demilitarized zone, e.g., Cyprus, have, in general, given way to the more complicated dispersion of peace-keepers as peace enforcers throughout a country, e.g., Sierra Leone. Only the more recent placement of peacekeepers in the cross border war between Eritrea and Ethiopia harkens back to the clearer, simpler times of years gone by. Further complicating the UN role are the cases of Kosovo and East Timor, where UN administration accompanies peace-keeping and peace enforcement operations. The following historical look begins with the Congo intervention of the 1960s.

Congo

In 1960, the UN entered its first quagmire with the new nation of Congo (later to become Zaire). Although 20,000 troops were sent, they could not deal with the dangers that resulted from postcolonial recon-struction. Competing governments, an ugly civil war, and a series of secessions and assassinations mixed with superpower rivalry and bands of ruthless mercenaries created a situation that left 234 peacekeepers dead.[21] This was the first case in which it became clear that the UN knew very little about what to do when there was not a government that it could deal with. Ironically, we have come full circle to the Democratic Republic of the Congo of today, where a weak state in partial control of its territory, with several opposing groups, presents a similar challenge, buoyed only by a fragile peace agreement experiencing daily violations.

Namibia

A model of UN peacekeeping. In 1989–90, Namibia was part of South Africa; by the 1990s, however, South Africa realized that Namibia would soon become independent. Nevertheless, South African troops continued fighting against rebel guerrillas up to the day of Namibia's official separation (and even briefly thereafter). UN peacekeeping forces were sent in to supervise Namibian elections; to nobody's surprise, the rebels won handily over a South African party. The peacekeeping forces were, by all accounts, extremely effective at keeping both sides at bay, and since the independence of Namibia the new government has been able to avoid much of the chaos endemic in other postcolonial nations, such as Sierra Leone. Although the UN claimed responsibility, their operations were aided by the relative placidity of both sides and the common desire for peace.

Cambodia

After a decade of violent civil war culminating in a genocide under the reign of the notorious Khmer Rouge and their final defeat by a Vietnamese-led "liberation" force, the Vietnamese withdrew in 1989, the country was renamed Cambodia, and Prince Sihanouk returned after 13 years of self-imposed exile. A transitional government was established until the Paris Peace Accord in October 1991, when the United Nations Transitional Authority in Cambodia (UNTAC) took over to oversee the peace process, reconstruction and national reconciliation. In 1993, elections led to the formation of a coalition government of Prince

---

[21]   David Morrison, "Make Peace—Or Else," *The National Journal*, 3 October 1992, p. 2250.

Norodom Ranarridh and Hun Sen. This was later followed by a coup attempt and the eventual consolidation of power by the Hun Sen government following the July 1998 elections. The UN experience was a mix of peacekeeping and peace enforcement, with the latter effectively handled by the Hun Sen Vietnamese-backed forces. A failed demobilization in the early 1990s compounded by an expensive UN presence left an uneven mark on the UN's ability to deliver.

Somalia

What began as a crusade for humanitarian aid in 1992 (a supposedly easy win for then-President George Bush), led by the United States, turned into disaster when the absolute breakdown of government (a parallel to Congo) left the UN troops unable to cope with the onslaught of chaos. The final straw came when 18 Americans were killed in Mogadishu and one of them was dragged through the streets at the end of a rope. The most important consequence of the Somalian experience the strengthening of America's resolve to never again risk the lives of its own soldiers for something not of pressing national concern. This severely limited the ability of UN peacekeeping to count on US support for funding or troops. However, the operation had positive consequences as well: starvation was mostly eliminated while the UN was present, and basic infrastructure (such as Somalia's largest water pump) remained functional. But once the UN withdrew the country again collapsed into chaos amidst the resurgence of warring clans.

Rwanda

Although it has been argued that the Rwandan genocide's blinding efficiency prevented an international response, few can argue that the UN did enough to help once reports of "ethnic cleansing" emerged. The UN operation was plagued by the freshness of Somalia. Force Commander General Dalaire, handcuffed with rules of engagement under Chapter VI, pleaded in a last minute cable to the Department of Peacekeeping Operations for the Secretary-General to seek a new mandate to engage with force under Chapter VII, only to be rebuked as the Security Council refused to enlarge. Years later UN Secretary-General Kofi Annan and President Bill Clinton would come to Rwanda to personally express their apologies for the road not taken.

Bosnia

Bosnia, formerly a part of Yugoslavia, was dominated by Muslims by the time Yugoslavia's breakup was taking place. In a referendum on independence held in 1992, the vast majority of voters chose to break away from Yugoslavia. The recognition of an independent Bosnia by the US and several European countries led Serb paramilitary forces to begin firing artillery shells, besieging Sarajevo and other cities. Soon, Serb-led paramilitary and military forces took over most of Bosnia, beginning a process of "ethnic cleansing," the new language of post-Cold War genocide.

The UN refused to take sides in the conflict; instead, it sent forces that supervised humanitarian aid, protecting aid workers and aid shipment. However, the UN soon decided that it would also protect designated "safe zones" where UN forces would actively preserve the peace. This idea would prove fatal to UN operations. Although UN forces had been trained and equipped merely to serve defensive functions, maintaining safe zones and implementing action against Serbs (which they were soon called upon to do) entailed peace enforcement actions—actions that UN forces both could not take (due to lack of equipment, training, and manpower) and were not allowed to take (since a political consensus could not be formed around authorizing UN force).

A cease fire was negotiated in 1994, but when the Serbs refused to comply with certain provisions (such as pulling their weapons out of Sarajevo), NATO came in and bombed Serb installations. In retaliation, Serb forces began attacking Bosnian cities and UN safe zones. These attacks led to the UN's withdrawal from many safe zones, including the now infamous Srebenica, where Serb forces slaughtered almost every Bosnian within the city. This marked the shift from peacekeeping to peace enforcement, and also signaled a shift from UN to other agents of force (in this case a regional security alliance in the form of NATO), essentially condoned by the UN. This model of peace enforcement was later to be repeated with the Economic Community of West African States Cease Fire Monitoring Group (ECOMOG) in Liberia, Sierra Leone, and Guinea Bissau, and again with NATO in Kosovo and the Australian led regional peacekeeping force (INTERFED) in Timor.

Finally, the Dayton Accords were signed, whereby a slim majority of Bosnian territory became the Croat-Bosniac Federation and the rest was constituted as the Serb Republic. Since then, the nation has been plagued by the inability to bring key individuals indicted for war crimes to justice and by continuous spates of violence.

Sierra Leone

The conflict began in 1991, when Foday Sankoh (a former army colonel) and his rebel army, the Revolutionary United Front (RUF), began the attack against then-President Joseph Momoh. The rebels wreaked havoc on Sierra Leone; victims and observers soon came to believe that the rebels had no objective but chaos on their minds. Most of the rebels' money came from smuggling diamonds through Liberia. Indeed, the rich mineral deposits of Sierra Leone quickly became easy pickings for rebels ravaging the countryside. Interestingly, mercenaries were used by the "government" (loosely defined) to stop the rebels, but often their merciless pursuit demoralized more than it helped.

In 1996, after a surprising democratic election of a civilian government to replace a succession of power-hungry army officers, a cease fire (and later a peace treaty) was signed by the government with the rebels. By the next year the peace deal had broken down. The democratically elected president, Ahmad Tejan Kabbah, was overthrown in a military coup led by Johnny Paul Koroma, a young officer. Unfortunately, Sankoh's rebel movement joined the military in its battle against the democratic government, leaving the deposed government vulnerable to this alliance of former enemies.

An African regional security alliance (ECOMOG) led by Nigeria soon intervened on behalf of Kabbah and ousted the rebels from Freetown. (Former mercenaries, now referred to as a private security firm—Sandline International, in particular, were also vital for this operation.) Unfortunately, the rebels still scourged the countryside with a reign of terror. Slowly the rebels gained strength, until in January 1999 they attacked Freetown. Although this attack failed to capture the city, the rebels wreaked a massive amount of destruction. Another peace treaty, led by the UN, was signed in July 1999, but the rebels did not follow through on their end of the deal (disarmament and return of diamond mines). Killings and abductions (including 40 UN observers) continued. In October six thousand UN peacekeepers were dispatched to Sierra Leone (under the UN Mission in Sierra Leone—UNAMSIL), where they joined Nigerian forces from ECOMOG.

By the end of the year it became clear that the rebels were not honoring the peace. Early in 2000 the UN increased the number of peacekeeping forces to 11,100, but fighting soon broke out between peace-keepers and rebel factions, and the rebels continued to inflict atrocities upon Sierra Leonian citizens. The UN forces were plagued with problems. Many units disobeyed orders; others were badly equipped or poorly trained; and still others fled in fear when reports of rebel attacks came in. There was also a lack of coordination between the African and non-African representatives from the UN.[22] Funding was also lacking, especially from the United States. The chain of command was broken, as officers telephoned home rather than obey the commands of their superiors. No fallback plan was implemented for worst-case scenarios. But perhaps the biggest problem was that the UN was dealing with a warlord who was conducting a campaign of pure horror: the more he terrorized the population, Sankoh reasoned, the more likely that an acceptable compromise could be reached.

The ultimate manifestation of the UN's difficulties came in May 2000 when 500 UN peacekeepers surrendered to a band of armed rebels and were held hostage. As some observers noted: "Once again the organization allowed itself to be used by the United States and other major powers to provide a thin blue fig leaf to cover their refusal to commit their resources to a solution."[23] British peacekeepers who came in shortly after the hostage situation repelled an attack on Freetown and were instrumental in preserving some semblance of security in a nation whose peacekeeping forces had almost completely broken down.

Most recently, the UN called for a ban on diamonds from Sierra Leone, in an attempt to cut off the rebels' source of income. Estimates vary, however, on how much of an impact this ban will have, especially since Liberia—whose president, Charles Taylor, is a supporter of the rebels—allegedly continues to launder the diamonds of their origin. Life expectancy in Sierra Leone is still hovering around 26 years.

Kosovo

In Kosovo, yet another unique situation emerged within the formal national boundaries of the Republic of Yugoslavia, the sovereign remnant of the former Yugoslavia. Here, principles of humanitarian intervention justified the entry of NATO forces to protect a people against

---

[22]   "Staying On," *The Economist*, 17 June 2000.
[23]   Ian Williams, "The UN as Fig Leaf," *The Nation*, 12 June 2000, p. 6.

the brutality of its own state. As Yugoslav Serbs resorted to the familiar tactics of ethnic cleansing, this time targeting Albanian Kosovars, the international community first watched in horror and then authorized NATO intervention. The Albanian Kosovars were protected after a protracted bombing campaign directed against Serbia, but still, peace for Kosovo came at a price: the continued recognition of Kosovo as a part of the former Yugoslavian State, albeit returning to its legal status of broad autonomy under the 1977 Yugoslav constitution. UN Resolution No. 1244 of June 12, 1999 confirmed this status and established the United Nations Mission to Kosovo (UNMIK) as a transitional administering body. Its legal authority has remained clouded ever since. For a discussion of the suggested legal status of the UN role in Kosovo, see Annex II.

Timor

Timor presents yet another twist on the use of international force in peace operations. Following a UN-sponsored referendum on the future of the former Portuguese Colonial Territory in which over 80% of the population voted for non-integration with Indonesia (in effect, independence), violence and destruction quickly ensued, led by a dissenting Timorese militia, allegedly supported by the Indonesian National Army (TNI). An Australian-led regional intervention force (INTERFED) finally intervened, again supported by a UN resolution (No. 1272 of October 4, 1999) to enforce peace. The UN subsequently established yet another transitional administration (UNTAET), but this time with a clear mandate to lead to the formation of an independent state. Once more, nation-building reemerged in the wake of decolonization. However, unlike the post-World War II decolonization process involving foreign empires, this time it takes the form of the deconstruction of "domestic colonial empires" such as Yugoslavia, Indonesia, and the former Soviet Union.

The above cases illustrate a number of lessons. First, when the use of force is required, the UN has increasingly deferred to national or regional security forces such as NATO, INTERFED, or ECOMOG. Second, peacekeeping—blue helmets patrolling and monitoring a clearly demilitarized space based upon agreed terms and conditions of cease fire and peace—is quite a different matter from peace enforcement. Third, every situation requires a case-by-case assessment and response. A number of initiatives are now under way to establish regional peace enforcement such as the "rapid reaction forces" of the EU (about 50–60,000 troops by 2003) in Europe.

Privatization is not intended to replace multilateral authority in either peacekeeping or peace enforcement operations. But, as subsequently discussed, it offers the distinct advantage of partnering between private security and multilateral and regional operations, providing there is full transparency and accountability.

Chapter 7

PRIVATIZING SECURITY:
A DOUBLE-EDGED SWORD

In the Fall of 2000 a senior UN official was approached to discuss United Nations initiatives in partnering with other international institutions. Near the end of the discussion he was asked: "What do you think about *privatizing* peacekeeping?" He reacted with dismay, recounting horror stories of mercenaries run amok in Africa. "The United Nations is a public institution," he remarked. "Giving its functions over to private companies would be irresponsible and dangerous."

The response is symptomatic of a much larger problem. Although the United Nations has for the last four years eagerly pursued the idea of partnering, not one of its historical peacekeeping initiatives mentions the idea of privatization. And yet without privatization of certain security functions, prospects for meaningful improvement of peacekeeping operations are slim.

The private sector can play a role in peace processes in myriad ways. The process of peace is complex and multi-staged, from peacemaking to peacekeeping, and from peace enforcement to peacebuilding. In varying degrees of effectiveness, the private sector role can be important at each stage.

Peacemaking

The peacemaking process has always, at root, been a matter of incentives and disincentives. Peace cannot be legislated. In any peace process all sides are continually calculating the costs and benefits of war and peace. These can come down to financial and material aspects, as well as psychological and ideological elements. Both pride and money played huge roles in the success of the first Camp David peace arrangements between Israel and Egypt. Both parties were assured over $2 billion per annum in combined military and economic aid assistance packages as the benefit of peace.

In the Dayton Peace Accord for Bosnia and Herzegovina, World Bank economists played a major role in specifying the economic and financial terms of the agreement, from revenue generation and sharing principles to budgeting and accounting, while State Department representatives concentrated on the ethnic politics of federalism and democratic processes as well as judicial and legal terms and structures.

In the last Abuja Accord, the final element that turned the peace process was not the political power-sharing arrangements, but the wealth-sharing arrangements, as Foday Sonkah, the RUF leader, was given the position of State Minister for Mineral Resources, in effect giving him de jure control of the diamond mines which he already controlled de facto. Of course, this initiative proved short-sighted, with its assumption that bringing his efforts above ground would eventually lead to government regulation and growing domestic resources for reconstruction and development. Unfortunately, this intent did not materialize. The important point is that incentives and disincentives, including promises of aid and private investment, can be critical to making or breaking a peace process.

In addition to the above, sanctions can play a role, albeit controversial, in providing incentives and disincentives to war. Criticisms abound that sanctions do not work, and that the brunt is borne not by governments, but by people. Many fear that sanctions can actually prove counter-productive, resulting in increased tension and hatred that intensifies the potential for violent conflict. Corporations doing business in war-torn regions can face deep conflicts of interest in balancing the bottom line of profits with national interests.

Targeting Sanctions and Incentives for Peace

Sanctions as "economic warfare" have been enforced through arms embargoes, foreign assistance reductions and cut-offs, export and import limitations, revocation of most favored nation (MFN) status, investment prohibitions, and the like. Sanctions have aimed to eliminate weapons of mass destruction in Iraq, to bring the Serbs to accept the Dayton agreement and cease fighting in Bosnia, to force Saddam Hussein's withdrawal from Kuwait in 1990, and to damage Fidel Castro's stronghold in Cuba. These sanctions, however, have resulted in only partial solutions and civilian suffering. They are also costly for corporations that do business in the countries affected.

Richard N. Haass, currently the Director of Policy Planning at the US State Department and formerly the Director of Foreign Policy Studies at the Brookings Institution and Editor of *Economic Sanctions and American Diplomacy* (Brookings Institution Press, 1998), suggests the use of targeted sanctions that correlate penalties more directly with the offenders to minimize ancillary civilian damage. In this way the humanitarian ramifications of broad-based sanctions could be avoided. David Cortright, research fellow at the Joan B. Kroc Institute for International Peace Studies at the University of Notre Dame and President of the Fourth Freedom Forum (Goshen, Indiana) supports this view. In a 1998 presentation to the World Bank, "Targeted Financial Sanctions: Problems and Prospects," Cortright noted the potential for targeted, or "smart" sanctions to be effective in promoting political transformation. Restricting loans and credits, blocking international financial transactions, banning travel, restricting the sale and trade of property abroad and freezing overseas assets, should, he maintained, be focused on decision makers as was done in South Africa during apartheid and in Iran in 1979 during the hostage crisis. The World Bank, he noted, could encourage sanction compliance through conditionality provisions in its lending practices.

Targeted sanctions may promote good governance while, by contrast, open-ended sanctions can erode it. In Cortright's *The Price of Peace: The Role of Incentives in International Conflict Prevention* (Rowman and Littlefield, 1997), edited for the Carnegie Commission for Preventing Deadly Conflict, strategies for targeted sanctions are mapped out, acknowledging the political and administrative hurdles to their implementation.

Haass, Richard N. "Sanctioning Madness," *Foreign Affairs*, November/December 1997, Vol. 76, No. 6, pp. 74–85

Peacekeeping

Although peacekeeping and peace enforcement may seem similar, the role of the private sector in each is different. Whereas in peacekeeping, military action is not key since a cease-fire has already been reached, by contrast, in peace enforcement operations, armed force is required. Both belligerents generally look to go beyond a cease-fire or truce to a negotiated peace agreement. In peacekeeping operations, military force is only required for monitoring the cease-fire, and lethal action is only used in self-defense.

Although adherence to the terms of mandate for engagement is as important in peacekeeping as in peace enforcement, flexibility often becomes the necessity. All too often, peacekeeping situations disintegrate into renewed conflict, requiring peace enforcement to maintain order. Here, the private sector can step in to provide flexible yet accountable security.

With advances in technology, the private sector's role in the technological aspects of peacekeeping has also become more important. For example, aerial photography using drones and satellite imagery has now become a fairly standard part of intelligence gathering in technologically advanced warfare. Also, miniaturization has led to the development of tiny cameras that can surreptitiously record the actions of both parties. Because surveillance is of the utmost importance in the interval between the signing of a cease-fire and the signing of a peace agreement, such cameras play a vital role in the peacekeeping process.

A combination of public and private parties can work well in peacekeeping operations. The UN can provide the personnel to monitor clearly demarcated demilitarized zones; examples range from Cyprus to Southern Lebanon to the recent positioning of UN soldiers between Eritrea and Ethiopia. On the other hand, the more sophisticated technological needs of training, communications, command and control, intelligence gathering, and supply logistics can be readily "outsourced" to the private sector for efficient and cost effective delivery.

Peace Enforcement

Peace enforcement, the harshest stage of the peace process, occurs when none of the belligerents wish to stop fighting. Without outside intervention, violence is likely to continue until one side claims victory or until both sides are exhausted. When such conflicts harm regional or international security, however, or when such conflicts create horrendous humanitarian crises, intervention becomes necessary.

Peace enforcement operations have traditionally troubled multinational armed forces. The chain of command in institutions like the United Nations has often been at odds with the tactical decisions demanded by the commanders of ground forces; as a result, in times of great peril, subordinates in a battlefield have been known to radio up to their national rather than international superiors. The result is a mess of contradictory and ultimately self-destructive commands that contribute to chaos. In Sierra Leone, it was not atypical for Nigerian units to take commands only from the deputy force commander, a Nigerian, and not the Indian Force Commander. This situation eventually led to the resignation of the Indian Commander.

Another problem lies with the mandates that multinational forces follow. Typically, these mandates—rules of engagement for the mission—are detailed and lengthy, and the word of the mandates is (unfortunately) less than gospel for many soldiers. Multinational troops have failed time and time again to fulfill their given mandates when their personal safety was put on the line—an understandable reaction in human terms, but unacceptable for any international body that seeks to restore peace. In Srebenica, Dutch units failed to protect Muslim Bosnians from slaughter abandoning the formally established safe zone to rampant massacre by the Serbian forces. In Sierra Leone, Jordanian troops were accused of providing fuel and rations to the Revolutionary United Front soldiers in the neighboring bush, allegedly in exchange for not directly harassing their position. Moreover, even when soldiers hold fast, nations often fail to live up to their professed goals: more than once a member state of the United Nations has pulled its troops out of a peace enforcement operation, demonstrating openly that its own soldiers are more important than any UN mandate. No clearer example of this can be found than in Somalia, when, after a US ranger battalion was decimated, the US responded by pulling its forces entirely out of the Somalia peace operation. The repercussions of the Somalia experience still resonate, with the United States prepared to make only grudging contributions of US peacekeeping troops in Kosovo.

UN troops have proven far too narrow-minded in their interpretation of their various mandates. Security conditions can change overnight, as in Rwanda, where an assumed peace was undercut by a swift act of genocide following the sudden death of the Hutu President, Juvenal Habaryamana, when his aircraft was shot down as it was returning from the Arusha peace negotiations. When such cases arise, ground troops must be able to swiftly re-evaluate and revise their position so as to maintain the integrity of the operation. Here, the problem lies less with the soldiers in the field than with the United Nations Executive, specifically the Security Council.

In addition, peace enforcement has often failed because of a lack of adequate finances.[1] In these circumstacnes, the question arises: can or

---

[1]   Jakkie Cilliers and Peggy Mason, eds., *Peace, Profit or Plunder? The Privatization of Security in War-Torn African Societies*. Pretoria: Institute of Security Studies, 1999.

should peace enforcement be privatized; and if so, to what degree? What are the benefits and risks in doing so? Can private peace enforcement be "regulated" like any other commercial enterprise?

Max Weber defined the authority and legitimacy of the State by its monopoly over the means and instruments of violence. As seen from the African experience in particular, private security companies are increasingly supplanting this primary responsibility of the State to provide security for people and investment. Globalization, coupled with the weakening of the State—particularly in Africa due to the changing patronage systems in the wake of the end of the Cold War, and in Asia due the economic shocks of the financial crisis—has led to an uncoupling of the West's security reach and its business engagement. This vacuum has led to the increased privatization of violence to obtain and sustain political power. Private security companies (PSCs) have flourished under these conditions—Executive Outcomes and Sandline in Angola and Sierra Leone, Military Professional Resources Incorporated (MPRI) in Croatia and Bosnia, to mention two of the most prominent. PSCs have become the modern embodiment of mercenary forces, protecting governments and multinational business interests alike. Globalization has made its mark on the security field as arms proliferation, illegitimate resource appropriation, transnational corporate greed, and the rise of multinational private security firms became inextricably linked.

By privatizing peace enforcement, many of the problems of PSCs can be addressed. In a private company the chain of command is clear. One end of the chain—the United Nations or another international organization or government deals with how its mandates will be implemented, while the other end of the chain—the ground troops—knows precisely where it receives its commands. Few better examples of this understanding exist than the Sierra Leone experience. When the Kabbah government had Executive Outcomes under its employ in Sierra Leone, the RUF were brought to the bargaining table, where the rebels made the withdrawal of EO from the country a key condition of a cease fire. Kabbah reluctantly agreed, under pressure from the international community. Unfortunately, Freetown and its defending ECOMOG forces were subsequently overrun by the unforeseen combination of rebelling government soldiers and the RUF. Kabbah was only returned to power when Sandline joined forces with ECOMOG.

Here, a bad situation was compounded by bad policy advice from the IMF. Its call for a reduction of state subsidies, a condition aimed at reducing the expenditure side of the government ledger and balancing the budget in exchange for a desperately needed injection of foreign exchange, led instead to a misguided reduction in the army's food subsidy. This was particularly offensive to the army insofar as had not been paid for months. This grievance became a major cause of the subsequent defection of a large number of the Armed Forces of Sierra Leone (AFSL) troops to the rebel Revolutionary United Front (RUF) cause, which led to the fall of the Kabbah government and a junta takeover.

Private security companies (PSCs) are less likely to defect. First, every member of the company, from commanders to soldiers, has a financial incentive to complete his tour of duty. It is, after all, a contractual obligation. As a result, soldiers are less likely to desert as they have a stake in "seeing it through". In many instances where remuneration is tied to shared profits from a mineral resource such as the diamond mines in Sierra Leone and Angola withdrawal is tantamount to foregoing payment as well as a breach of contract. Secondly, the security company has an incentive to complete its objectives. As a private company it has a reputation to protect, and a failure in one campaign could easily adversely affect the prospect of future contracts.

Before examining the benefits and risks of private security companies, it is important to first define and differentiate between private military companies (PMCs) and private security companies (PSCs). This distinction is essential to an assessment of the role the UN and other multilateral agencies play in addressing problems which require both political neutrality and the application of military force.

Abdel-Fatau Musah, of the Center for Democracy and Development in London and a long-time student of private military and security groups in Africa, defines PMCs as follows: "Private Military Companies are corporate entities comprising military and intelligence entrepreneurs whose activities include but are not co-extensive with: organizing mercenaries into temporary armies for combat operations in foreign conflicts on behalf of a party to the said conflict; procuring war material and logistics; providing military training and advice and acting as force multipliers to clients' armies; intelligence gathering on behalf of the client state/party to conflict and or foreign states; and guarding installations and providing VIP escort. PMCs usually pay cash to their personnel and receive payment both in the form of cash and in kind typically in the form of mineral concessions from their clients. Gurkha Security Guards, Sandline International, and the now defunct Executive Outcomes are examples of PMCs."

Musah goes on to classify such UK-based firms as Defense Systems Ltd. and US-based groups as Military Professional Resources Incorporated, DynCorp and the International Chartered Incorporated as in a gray area between PMCs and private security firms. The distinction drawn is that these firms provide all of the services of PMCs, with the exception of engaging in direct combat. In addition, Musah points to local security firms such as Saracen in Uganda and Teleservices in Angola, which are joint ventures between government officials and PMCs.[2]

Problems that are global in nature demand an honest broker to seek resolution. Ideally, a United Nations force can rise above national sovereignty to play such a role. Or it can sponsor other neutral parties to do so through sanctioned and regulated employment of private security firms.

Once the decision to use force is made, the next step is to decide how to implement it. The force of a single strong nation may suffice. In this case the United States or the European Union may implement international action pursuant to a UN resolution as the Australians did in leading the peacekeeping force in East Timor. Often a single nation of regional coalition is too weak, or lacking in moral authority to accomplish international goals. One must then turn to a broad based multinational force under UN auspices. Here too there is room for a supplementary role by private security operations.

The UN serves as a forum for discussion, and in the Security Council as a venue to forge consensus regarding the use of force. Any subsequent military action by the UN is accountable to the terms of the enabling UN Security Council resolution, rather than the broad constituency of all the member states. But, lacking both a standing army and a self-sustainable budget, in authorizing the use of force the UN must rely on its member states for personnel, money, and legitimacy. Yet, only a few nations consider the UN authorization of military force or call for military personnel a high priority on their national agenda.

The immediate evacuation of US military personnel following the death of eighteen soldiers in the UN's peacekeeping operation in Somalia is an example of the low priority that many nations accord to provision

---

2   Abdel-Fatau Musah, "Private Military Intervention, Arms Proliferation and Resource Appropriation in the Process of State Decay," paper presented at Conference on State Collapse and Reconstruction: Lessons and Strategies. Graduate Institute of International Studies, Geneva, and the International Committee of the Red Cross (ICRC), Geneva, December 7–9, 2000, pp. 1–21.

of military personnel to the UN. This is not the case uniformly. Canada and the Nordic countries, in particular, have contributed heavily to UN military operations. However, without the support of the US, few operations are able to sustain themselves. Rwanda is a case in point: Canada led the formation of a renewed peacekeeping effort after the genocide, but could not sustain the effort when consensus could not be reached on a joint disarming of the Intrahamwe in the Goma refugee camps. The Rwandese Patriotic Army eventually took matters into its own hands, attacking the camps before the UN force could be formed. Thus a violent conflict in the region was ignited, leading to a prolonged Congo war involving several African nations fighting on multiple fronts with different proxy rebel armies.

Today, the UN's endeavor to patch together complex peacekeeping operations is continually dogged by the fact that peace enforcement may be a necessary prerequisite to achieving sustainable cease-fires. Nowhere is the tension and interplay between peacekeeping and peace enforcement more clearly revealed than in the UN's effort to cope with the crisis in West Africa and the African Great Lakes region.

The Limitations of Private Security

Seen in this context, it is possible to postulate the following limitations on the use of private security to augment the UN's role in peacekeeping and peace enforcement:

1) The resort to private security firms can raise questions about the necessity of UN operations in which they are employed. On the other hand, the use of private security, rather than national military personnel, can also allow states to better tolerate losses and thus dampen public debate.

2) Use of private security firms does not guarantee better implementation. Many of the mistakes in peacekeeping or peace enforcement come not from misapplication of resources, but from mistaken objectives or unclear objectives. Military missions are often confused by the conflicting demands of interested parties. When this confusion is transmitted down the chain of command, military forces necessarily become ineffective, regardless of whether they are private or public entities. This was evident in Bosnia, where UN peacekeeping forces received contradictory messages from their superiors about how to respond to various

situations. Private security forces would have to be monitored closely and could thus be expected to behave more cautiously.

3) Private security forms cannot force the UN into action. When nations try in this manner to bypass the UN-for reasons such as pressing national security or ethnic pride - they inherently complicate UN operations. This occurred in Sierra Leone, where ECOMOG, staffed mostly by Nigerians, was unable to work with a contingent of UN forces, resulting in confusion and charges of deliberate misinformation.

4) The biggest obstacle to the use of private security forces is the difficulty in regulating their performance, particularly in regard to human rights violations and conflicts of interest. In effect, as war is profitable for a security business, there is a "moral hazard" in employing forms whose profits depend upon the continuation, rather than termination, of war.

From Anarchy to Order: Somali Businessmen in Search of Government Security Function

In the anarchy that replaced the military dictatorship of Muhammad Siad Barre, who was overthrown in Somalia almost a decade ago, businesses seem to be flourishing. "There are five competing airlines here; three phone companies, which have some of the cheapest rates in the world; at least two pasta factories; 45 private hospitals; 55 providers of electricity; 1,500 wholesalers for imported goods; and an infinite number of guys with donkeys who will deliver 55 gallons of clean water to your house for 25 cents." However, without some sort of government they will not be able to prosper for much longer. All these businesses have to provide everything for themselves, including services such as security that would be normally provided by a government. In the current Somali environment this means hiring a gunman with an AK-47 who will defend a business from local warlords.

What could be the way out? Over 2,000 Somali businessmen who would "love to pay taxes" in exchange for "law and order" are backing various candidates for leading positions in a future government. The rest of the population is worried about what kind of influence these businessmen will have on the new government and, therefore, whether or not law and order will be the same for everybody?

Somalia is one of the few war-torn countries in Africa that has achieved this booming business climate on its own. It is also true that with an efficient form of government, Somali people could be even *better off*. For example, in Somalia there are three phone companies, each of which operates independently from the remaining two. In order to have access to all people with a phone, one would have to get three phone lines! In this situation government intervention/regulation could force these three companies to merge. Perhaps there is a need for government after all!

Reference: *The New York Times*, August 10, 2000; Ian Fisher, "Somali Businesses Thwarted by Too-Free Enterprise," *Mogadishu Journal*.

The Advantages of Privatizing Security

Once political consensus has been reached and once military objectives have been clearly identified, employing private security companies could have the following advantages:

1) *Lower costs.* Specialized firms, with their own equipment, training, and common experience, can easily lower the costs of using military force. EO cost Sierra Leone's government $35 million for the 22 months it worked there, compared to a planned UN operation budgeted at $47 million for eight months. Similar cost comparisons can be established for the costs of private security as contrasted with those of the UNAVEM operation in Angola.

2) *Better training.* This includes not just the training in the security firm itself-which is likely to be superior to the training in other groups as security firms are specialists-but also includes the ability of the firm to train other firms.

3) *Better command and control.* A clear chain of command is set up: soldiers report directly to the firm, which then reports to the UN. This avoids the problems in the field where nationals would report to their domestic superiors first rather than to their UN field officers. The use of standardized stat-of-the-art communications equipment across units also enhances command and control.

4) *More determined forces.* PSCs generally pay significantly more than what the UN offers its troops. Indeed, UN troops often have little stake in the conflicts or the lives of the people they are sent to protect. A private security firm, on the other hand, has a financial interest in achieving results, and thus is likely to be more determined to succeed in performing the task at hand to preserve its current contract and enhance its potential for future contracts with the UN.

5) *Speedy delivery.* Fast action is a major UN challenge. It cannot summon troops until a resolution has passed the Security Council. Often this is long after a crisis has begun. This occurred in Rwanda, where genocide was carried out with blazing speed. The UN could have stepped in once word of the killings came out, but the political process of moving resolutions through the Security Council made early intervention impossible. While the use of private security firms would not, in and of itself, reduce the political process, it could diminish the lag between the passage of a UN Security Council resolution and the deployment of troops.

6) *Greater willingness to act.* When all that is at issue is relatively small financial risk, a nation's proclivity to act is enhanced, especially where the risk of casualties is severe. For example, in providing for the protection of humanitarian aid workers, or the monitoring of elections, only a small force may be necessary. But even here the mustering of a small number of soldiers can be difficult politically if the situation is still fraught with physical danger. By contrast, private security operations take advantage of the narrow gap between a nation's willingness to spend lives and its willingness to spend money.

The Risks of Privatizing Security

In addition to the inherent limitations of employing private security forces, there are several special risks. First, member states, not being involved in the conflict themselves, may not be able to accurately determine the amount of funding that should be given to private security firms. If the private security firm receives less than it needs to protect itself, it could withdraw or forego achieving its objectives. And if the PSC is dishonest, it could inflate the risk. Still, UN force faces similar hazards. Setting standards for gauging performance in peacekeeping or peace enforcement thus becomes necessary where private security forces are to be used.

Secondly, the legitimacy of private security companies remains open to question. How should they be registered and regulated? Should only the UN be allowed to use them? If the UN, why not NATO, OSCE, other regional bodies? Some Security Council resolutions ban the use of mercenaries, albeit in an unregulated context.

Mercenaries were used in Sierra Leone and various other African conflicts with mixed results. Being professional soldiers, they were merciless in combat and in the field; while effective, they were not well-liked. Moreover, the violence that mercenaries inherently engender could produce lingering problems, contributing to further violence and extensive conflict.

Privatizing Peace Enforcement: A Necessary Evil?

Regulating the use of private security has become a necessity. This involves setting clear standards to guard against conflict of interest, govern entry and exit, establish human rights criteria, and provide guidelines for costs and pricing of the services. Pre-certification and or licensing of private security firms would be required condition for entry. While the UN has acted to ban mercenaries—as early as 1968, Resolution 2465 condemned the use of mercenaries; international humanitarian law reinforced this man with the adoption of Article 47 to the Additional Protocols to the Geneva Convention of 1977 and, more recently, with the 1989 International Convention against the Recruitment, Use, Financing, and Training of Mercenaries.[3] It is, at best, questionable that these measures were meant to apply in the context of a regulatory framework for the certification and governance of private security firms.

The use of private security is as old as mercantilism itself. The United East India Company of the Netherlands was granted powers to make war, conclude treaties, acquire territories, and build fortresses as part of it service to the government or crown. Chartered companies such as the British East Africa Company, which extended the imperial power of governments and royalty, were common in the age of imperialism. The United Kingdom is reputed to have hired 30,000 Hessian soldiers to fighting the American revolutionary war in order to avoid conscripting its own citizens.[4] Lord Lugard observed that these "empire-building" companies were, at best, an imperfect form of government. Today, however, the use of regulated private force may prove essential to meeting contemporary needs.

With post-Cold War downsizing there is an abundance of inexpensive military hardware on the international market, and numerous well-

---

[3]   See Damian Lilly, "The Privatization of Security and Peacebuilding: A Framework for Action," *International Alert*, September 2000. Also see Herbert Howe, "Global Order and Security Privatization," *Strategic Forum*, No. 140, May 1998, pp. 1–5.
[4]   See David Shearer, "Outsourcing War," *Foreign Policy*, No. 112, Fall 1998.

trained military personnel.[5] In weak states, possessing less than effective and loyal armies, private security firms are in demand. This combination of global market supply and State failure has led private security firms to become more active on several fronts: protecting assets of multinationals; protecting humanitarian workers, and assisting, sometimes even supplanting, state security forces. Given this global dynamic, it is increasingly likely that the United Nations will choose to expand its capability in peacekeeping and peace enforcement by acknowledging and properly regulating private security. International law permits states to employ necessary measures to maintain effective control over their territory, and as recently affirmed by the Organization of African Unity thus includes necessary measures to "respect the frontiers existing on their achievement of national independence."[6]

Regulation of private security, when it comes, should extend to weapons and munitions procurement and intelligence and logistics support, as well as the use of force. The UN would have to clearly delineate limits beyond which private security companies cannot stray. The real challenge will then lie in integration of private security in UN peace monitoring and enforcement functions. As John Donahue has observed, the privatization of defense is likely to be most successful when the mandate or talk at hand has clear and measurable goals, and when those goals are more important than the means by which they are achieved.[7]

Global regulation would need to be complemented by regional and national regulation to ensure coherent policy and effective enforcement. Many governments, including the United States and the United Kingdom, which already have laws governing international arms trafficking, do not deal with the subject of private security. South Africa, in the wake of international criticism over the activities of Executive Outcomes in Sierra Leone, also passed laws governing the establishment and activity of private security companies. Regional bodies such as the Organization of American States (OAS) and the Economic Community of West African States (ECOWAS) have laws regulating the flow of arms and munitions across borders but do not regulate private

    5   Deborah Avant, *The Market for Force: Exploring the Privatization of Military Services.* New York: Council on Foreign Relations, 1999, pp. 1–24.
    6   See Jeffrey Herbst, "The Regulation of Private Security Forces," paper prepared for conference on Privatization of Security in Africa, South African Institute of International Affairs, Pretoria, December 10, 1998, pp. 1–28.
    7   John Donahue, *The Privatization Decision: Public Ends, Private Means.* New York: Basic Books, 1989.

security. Codes of Conduct and self-regulation are always welcome additions to global, regional and national regulation, but unlikely to be effective without oversight by NGOs and civil society as well as governments and multilateral and regional institutions.

Once security is attained, by whatever means, attention can shift more fully to state rebuilding. Often there will not be the luxury of being able to wait for one state (physical insecurity) to end before the other (development) can begin. This is especially true in civil wars where the legacy of war can be devastating long after the shooting has subsided. Massive displacement of populations, unemployment, a breakdown in basic services, food insecurity, physical destruction, and a weakening of the social fabric have become the special characteristics of prolonged civil war. Multilateral and regional institutions have been able to effectively handle this legacy and to assist in the transition from a state of relief and risk of war to sustained reconstruction and development. Too often humanitarian relief and volunteer efforts coupled with stationing peacekeeping troops in a war-torn nation is seen as the solution. But this only thereby extends the occupation and militarization of a country. In effect, it creates a form of suspended or frozen emergency peacekeeping operations. The experiences of Afghanistan, Sudan and Cyprus are illustrative. Shifting from relief or saving lives to development or sustainable livelihoods is a difficult undertaking for the international community. What does it take for a country to be weaned from dependency to self-sufficiency? For a government to get back on its feet, for revenues to once more be regenerated, and for foreign investment to replace the largesse of relief and development aid? Before we turn to the role of the private sector in this enterprise, let us first draw some lessons from the impact of humanitarian relief on enabling this process of moving from relief to development to go forward.

Chapter 8

HUMANITARIAN ASSISTANCE: SAVING LIVES AND DISTORTING MARKETS

Sovereignty is no longer a guarantee of unqualified membership within the international community. As Mark Duffield has noted, there has in the last decade been an opening up of "humanitarian space." Kosovo and East Timor are the most recent examples of the fact that time-worn conceptions of sovereignty will no longer be allowed to stand in the way of protecting lives put at risk by the excesses of government.[1]

In these circumstances, particularly where warring factions disregard fundamental humanitarian principles and put a civilian population at grave risk of displacement, starvation and death, humanitarian agencies have sought to provide four basic types of assistance:

(1) save lives by meeting food, shelter and other basic survival needs;
(2) promote a social welfare safety net in the wake of weakened traditional support systems;
(3) protect human rights; and
(4) enable rehabilitation and livelihood development. In the latter case, humanitarian agencies have now stretched their mandate to venture into reconstruction and development, or what are now called "gray zone activities."

In places like Rwanda, UNHCR now finds itself not simply repatriating refugees but engaged in shelter and income-generating and

---

[1] See Mark Duffield, "Complex Emergencies and the Crisis of Developmentalism," *IDS Bulletin* 25:37–45, 1994; also see Mark Duffield, "Aid Policy and Post-Modern Conflict: A Critical Review," Occasional Paper 19, The School of Public Policy, University of Birmingham, 1998.

resettlement activities. These are tasks it is ill-equipped to handle. But in the absence of others coming in to do the job, it has assumed these additional responsibilities. The result, unfortunately is to often inadvertently plant the seeds of further conflict. In Afghanistan, the ICRC now finds itself managing and financing the operation and maintenance of hospitals and clinics, although it started by simply providing emergency medical supplies. The UN World Food Program now often finds itself supplying seeds and planting tools along with food. Development aid is surely needed in this gap between relief and development. But without a legitimate governmental authority or well-equipped institutional partner, measures like those of UN HCR and the UN World Food Program are severely handicapped. Traditional development performance standards are not utilized nor conditionalities made to prompt the collapsed state entities to recovery.

Operating under these conditions, humanitarian agencies have been vulnerable to a range of setbacks. Most prominently is the difficulty in maintaining core values of neutrality and humanity as they are subjected to increasing manipulation and politicization. For example, in the UN's Operation Lifeline Sudan (OLS), access is continually negotiated with both government and rebel sides with the result that agencies have been directly or indirectly assisting different warring factions.[2]

Margaret Buchanan-Smith[3] summarized several important ways in which relief can be manipulated. These include management of access to relief, use of malnourished populations to attract humanitarian resources, siphoning off of goods and services to support armed fighters or personal ales, taxation of relief goods, monopolizing procurement, and contracting for the transportation of illicit as well as licit goods and services. The unintended consequences of relief when it becomes politicized are great. This is especially true with regard to distortions which humanitarian relief, despite all its good intentions, can create in a local economy.

Humanitarian assistance has become big business. The OECD recorded a growth in expenditure on emergency relief from $600 million in 1985 to over $6 billion in 1995. That marks a growth of over 1,000% in less than a decade. The relief industry has grown to such pro-

---

    2   Karim, A., et al., "Operation Lifeline Sudan: A Review," Report, 1996, UNICEF.
    3   Margaret Buchanan-Smith, "Humanitarian Aid in the Political Economy of Collapsed States: Changes, Dilemmas and Unintended Consequences," paper presented at Conference on State Collapse and Reconstruction: Lessons and Strategies, ICRC/PSIS, Geneva, December 2000, pp. 1–13.

portions that there are now annual trade fairs marketing the wares and services of a multitude of private firms ranging from mine removal equipment to packaged foods, mini portable water purification facilities to instant tent cities and solar driven communication equipment. Such trade fairs, moving between Geneva and New York, reflect an entire industry. The WorldAid directory lists more than 2,000 commercial suppliers and over 500 aid agencies that exhibited at the UNOPS-organized international Aid and Trade Conference held in New York May 31—June 1, 2000. With the emergence of a global contract culture in pursuit of the spoils of humanitarian relief, it is understandable that relief agencies have been accused of perpetuating greed and fueling conflict in the name of altruism and peace. Bilateral donors have joined the bandwagon of advertising their largesse, anxious to demonstrate that they are responsive to CNN images of starving children. In so doing they also seek to portray themselves as having "legitimately" intervened in a "humanitarian" crisis, thus enabling relief to emerge as a subtle but important arm of foreign policy.

Robin Davies brilliantly captures the unintended distortions that humanitarian assistance, in concert with a large contingent of peace-keepers and international civil servants, can have on a local economy. He notes the purely inflationary impact wrought by the injection of such massive amounts of capital, from Cambodia to Mozambique and most recently the Balkans and East Timor.[4] With foreign money surging into the local economy, the local currency quickly becomes depreciated due to inflation in local prices for goods and services. Those sectors of the population living off the local economy are faced with exorbitant prices and the necessity to retreat into subsistence agriculture to survive, unless they are one of the few fortunate nationals to land a job in the UN administered economy. In terms of macro economic policy, the increase in the money supply without a proportional increase in products and services offered leads not only to runaway inflation, but also to rendering ineffective the traditional methods of controlling the money supply (i.e., by buying and selling government bonds). In the medium to long term, the power of the domestic government to maintain GDP growth with low inflation can be severely crippled.

Inevitably massive distortions occur, affecting wages and the local labor market. Suddenly, teachers in the Balkans traditionally making

---

4   Robin Davies, "The Dynamics of Large-Scale Humanitarian Assistance," paper presented at World Social Summit, Geneva, July 2000, pp. 1–16.

$30 per month in the classroom are abandoning their students to take up jobs as drivers and office clerks of the various relief and peacekeeping bodies at $300 per month. This internal brain drain has the additional negative effect of diverting much needed scarce local capacity away from the necessary task of reconstructing the public sector. Of course, the consequence of not hiring local labor is also problematic, as it gives many in the indigenous population the status of "aid recipient." The result can often be to subtly create an "entitlement" welfare-oriented mentality which is difficult to overcome when the aid is no longer there, turning to bitter resentment against the hand that fed. Compounding the difficulty of transition to a self-reliant, sustainable economy are the following ubiquitous factors: a) the external brain drain faced by fledgling states, b) the reduction in the labor force due to refugee streams, and c) the illusion of a sustainable economic boost that humanitarian assistance often creates before being burst upon withdrawal.

There are more often than not long-term budgetary and human capacity implications of such short-term relief assistance. First, successful implementation of many projects requires long-term funding and capacity, most of which must be undertaken by local actors. Thus the entire issue of sustainability is left up in the air, as neither the capability to raise revenues for continued financing nor the human capacity has been transferred or put in place locally to sustain institutions and operations.

Bridging the "Ingenuity Gap"

Thomas Homer-Dixon, Director of the Peace and Conflict Studies Program at the University of Toronto, and author of *Environment, Scarcity and Violence*, contends that scarcity of natural resources increases risk of insurgency, ethnic clashes, urban riots and coups d'état.[5] In his latest book, *The Ingenuity Gap* (Knopf, 2000), he asserts: "Environmental problems cannot, by themselves, cause violence. They must combine with other factors, usually the failure of economic

---

[5]   Homer-Dixon poses that environmental scarcity in coming decades could produce five general types of conflict: "(1) Disputes arising directly from local environmental degradation caused, for instance, by factory emissions, logging, or dam construction; (2) ethnic clashes arising from population migration and deepened social cleavages due to environmental scarcity; (3) civil strife (including insurgency, banditry, and coups d'état) caused by environmental scarcity that affects economic productivity and, in turn, people's livelihoods, the behavior of elite groups, and the ability of states to meet these changing demands; (4) scarcity-induced interstate war over, for example, water; (5) North-South conflict (i.e., conflicts between the devel-

institutions or government."[6] Societies that adapt well to the problems of scarcity, he says, tend to deliver sufficient ingenuity to address associated social and technological problems. Innovations that address these problems can potentially alleviate—even prevent—conflict, bridging the "ingenuity gap."

Homer-Dixon notes: "The information revolution has contributed to a shift in power from states and governments to individuals and subgroups, complicating the abilities of governing powers to coordinate and enforce solutions and problems."[7] Here, the business community can provide incentives for learning, training and alternative economic opportunities to bridge the ingenuity gap.

One example of private sector involvement in bridging the ingenuity gap is seen through a partnership between Intel Corporation, Conservation International, and UNESCO (UN Educational, Scientific and Cultural Organization). Since 1996, Conservation International and Intel Corporation have partnered with UNESCO to provide computers, geographic information system (GIS) software, Internet connections, and hands-on training to managers of 25 biosphere reserves worldwide. The biosphere reserve network, created in 1976 by UNESCO, encompasses protected areas in 82 countries. Through partnerships like this, both the digital divide and ingenuity gap are lessened and human capital is strengthened as scientific research is conducted, conservation methods adapted, and sustainable natural resource practices are implemented.

It is not unusual for informal, or "black," economies that develop during the survival mode of armed conflict to become so deeply entrenched that it outlasts the end of the fighting. Indeed, often at war's end it is endemic as opportunistic thinking prevents a long-term approach compounded with the rise in corruption. This shadow economy pays little or no taxes, thus depriving the reemerging state of much-needed revenue sources. This occurs as scarce local capital and skills are diverted away from productive investments to provide more immediate and profitable services to UN or other international administrators. This tendency is in turn exacerbated by the collusion of interests amidst donors who

---

oped and developing worlds) over mitigation of, adaptation to, and compensation for global environmental problems like global warming, ozone depletion, threats to biodiversity, and decreases in fish stocks." Homer-Dixon, Thomas F., *Environment, Scarcity, and Violence*. Princeton University Press, 1999, p. 5.

  6   Homer-Dixon, Thomas F., "The Ingenuity Gap: How Can We Solve the Problems of The Future?" *The Washington Post*, November 16, 2000.

  7   "The Ingenuity Gap," Carnegie Endowment for International Peace, November 13, 2000. http://www.ceip.org/ files/events/IngenuityGap.asp?p=7.

need to disburse aid commitments as indicators of performance, relief agencies whose very existence depends upon the next emergency, contractors whose bottom line is profit, and corrupt officials, warlords, and bureaucrats whose greed and personal survival is more important than their commitment to their country or their people.

Unregulated and out of control, the private sector can just as easily collude with humanitarian and local actors in Kosovo as it can with warlords in Liberia to plant the seeds of recurring conflict and ensuing chaos. Privatizing a state-owned company in Croatia or the former Soviet Union in a vacuum of responsible business leadership is likely to lead to no better result than the demobilizing of youthful unskilled and unsupported combatants in Sierra Leone in a security and employment vacuum. Privatizing peace must mean more than simply opening up channels for rapacious companies. What needs to be done?

First and foremost, the new rules of the game must be established. With property rights and contractual obligation not respected, it is little wonder that foreign investment, the engine of reconstruction and development, is wary of entry into war-affected areas struggling to break from the past. It took two years for UNMIK to establish a viable commercial law in Kosovo. Only recently has the idea of emergency legal teams begun to take root as being of nearly equal importance to provision of shelter, food and security. Still, the preoccupation with establishment of criminal and human right law overshadows attention to business and commercial law. Political and military stability needs to be balanced by economic and social stability. Privatizing peace, if anything, means putting in place a transparent, accountable, and enforceable set of rules, laws and norms of behavior, as well as the institutions and human capacity to implement them. With three different types of uncertain and unenforceable property rights (state, communal and individual) operating in Kosovo, there is little likelihood that even a citizen will invest in his own area, never mind a foreign investor. With poor to no contract or bankruptcy laws, there is little to ensure the security of assets, and little to impede their transfer out of the country.

Relief agencies need be driven by local needs, and not by donor and NGO perceptions. Like commercial enterprises, they must be held to a code of operation, a set of standards and a high degree of transparency and accountability. The Sphere Project, launched in 1997 by a number of humanitarian agencies, has developed a Humanitarian Charter and a set of universal minimum standards for humanitarian assistance and disaster relief in the areas of water supply and sanitation, nutrition, food aid, shelter and site planning, and medical services. The Charter is based on international humanitarian law, as well as on the principles of the Code of Conduct for the International Red Cross and Red Crescent Movement and Non-Governmental Organizations in Disaster Relief (1994). By focusing on promoting sustainable livelihoods rather than being exclusively centered on saving lives, they will be able to avoid the longer-term implications of their initial quick fixes. For example, by moving from food aid to cash aid as the response to agricultural crises, they can avoid undercutting local production. As local farmers cannot compete with a price of zero, that of free food, it is better to provide cash aid to enable them to work their own fields.

Similarly, utilizing local skills such as carpentry to build windows and door frames, rather than contracting to external suppliers, can enhance rehabilitation and revitalize local human capital and small enterprises. In Krajina, Croatia, the Catholic Relief Services (CRS) provides an excellent model: they give returning local carpenters tools and building supplies, guaranteeing them a market by providing orders for goods they might otherwise buy on the external market (such as school desks, chairs, windows, and the like), and pay them back in kind through goods produced until the cost of tools and materials are paid for. Meanwhile, the local craftsman is back in business, generating demand while enabling the CRS to transit from relief to development.

In Kosovo and Bosnia the Mercy Corps, an international NGO, works to not only bridge the divide between warring sides by integrating them into shared credit unions, but also works through micro-financing to all both sides to repay loans in kind. Gradually, as borrowers get their enterprises up and running, they can earn, save and repay in currency, shifting from the in-king loan servicing to normal banking practices.

By building local capacity and procuring local goods, rather than substituting for local labor and materials, unintentionally undercutting capacity-building and local markets in the process, relief agencies can contribute to the development of medium to longer term human resources required to resurrect the economy.

Because humanitarian assistance is often fungible, especially budgetary support through structural adjustment operations, it can, if placed in the wrong hands, fuel conflict as well as support reconstruction and development. Humanitarian relief in Goma (Rwanda) ended up feeding an army in training, the Intrahamwe; while aid to the treasury in

Rwanda freed up local resources to support armed struggle in the Democratic Republic of the Congo. These problems call for greater accountability and transparency. They also call for a review of budgeting and planning procedures for relief and development work.

Trade, too, can be linked to conflict. As Neil Cooper explains: "Conflict goods are non-military materials, knowledge, animals or humans whose trade, taxation or protection is exploited to finance or otherwise maintain the war economies of contemporary conflicts. Trade can take place by direct import or export from the conflict zone or on behalf of military factions (both government and non-government) by outside supporters. Arms, military aid and services of mercenaries, as they may be paid in kind, concessions, or cash could be included as conflict goods."[8]

Privatizing peace in the context of trade requires regulating the illicit flow of conflict-enabling highly-valued, easily tradable commodities like diamonds, gold, and precious gemstones. Similarly, goods which are only slightly less tradeable—like forest woods, oil, drugs and arms—call for trafficking controls. Yet another aspect of the illicit trade that fuels conflict needs to be arrested and controlled is illicit traffic in people, whether children used as cooks, porters or soldiers, or women held in bondage for prostitution. Once such example is large-scale prostitution trafficking out of Macedonia to the Balkans. In Badme, on the border of Ethiopia and Eritrea, it was discovered in late 2000 that some 5,000 prostitutes had been brought to this small border town to serve the troops; thus increasing the risk of AIDS throughout Ethiopia as many of the front line troops returned to their villages throughout the country after demobilization. Fortunately, the World Bank-assisted demobilization program in Ethiopia has a sizable AIDS screening, education, and protection component.

To prevent the criminalization of war economies through informal taxes in the form of protection money, the illegal sale of state assets for personal gain, and the improper provision of trade and mining concessions, these activities must be brought under official transparent control and regulation if peace is to be sustained. In this regard, closer collaboration of the private sector with humanitarian agencies offers distinct advantages. The new relationship can transcend commerce.

---

[8]   Neil Cooper, "The Role of Conflict Goods in State Collapse and Reconstruction," paper for conference on State Collapse and Reconstruction, ICRC/PSIS, Geneva, December 6–10, 2000.

Business can provide technology transfer, management, marketing and organizational expertise, and practical cost-conscious approaches to problem-solving as positive features of a new business-humanitarian partnership.

Ericsson Response: First on the Ground

In April 2000, Ericsson, a leading telecommunications corporation, announced Ericsson Response, a global initiative aimed to alleviate suffering in the wake of disaster. In conjunction with various UN entities including the Office for the Coordination of Humanitarian Affairs (OCHA) and the UN Development Program (UNDP), and the International Federation of Red Cross and Red Crescent Societies (IFRC), Ericsson has begun to establish disaster preparedness programs, rapid deployment communications technologies, and a volunteer program.

Later that year the partnership was extended and the "First on the Ground" project was announced. Ericsson, operating in over 140 countries, claims that because communications systems are among the first casualties of disaster, and because humanitarian efforts are using various communications systems prohibiting their overall organization and efficiency, its capacity to assist rescue missions and relief operations is much needed. The multinational will now provide and maintain mobile communications equipment and expertise for humanitarian relief operations and will help to improve existing networks where appropriate.

Ericsson's history in disaster response includes providing mobile base stations for refugee camps during the Kosovo crisis, reinstalling damaged telecom equipment for earthquake victims in Turkey, and providing phones for flood victims in Vietnam. Whether it be a disaster-to-peace or war-to-peace transition (often interchangeable scenarios), the presence of such infrastructure and focused attention forecasts a recovery that achieves the peace phase.

"Ericsson pledges support for improved disaster response," Press Release, 11 April 2000; "First on the Ground: Communications in Disaster Relief Operations," Media Release from the Office of the United Nations Resident Coordinator, UN Viet Nam, 2 September 2000.

Chapter 9

BRIDGING RELIEF AND DEVELOPMENT: THE CHANGING ROLE OF Ngos AND THE EMERGENCE OF THE GLOBAL CIVIL SOCIETY MOVEMENT

Non-governmental organizations which play an important role in relief are becoming increasingly attuned to the changes required to play an even greater role in bridging the gap between relief and development. They are emerging at the forefront of advocacy for transparency and accountability with regards to corruption, environmental degradation and human rights abuses.

In the wake of the tumultuous WTO meeting in Seattle, and the subsequent protests at the IMF and World Bank in Washington by a coalition of civil society organizations, the Edelman Group, a New York polling agency, surveyed opinions of five hundred individuals active in the media, between the ages of 34 and 64, from each of five industrialized countries (United States, United Kingdom, France, Germany and Australia) regarding attitudes toward NGOs, global multinational corporations, and the G7 governments. It found as follows:

1) NGOS are trusted nearly two to one to "do what is right" compared to governments, media and corporations;
2) NGOs rank significantly higher as a source of credible information than media outlets or companies on issues such as labor and human rights, genetically modified food, and environmental and health matters; and
3) NGOs such as Amnesty International, Greenpeace, the Sierra Club, and the World Wildlife Fun have greater credibility than

such corporations as Exxon, Ford, Microsoft, Monsanto, or Nike. Eighty percent of US respondents view Greenpeace as highly effective, 78% for Amnesty International. Only 11% see government or companies as "making the world a better place."[1]

Clearly this lack of trust in media, corporations, and government is widening, as respect for the role of the global emerging civil society movement increases despite recent excesses. It is not surprising in this light that the State of the World Forum, a leading global civil society body, recently launched a Commission on Globalization. The overarching theme set for further study by the forum is the effect of globalization on peace and security.

The NGO Experience in War-to-Peace Transitions

There is general consensus that NGOs play an enormously valuable role in relief, and that they could be even more instrumental in facilitating war-to-peace transitions. In his Agenda for Peace, former UN Secretary-General Boutrous Boutrous-Ghali emphasized that peace in the largest sense cannot be accomplished by the United Nations system or governments alone: "Non-governmental organizations, academic institutions, parliamentarians, business and professional communities, the media and the public at large must all be involved."[2] In terms of preventive diplomacy, non-governmental organizations are well-placed to play a part in early warning by drawing the attention of governments to nascent crises and emerging conflicts; and in post conflict peace-building they can do much to assist fragile governments and destitute populations to find the means to make peace last. On a day-to-day basis it is the non-governmental organizations, through their emphasis on popular participation and inclusiveness, that best link democracy to peace.

---

1   Edelman PR Worldwide is the world's largest independent, privately-held public relations firm and the sixth-largest overall, with 2000 revenues of $225 million, 40 offices, and 2,000 employees worldwide. Strategy One is the division of Edelman which conducted the survey. See full press release and report: "Non-Government Organizations More Trusted than Media, Most-Respected Corporations and Government," December 1999.

2   Boutrous-Ghali, B., Agenda For Peace. UN Document A/477-277, October 3, 1992.

NGOs and their Relationship to the Multilateral System

Non-governmental organizations represent civil society participation in the international system. Traditionally, the UN had no institutional or informal framework for citizen representation. NGO active engagement with the UN system derives from UN Charter Article 71, which empowers the Economic and Social Council (ECOSOC) to make suitable arrangements for consultation with non-governmental organizations. Today non-governmental organizations can be accorded consultative status. The proliferation of non-governmental entities calls on the UN system and the international financial institutions to facilitate better coordination. This has proven a challenge. NGOs are notorious for their independence and coordination is not their hallmark. While greater collaboration would be helpful in limiting random activity, overlap and duplication, formal UN-led efforts at coordination are not viewed by NGO leaders as desirable. They generally believe that left to their own devices, they can push harder and more openly for drastic changes based on their relationships with governments, sometimes adversarial but at other times cooperative and businesslike. At the local level, NGOs often develop deep relationships and establish significant bases of popular support; and at an international level, bilateral and multilateral organizations increasingly rely on them as project subcontractors and a public consciousness.

NGOs have worked in close collaboration with the UN and the World Bank in responding to complex humanitarian crises occasioned by the collapse of governments, ethnic or religious conflict, and natural disasters. They provide technical expertise in the field, mediate between local communities and the state, and, as in the case of West Bank/Gaza, have taken a leadership role in reconstruction. Moreover, the World Bank and NGOs have worked together on the issue of structural adjustment policies, a matter of central concern for many NGOs. As part of the Bank's commitment to engaging the NGO community it has undertaken a joint initiative with some of its strongest critics to review the Bank's structural adjustment policies through a multi-country civil society assessment. The Structural Adjustment Participatory Review Initiative (SAPRI) was proposed to the Bank by the NGOs as part of a comprehensive review of adjustment programs in conjunction with NGOs. The Bank accepted that challenge and over one thousand civil society organizations have formed part of the SAPRI network in a process that involves eight different countries. The Bank has also made special efforts to engage local NGOs in ground operations and has established a special unit for that purpose.

Nonetheless, there are substantial obstacles to NGO-UN-World Bank partnering arrangements. There remains a widely held view that "there is no NGO community. They are extremely diverse and cannot simply be lumped and institutionalized as one group." Antonio Donini, a senior officer in the Executive Office of the Secretary-General of the United Nations, writes, reflective of this view, in an article on "The Bureaucracy and the Free Spirits," that the evolving "NGO galaxy" is an extremely diverse and sometimes fractious universe crisscrossed by contradictory forces.

Andrew Nastsios, named Administrator of US Agency for International Development (USAID) in April 2001 and former Vice President of World Vision and Executive Director of World Visions Relief and Development, observes that absent complete reorganization of the relief response structure, which is politically and administratively unfeasible, incremental reform through greater NGO unity provides the best answer. He suggests that NGOs could better organize themselves through InterAction, an umbrella NGO group, and the International Council of Voluntary Agencies (ICVA), and that operating on the basis of a unified strategy among themselves, they could substantially increase the chances for successful partnership between them and the UN system. However, questions remain as to the extent that NGOs are ready and willing to be involved in such global partnerships.

NGOs, which have also been referred to as the "Civil Society Community," reflecting the diversity of these organizations, have played an increasingly significant role in peacebuilding, particularly in Mozambique, the West Bank and Gaza, and in Bosnia. This experience the advantages of particular NGO involvement in peace-making as well as peacebuilding. The experience of NGOs in Gaza and the West Bank illustrates the difficulties which often arise between NGOs and emerging governments, and how those tensions can be dealt with successfully.

In Bosnia, there has been a general lack of cooperation between the UN and NGOs. For example, efforts by NGOs to engage in rule-of-law reform and restructuring of judicial institutions have not been supported by the UN High Representative. On the other hand, Mozambique's development and economic growth can in large measure be attributed to the structure of coordination between the international community, NGOs and the government of Mozambique. In the West Bank and Gaza, NGOs and the Palestinian Authority often failed to find common ground, but World Bank intervention and cooperation through regular communication helped smooth many of these difficulties.

Mozambique: NGOs and the Peacemaking and Peacebuilding Nexus

The Mozambique civil conflict raged for 15 years (1977–1992) at tremendous cost in human lives and refugees. Its resolution stands out as one of Africa's, and indeed the world's, great success stories. Its history provides valuable lessons for peacemaking and for peacebuilding, and demonstrates that the two stages are closely linked: how a war ends can often be instrumental in determining the success of peacebuilding. It also shows that NGOs can play a critical role in both phases.

Peacemaking in Mozambique was made possible by the active involvement of the government of the United States, although largely behind the scenes, and a respected NGO, the Community of Sant'Egidio, an Italian Catholic lay order. Peacemaking efforts by the key outside government actor involved, the United States, was hampered by the Cold War. Within the US Administration it led to conflicting views—beyond agreement on the supply of about $100,000 million per annum for humanitarian aid—over which side to support. The ruling FRELIMO government was supported by the State Department. The Department of Defense and the CIA tended to align Mozambique with Angola and Ethiopia, as a Soviet client state, pointing to its embrace of Marxist principles, and instead campaigned for US aid and military assistance to the RENAMO insurgency, which they viewed as "the wave of the future." In this political cauldron, which might otherwise have resulted in a stalemate among contending bureaucratic forces, the Sant'Egidio played a critical role which helped push President Reagan, on October 7, 1987, to urge President Joaquim Chissano of Mozambique to accept negotiations aimed at transforming RENAMO from a guerrilla army into a political force through free elections.

In the effort at encouraging dialogue and reconciliation, the United States was aided by a number of governments who had interest in Mozambique: Portugal, Kenya, Zimbabwe, Italy, and the Vatican. But it was the Sant'Egidio, which had become a non-threatening link to RENAMO, which was destined to played perhaps the most critical role. Through Assistant Secretary of State for Africa, Henry Cohen, Sant'Egidio's peacemaking role was actively supported. Thus the United States played virtually no public role in the pre-negotiations during 1989, although it followed them closely through its embassies in Maputo,

Nairobi, Pretoria, and Rome, and left to Sant'Egidio, away from the spot-light, the principal task of urging President Chissano to enter into direct talks aimed at a pluralistic multiparty system government.

On October 4, 1992, 27 months after having seriously negotiated in Rome in July 1990, the two protagonists signed a final cease fire and set-tlement of claims. A Joint Political Military Commission was established to oversee implementation, with the UN Special Representative in Mozambique who had been present at the peace talks working as the tie-breaking chairman of the Commission. Whereas in Angola the UN representative was a mere observer with no power, in Mozambique he had become the virtual czar of implementation. UN peacekeeping forces consisting of 7,000 persons were brought in to keep the peace, compared to only 500 that had been sent in earlier to Angola to maintain the peace there. The United States, Portugal and a number of other governments had become official observers to the peace negotiations, and their inter-est in the subsequent phase of peacebuilding was enhanced by their par-ticipation in the earlier phase.

The lesson of Mozambique is clear: NGO intervention in the role of trusted intermediary and mediator, a role which the Sant'Egidio played to great effect, combined with US and other regional power involvement, facilitated both peace negotiations and a head-start in post conflict reconstruction. It is a model of what can be done by NGOs, in concert with other institutional partners, in the peacebuilding process.

Gaza and the West Bank: Easing NGO-Government Tensions

The 1993 Oslo Peace Accords enabled peacebuilding for the Israel-Palestinian track of the Arab-Israeli conflict. Prior to that, largely indige-nous NGOs in conjunction with UNRWA, the United Nations Relief and Works Administration for Palestinian Refugees, played an important role in the provision of services that normally would have been accorded by a government. Thus between 1967 and 1993, when Israeli military occupation ended, and for many NGOs during the period of Jordanian and Egyptian rule over the West Bank and Gaza (WBG) between 1949 and 1967, as documented by Barbara Balaj of the World Bank in her excellent study on the subject, NGOs were responsible for provision of the bulk of primary, secondary and tertiary health care services. Before 1993 they were responsible for 100 percent of disability care, 100 percent of pre-school programs, and a large proportion of agricultural training, welfare, housing and other services in the area.

As of 1994, there were over 1,200 domestic and 200 international NGOs in the WBG. Of the latter, many were created during the Intifada (1994–1998 Palestinian uprising against Israeli occupation). In her study, Balaj concludes that many NGOs "were highly politicized and served as little more than political fronts, with the service provided being of secondary importance"[3] insofar as promotion of Palestinian national autonomy had assumed parallel, if not superseding, importance to service delivery. In this intensified political climate, rivalries among international NGOs emerged as they competed with each other over political goals and coordination with indigenous NGOs. The result has been an NGO sector that tends to be very unruly and large in relation to the small geographic size of the West Bank and Gaza, with poor coordination among the various organizations. The beginning of the Israel-Palestinian peace process only further aggravated matters, as the transfer of service responsibilities to the new Palestinian Authority (PA) was seen as threatening the NGOs preeminence in this field. And with donors to NGOs switching to financing the PA, a funding crisis loomed for many NGOs which had been providing critical health, education and social welfare services. In this context, NGO-Palestinian Authority relations inevitably became strained, as the PA wanted to be seen as the direct deliverer of "peace dividends," and became distrustful of many NGOs, viewing them as critics and/or political opponents.

Several lessons emerge from this experience in Gaza and the West Bank. The first relates to tensions between an emerging government and a strong NGO community with substantial links to outside funders—as community which, unlike its counterpart in Mozambique, had not been involved in the peacemaking phase, but rather saw itself as being uprooted by the peace process. Here there is a need for intervention to ensure no disruptions in public service delivery as the sometimes difficult modalities for transition are worked out. The World Bank, in conjunction with donor governments, can enable a smooth transition by selecting high-quality NGO programs for funding and letting others go. It can use its expertise to make assessments of NGO activities and establish a clear legal and regulatory basis for governing their activities, including registration and possibly assistance in creation of a PA liai-

---

[3]   Balaj, Barbara, "NGOs in the West Bank and Gaza," The World Bank, 1999.

son office for NGO dealings. In this way the World Bank can contribute to diminution of government-NGO tensions, and aid in elimination of NGO duplication of effort and inefficient use of resources.

In fact, the World Bank has played that role in the West Bank and Gaza, going beyond the more hesitant and cautious approach (previously advocated as Bank policy) of serving merely as a useful interlocutor between the government and NGOs. In bringing them together, the Bank facilitated joint efforts for economic recovery and development by enabling international and local NGOs to become more professionalized, transparent and accountable in their financing and programs. Recognizing the key role played by NGOs, the Bank's Emergency Assistance Program for the West Bank and Gaza (1994–96) included additional assistance of $120 million for incremental budget support for NGOs. In addition, the World Bank provided further assistance by creating the Palestinian NGO project, which helped to ease the shift in donor funding away from NGOs to the Palestinian Authority during the transition to peace. The Bank proposed the establishment of a NGO trust fund to provide funding for NGOs over three years, and to enable the best of them to restore their programs. Development grants to NGOs range from $5,000 to $1 million in health, education, agriculture and social welfare services.

The World Bank can do more, in coordination with the PA, to strengthen institutional capacities and to professionalize the operations of NGOs receiving grants under the project. Clearly, both the PA and the NGOs would be the beneficiaries of an improved legal and regulatory framework for NGO operations. Enabling such NGO-governmental coordination will put to the test the World Bank's evolving political skills. The IFC track record in establishing good government and good NGO relations while encouraging reform in the West Bank and Gaza augurs well for future Bank-NGO relations in Gaza and the West Bank and elsewhere.

InterAction: Coordinating NGO Operations

InterAction is the umbrella group for NGOs operating in the United States. It has sought to act as a unifying element and also to ease the inhibitions of many American NGOs in reaching out to the private sector.

Enhanced NGO cooperation is, however, difficult to achieve. Most NGOs are fiercely zealous in protecting their independence and separate sources of revenue. They also tend to be suspicious of the private sector and the World Bank, and to aggressively challenge multinational corporations' influence and power, demanding that business recognize a broader set of stakeholders and become more accountable to civil society. The action of the NGO community during the disruption of the Winter 1999 WTO meeting in Seattle was indicative of this attitude. Although the NGO community distanced itself from the destructive elements that led to street violence in Seattle, the NGO community tended to support the demands of the most vocal protesters, echoing their sentiments that international business is not to be trusted and that international organizations must be subjected to public scrutiny.

In many respects NGOs, in their interaction among themselves and in their outreach to the private sector, have reached a more advanced level in the United Kingdom. International Alert, in particular, has done an exemplary job in working with the international NGO community to coordinate activity, and in reaching out to the private sector in conjunction with the Prince of Wales Business Leaders Forum and other corporate groups. As a result, it has in a very short time since its inception in 1985 come to be respected by all players in the field, including governments with whom it has cooperated in a variety of settings establishing the neutral space for negotiations. Its basic position, which serves as a model for an often fractious NGO world, is set forth in its Code of Conduct for Conflict Transformation Work (1998): "International Alert (IA) believes that in partnership the 'whole' is greater than the sum of its parts. It aspires to be an organization able to network across regions and cultures, building coalitions among non-governmental organizations and other institutions." Moreover, it brings to bear extensive knowledge in understanding the history and socio-economic context of conflicts, plays a constructive role in planning programs coherently, and has a proven track record of working in tandem with the private sector.

By participating in innovative partnerships, NGOs may be better able to influence national and international dialogues on peacebuilding and on reforms that support sustainable development. Peter Sollis, in *The UN and Global Governance* (1996), asserts that in post-war conditions "NGO fragmentation is a liability . . . fragmentation hinders the effectiveness of resource-starved NGO associations. With their narrow base, NGO associations are unable to play an influential role in creating real commitment to greater coordination . . . this is particularly true at the program level."[4] A framework for NGO collaboration would thus

---

[4]   Sollis, Peter, "Partners in Development? The State, NGOs and the UN in

strengthen the contribution that NGOs can make through lessening their tendency to fragmentation. In demonstrating that good working relations by selected representatives of the NGO community can be established with the other players in peacebuilding efforts, a ripple effect can be created enabling more constructive across the board dealings between NGOs, the World Bank and UN officials, and representatives of the private sector.

Central America," in *The UN and Global Governance*. New York: United Nations, 1996, pp. 189–203.

Chapter 10

PUBLIC-PRIVATE-CIVIL SOCIETY PARTNERSHIPS: THE NEW PEACEBUILDING TRILOGY

Peacebuilding commonly refers to reconstruction and reconciliation as leading to the consolidation of peace, prevention of recurrent
violent episodes and the transition to normal development. This is far
too complex and important a task to be left solely to the United Nations
and the Bretton Woods Institutions. Surely it is not something that weak
governments, divided societies, or NGOs can take on alone. A far more
effective approach is to integrate the private sector into Peacebuilding
as private investment will remain the primary engine of sustainable
growth and development in war-torn societies. The largesse of the international aid community, or more mounting debt incurred by borrowing from multilateral financial institutions is a poor substitute for private
capital.

However, doing business in the global marketplace, many corporations soon find themselves working in areas rife with political, social
and environmental challenges, the most threatening being armed conflict. In this environment, multinational corporations cannot escape the
scrutiny of human rights and environmental advocacy groups, from
Global Witness reporting on the rape of the Cambodian hardwood forest and Angolan diamond mines, to Human Rights Watch criticizing the
abuses of warring factions in West Africa. Many companies now
acknowledge, through the formation of special divisions and staff, that
protecting human rights, attending to the social and environmental
impact of their investments, and doing good as well as maximizing profits must standard parts of their investment strategy.

In a recent congressional hearing on Security in a New Century, Juliette Bennett of the International Peace Forum summarized a range of investment activities, worldwide, which endeavor to promote peace and prevent conflict as an essential element of a successful investment strategy.[1] She recounts the work of companies like BP Amoco in partnering with local government and NGOs to eliminate corruption and promote the rule of law and the more equitable distribution of profits from their investments in Nigeria; and Freeport McMoran Copper and Gold Inc., working to promote community development in West Papua in Indonesia.

More recently, the US and the UK, working together with non-governmental organizations, sponsored an effort which led to a number of private companies agreeing to a voluntary standard on corporate security arrangements which focus on human rights. UN High Commissioner for Human Rights Mary Robinson has emphasized on an expanded human rights agenda which includes economic and social rights, and a rights-based approach to development. As a result human rights and peace organizations are now looking to the business community to play a key role. Groups like Amnesty International are working closely with companies like BP Amoco, Royal Dutch Shell and Rio Tinto in the development of a corporate human rights policy.[2] Others, like International Alert, the Prince of Wales Business Leaders Forum, and the Council on Economic Priorities, have recently conducted research on the private sector as a partner for conflict prevention and resolution, setting forth a framework of key questions and parameters against which private companies can assess the likely impact of their investments on conflict. The rising costs of security services to protect assets and avoid material losses from subversive activities such as the blowing up of oil pipelines in Nigeria and Colombia as well as litigation and reputational costs, and lost opportunity costs, have led to heightened concern by multinationals, particularly in the mineral extractive industries, about the positive as well as negative roles that businesses can play in conditions of violent conflict.[3]

---

1   Juliette Bennett, "Promoting Regional Stability through Public-Private Partnerships," presentation for the House Study Group on Security for a New Century, December 1, 2000, pp. 1–20.

2   Amnesty International UK, "Human Rights—Is it Any of Your Business?" London, 2000.

3   "The Business of Peace," *International Alert*, London: The Council on Economic Priorities and the Prince of Wales Business Leaders Forum, October 21, 2000.

The UN has become involved with Secretary-General Kofi Annan's 1999 "Global Compact" actively pledging support of improved governance policies which enhance human security as well as flourishing markets. A number of signatories have already formed effective partnerships with UN special agencies to promote these goals. Microsoft worked with UNHCR in Kosovo to develop a computerized refugee registration system to better service and track assistance to refugees. SAFIR, a South African aviation company, has worked with the World Food Program to improve drop technology for food distribution to internally displaced persons in high-conflict areas. Ericsson has worked with the UN Office for the Coordination of Humanitarian Affairs (OCHA) and the ICRC to provide state-of-the-art wireless communication for humanitarian relief workers. Lloyd Dumas said it best over a decade ago in his book *Economics and Alternative Security*: "There is no necessary reason why multinational corporations' decisions could not be geared to the pursuit of the broader and longer term goals that characterize the peacekeeping [and peacebuilding—authors' addition] international economy."[4]

Cisco and UNDP Launch Netaid.org

September 8, 1999. US President Bill Clinton, British Prime Minister Tony Blair, and former South Africa President Nelson Mandela logged onto http://www.netaid.org to launch the largest humanitarian Internet site in history. Cisco Systems, an international leader in Internet networking, donated over $10 million in 1999 to found, in conjunction with UNDP, Netaid, a web-based initiative that aims to relieve extreme poverty and aid in humanitarian relief efforts worldwide. Internet users are able to donate various packages of aid through the site to assist processes such as reuniting refugee children with their mothers, preventing the spread of HIV/AIDS in Asia and Africa, bringing safe drinking water and good hygiene to rural communities in Honduras, and providing safer environments for childbirth in Rwanda.

Netaid began with the Internet broadcast of three benefit concerts on October 9, 1999 in Geneva, London and New Jersey. A portion of the proceeds assisted refugees in Kosovo and relief work in Africa. Furthermore, the partnership has aimed to provide students in developing countries in the Asia Pacific region with Internet access. Netaid is also sponsored in part by KPMG and Akamai Technologies.

---

4   Lloyd Dumas, *Economics and Alternative Security*. Austin: University of Texas, 1990.

Lippman, Thomas W. "An Unlikely Net Alliance: Cisco, UN Plan Site to Fight Third World Poverty," *Washington Post*, August 12, 1999; Pareles, Jon. "Concerts to introduce humanitarian website," *New York Times*, September 9, 1999

The private sector can help address the legacy of war in four ways. First, the creation of jobs by the private sector will, socially and economically, reintegrate war-affected populations—returning refugees, internally displaced persons, and demobilized soldiers—into postwar society. When former soldiers are not reintegrated, the risk of their returning to a life of crime or exploitation behind the barrel of a gun are highly. In Uganda, where over 80% of ex-combatants were successfully reintegrated into agriculture and small enterprise, a study of violence among them confirmed that on average they committed fewer crimes than even ordinary citizens.

Second, private industry can accomplish the equally important task of rebuilding the institutions and culture of enterprise culture required to sustain peace. While the legacy of war is often obvious, the structural causes of war are less clear, and therefore too often ignored. Weak public institutions that precede and often cause war can persist even after peace has been established. For example, the legal institutions of post conflict nations are often in shambles. Aside from physical infrastructure such as courthouses and prisons, few post conflict nations have enough trained lawyers, judges, or investigators to restart their legal system. The private sector and a broadened notion of security, that is, human security, go hand in hand. The promotion of the rule of law, particularly as it pertains to property rights and the honoring of contractual agreements, is as essential to human security as is the promotion of human rights under international law.

Third, the private sector, through the conversion of military assets to productive civilian use, can dismantle the physical infrastructure of war. For example, the government can sell land to a private firm with the understanding that the firm will de-mine that piece of territory. Similarly, former combat installations—bases, field offices, and so on— can be sold to companies that might find use for these buildings. In South Africa over 1000 former military bases are now being targeted for conversion to civilian use, freeing land for former disenfranchised peoples, and providing ready infrastructure for investors to create industrial zones and promote employment and productivity. Clearly the private sector can help to accelerate the demilitarization of the country.

Fourth, the private sector can replace the war economy, giving people new sources of wealth and therefore new incentives to observe the peace. A good example is the Peace Parks Foundation in Southern Africa, which facilitates partnerships between the private sector, local communities and government to promote eco-tourism, conservation, and job creation along contentious borders. The World Wildlife Foundation has also been instrumental in promoting such peaceful uses of contentious space worldwide.

National reconciliation is difficult to achieve during the peace consolidation phase, but here, too, private institutions can help. By bringing together former combatants in an atmosphere that stresses both cooperation and strict discipline, private companies can contribute a little to encouraging them to live together peacefully again. PeaceWorks, a "not only for profit" food company, seeks to promote reconciliation and cultural understanding among diverse warring groups in the Middle East and South Africa by forming joint venture companies between Israelis and Palestinians. In Ireland, Oracle worked with the State of the World Forum to donate 100 Internet computer hookups to Catholic, Protestant, and non-sectarian schools in Belfast as part of a program to promote communication and peaceful coexistence.

The world will never be quite the same, post-Seattle. Demonstrations by a new cross-cutting array of civil society organizations encompassing environmentalists, labor unionists, human rights advocates, and peaceniks coalesced around what the Dalai Lama has called the "People Line and not the Bottom Line." Public consciousness about issues revolving around globalization, inequitable distribution of resources, and the role of international financial institutions was again heightened at the subsequent demonstrations surrounding the IMF-World Bank meetings in Washington, Ottawa, Geneva and Prague. The concerns of an emerging global civil society, fueled by the power of the Internet and CNN media coverage, emerged with a major public policy-shaping voice. No matter how badly promoted, the message was the same that Kofi Annan noted at the Business Humanitarian Forum in November 2000: "With Global power comes global responsibility."[5]

---

[5]   Quoted in John J. Maresca, "A New Concept of Business," *The Washington Quarterly* 23:2 (Spring 2000), pp. 155–163.

The Business-Humanitarian Forum Association seeks to "encourage dialogue and mutual support between the business and humanitarian communities."[6] According to the Association, the traditional conception of businesses as purely profit-driven enterprises is outdated. While profit may still be the primary motive for business actions, other factors—human rights, the environment, labor standards, and so on—now also play an important part in managerial decisions.

In part, this recent adjustment in the outlook of businesses stems from a globalized world that is increasingly becoming a single economic forum. Globalization has allowed businesses both to increase their power and to exercise that power over a larger geographic space. With power, however, have come greater calls for responsibility. Although these calls have almost always existed, two factors today make them difficult to ignore. First, revolutions in communications technology have forced businesses to endure continuous public scrutiny; second, the spread of democracy and of some level of wealth has increased public expectations about the minimum humane quality of life.

But contrary to the view proposed by some in the private sector, businesses are not being coerced to take into account humanitarian, environmental, and other factors. Instead, many companies—especially resources companies, which are tied to specific geographical areas—are choosing of their own free will to consider these factors in their decision-making process. A disrupted society means lost resources and more risk for businesses located in troubled areas; a stable, prosperous society, on the other hand, means healthier workers and more eager consumers. Furthermore, particularly in democracies, strong relationships between the company and the local community can advantage the company by way of favorable regulations and general good will as well as in maintaining a good reputation.

The fact that businesses increasingly find it in their interest to engage in humanitarian and other non-commercial endeavors bodes well for crisis areas. By employing young adults, businesses can prevent the growth of a disaffected and often angry population prone to mobs and riots. By paying salaries, businesses can give wealth and, more importantly, hope to the population. The economic integration of business into

---

6   This section is drawn primarily from an article by John J. Maresca, President of the Business-Humanitarian Forum Association, *supra* n. 125, and from a report on the findings of the first Business-Humanitarian Forum, held in Geneva on January 27, 1999 (available online: http://www.bhforum.ch/report/index.htm).

a society also ties the population's self-interest with the stability of society, further damping potentially destabilizing activities. Businesses can use their existing infrastructure in crisis areas, such as transportation equipment, to aid in humanitarian endeavors. And finally, businesses can donate funds to humanitarian causes, in a sense enlisting partners for a common cause.

Thus, in relation to the public sector, businesses have compatible interests and complementary capabilities. In recognition of this confluence, new strategies, such as the UN's Global Compact, have been developed to integrate business concerns with the concerns of others more directly focused on achieving social justice. In January 1999, UN Secretary-General Kofi Annan set forth a framework for responsible private sector involvement in humanitarian, environmental and labor issues: "We have to choose between a global market driven only by calculation of short-term profit, and one which has a human face. Between a world which condemns a quarter of the human race to starvation and squalor, and one which offers everyone at least a chance of prosperity, in a healthy environment. Between a selfish free-for-all in which we ignore the fate of the losers, and a future in which the strong and successful accept their responsibilities, showing global vision and leadership."[7]

Corporate Codes of Conduct: Bridging Bottom-Line Profits and People Line Impacts

The *UN Global Compact*, launched at the World Economic Forum in Davos, Switzerland in January 1999, recognizes that the private sector plays a role in development. The Compact suggests norms, based on international law, which corporations should incorporate into their daily operations. These norms are presented in nine principles that regard human rights, labor and environmental standards. The UN's goal is to have 1,000 corporations endorse the Compact by 2002 (as of Jan 29, 2001, approximately 300 had done so including 220 Brazilian companies, business leaders in Malaysia and India, and top companies like Unilever, BP, DuPont, Volvo Car Corp., and Nike).[8]

---

[7]   Holme, Richard, and Phil Watts. *Corporate Social Responsibility: Making Good Business Sense*. Geneva: World Business Council for Sustainable Development, January 2000.

[8]   Cone, Jason Topping, "Switzerland: UN Chief Enlists ABB CEO to Boost Global Compact," *Forum News Daily*, January 29, 2001.

The Global Compact does not require compliance, but is a voluntary set of guidelines. One watchdog NGO, Corporate Watch, complains that the Compact is too vague to serve as anything more than a chance for corporations to improve their public image and counter the backlash against trade and investment liberalization.[9] Critics of the Compact look to natural resource extracting companies that have endorsed the principles such as Shell, Rio Tinto, Statoil, and Norsk Hydro because they are likely to be in conflict zones and can potentially exacerbate conflict. The Compact does not specify protocol for investment in conflict regions, though some corporations, like DeBeers, are working to ensure they don't buy diamonds from those areas where the money purchases arms and fuels conflict. Statoil donated $115,000 to the Norwegian Refugee Council to support internally displaced persons in countries where it operates including Angola, Azerbaijan and Georgia.

Other strategies that provide guidelines for transparency, monitoring systems, and accountability for corporate activity include the following:

The first *OECD Guidelines for Multinational Enterprises* were adopted in 1976 in response to problems that emerged within the UN in light of corporate involvement in a 1973 coup d'état in Chile that led to a military takeover.[10] The guidelines aim to harmonize different national policies and to strengthen confidence between multinationals and government authorities on a voluntary basis, thereby preventing governments from discriminating against foreign investors or subjecting companies to conflicting national rules.[11] These guidelines reconcile job creation, global market expansionism and the need for foreign direct investment in developing regions with necessary investment patterns. Thus far, 29 OECD governments as well as Argentina, Brazil, Chile, and Slovakia promote the OECD Principles of Corporate Governance, which include five main areas: rights of shareholders and their protection, equitable treatment of all categories of shareholders, role of employees and other stakeholders, timely disclosure and transparency of corporate

---

9   *Ibid.*
10   Tapiola, Kari, "The Importance of Standards and Corporate Responsibilities—The Role of Voluntary Corporate Codes of Conduct," OECD Conference on the Role of International Investment in Development, Corporate Responsibilities and the OECD Guidelines for Multinational Enterprises, Paris, September 20–21, 1999. Tapiola is the Executive Director of the Fundamental Principles and Rights at Work Division of the ILO, based in Geneva.
11   Dale, Reginald, "Rules Even Businesses Should Love," *International Herald Tribune*, December 12, 2000.

structures and operations, and responsibilities of board to company and shareholders and stakeholders.[12]

The *ILO's Tripartite Declaration concerning Multinational Enterprises and Social Policy* focuses on the promotion of responsible corporate activity with regard to labor and employment practices based on internationally recognized human and labor rights codes. It supports the UN human rights declarations, advocates the elimination of child labor, and requires an annual report from member countries regarding measures taken to satisfy ratified Conventions and Recommendations. These guidelines, still voluntary, are signed onto by governments and implemented by corporations in tandem with workers. The ILO amended the Declaration in March 2001 to incorporate the four principles of the Declaration on Fundamental Principles and Rights at Work, and has recently expanded its programs to support corporate "best practices" by holding educational seminars, distributing promotional materials, offering surveys to governments to monitor the effectiveness of the Declaration, and through the launch of the Business and Social Initiatives Database.[13]

The *Global Reporting Initiative* (GRI) began in 1997 with the support of the UN Environmental Programme because stakeholders wanted not only increased engagement, but also tangible measurable and verifiable performance information. It is a long-term, multi-stakeholder, international effort to disseminate sustainability reporting guidelines for voluntary use on economic, environmental, and social activities. The GRI functions such that public expectations of corporations to be agents of equitable development and environmental stewardship be leveraged against proof of activity.[14] At the Second International Symposium of the GRI entitled "Leveraging Investment, Corporate Accountability, and Disclosure to Advance Sustainability," held November 13–15, 2000 at George Washington University in Washington DC, John Rintamaki, Group Vice President for Ford Motor Company, acknowledged that with shareholder resolutions, campus organizing, and media attention, there is "no place to hide." He noted that the GRI is a means to raise expecta-

---

[12]   Witherell, William, "Corporate Governance: A Basic Foundation for the Global Economy," *OECD Observer*, September 11, 2000. Witherell is the Financial, Fiscal and Enterprise Affairs Director.

[13]   "Corporate Responsibility in the Global Economy," *ILO News*, March 13, 2001. http://www.us.ilo.org/news/focus/0103/FOCUS-7.html.

[14]   Global Reporting Initiative (GRI), *Sustainability Reporting Guidelines on Economic, Environmental, and Social Performance*, June 2000. Materials attained at the November 13–15, 2000 conference held in Washington DC.

tions and to provide leverage for corporations such that more discussions occur within the MNE, consumers are engaged, and governments
are not solely responsible for instituting change.

The *Social Accountability International SA 8000* establishes a uniform
standard for third party verification of corporate responsibility with
respect to UN and ILO Conventions for workplace conditions. SAI, formerly known as CEPPA, the Council on Economic Priorities Accreditation Agency, is the accreditation agency for SA 8000 and is affiliated
with the Council on Economic Priorities, a social responsibility research
institute. Since 1997 it has sought transparent, measurable and verifiable standards for certifying the performance of organizations modeled
after the International Organization for Standardization's (ISO) 9000
and 14000 Series quality control certification processes.

As of May 2000, the International Chamber of Commerce noted there
were more than forty codes designed to govern global corporate activity.[15] Thus, while various strategies for promoting corporate social
responsibility are increasingly available, they are typically non-binding
and lack mechanisms for accountability and monitoring.[16] Still, self-reg-
ulatory codes, often preferable to direct regulation for corporations, have
served in many cases to identify and satisfy stakeholder demands for
responsible behavior.

While the Business-Humanitarian Forum and similar associations
have made many useful suggestions for private-sector/public-sector collaboration, they have often proceeded on the assumption that a sustainable basis for business in conflict areas already exists. However, in
post conflict situations a suitable business climate will often have to be
established *de novo*. In this regard, certain NGOs have played a useful
role in promulgating voluntary codes of business conduct and in otherwise creating an enabling climate for reconciling the divergent interest
of various actors in post conflict situations. Recognizing that "business
is profit-focused and competitive, the public sector *is* bureaucratic and
inflexible, and the governmental organization (NGO) sector *is* territorial
and combative," CIVICUS has worked hard to smooth these differences.[17]

---

[15]   Aaronson, Susan Ariel, "Oh, Behave! Voluntary Codes Can Make
Corporations Model Citizens," *The International Economy*, March/April 2001.

[16]   *Ibid.*

[17]   Tennyson, Ros and Alina Zyszkowski, "The Learning and Sharing Process:
Why Is Partnership between Sectors such a Challenge?" In CIVICUS, *Promoting
Corporate Citizenship: Opportunities for Business and Civil Society Engagement*.
Washington DC: World Alliance for Citizen Participation, 1999, p. 1.

Chapter 11

REVISITING "NATION-BUILDING"

Writing in the New York Times on February 13, 2001, syndicated columnist Tom Friedman put in perspective what has become increasingly clear to many policymakers: "Nation-building—helping others restructure their economies and put in place decent non-corrupt governments"—must, he contended, be a cornerstone of US foreign policy. To be sure, there is still little bipartisan consensus on the issue. However there is little doubt that the concept's vitality has been resurrected since the debacle in Somalia.

Much of the current thinking on "nation building" and the role of international organizations stems from the 1992 *Agenda for Peace*,[1] the landmark study by former UN Secretary-General Boutros Boutros-Ghali. The *Agenda* contends that the United Nations needs to transform itself— to go beyond the traditional missions of peace enforcement and peace-keeping. State failures, characterized by crumbling or abandoned democratic structures and the regression of economic self-sufficiency, have, according to the *Agenda*, been compounded by ethnic and tribal war. "Nation-building" is propounded to meet the underlying grievances that propel civil conflict. Despite its recent bad name in U.S. policy debates, the aim of nation-building is unassailable: to stop the unrest, and then to promote the rule of law and good governance. So too is the conclusion that nation-building may not be possible without the restoration of security through international peace enforcement, more heavily armed than traditional peacekeepers and authorized to use force in cases where "[c]ease fires have . . . been agreed to but not complied with."[2]

---

[1]   *An Agenda for Peace: Preventive Diplomacy, Peacemaking and Peacekeeping*, U.N. Doc. A/47/277 and S/24111 (Jun. 17, 1992), para. 22.

[2]   *Ibid.*, para. 44. On continuing implications for international organizations of Boutros-Ghali's pioneering suggestions, see J. Stremlau & F. Sagasti, *supra* note

In advocating expansion of the UN's security role, the *Agenda for Peace* was treading on soil entirely new to the UN experience. Though peace enforcement is the only military role explicitly authorized by its 1945 Charter, the UN's role first expanded to encompass a complex form of peacekeeping in response to the 1962 Congo crisis, an intervention supported by the United States. Despite Soviet objections, the right of the UN to perform this function was endorsed by the International Court of Justice in the *Certain Expenses of the United Nations* case.[3] Peacekeeping —even where a force is authorized by the General Assembly, rather than the Security Council—was justified as a legitimate UN activity insofar as it was tied to the Charter goal of maintaining international peace and security. In the view of the Court, the Security Council retained a *primary* but not exclusive responsibility in that area.

By contrast, "nation-building" has never received similar judicial endorsement. To be sure, various UN agencies like UNDP and UNICEF have always operated in the nebulous zone between humanitarian assistance and development, working to assist movements toward democracy and good governance. This is a part of "nation-building." But as contemplated by Boutros-Ghali, "nation-building" encompasses the deployment of international troops to support national transformations. The disastrous results of the UN intervention in Somalia in 1993 led, however, to American disillusionment and then hostility to the concept. The subsequent failure, at enormous cost, of UN nation-building efforts in Cambodia further shook the confidence of key states at the United Nations. Rather suddenly, the very term "nation-building" took on a somewhat odious air, and Boutros Boutros-Ghali, as its chief proponent, became the object of a concerted campaign by the United States and others to defeat his bid for reappointment.

Yet, at about the same time, and with far less fanfare, "nation-building" was gaining a more receptive welcome at the World Bank. Although criticism of local governance had been considered off limits for the Bank

---

25, ch. 1.1 ("Boutros-Ghali's readiness to acknowledge that the problems of governance are also a general and legitimate concern of the UN marked a significant departure for an intergovernmental organization. The nature and policy implications of this challenge for the UN and other international institutions—including the World Bank—will be difficult to delineate and address.") For a critique of the concept of nation-building and its expansion into a norm of humanitarian intervention, see E. Luttwak, "Kofi's Rule—Humanitarian Intervention and Neocolonialism," 58 *The National Interest* 57 (Winter 1999–2000).

    3   [1962] I.C.J. 150.

over the years, as a consequence of internal legal opinions reading its mandate as reaching only purely economic matters, increasingly the Bank came to realize that it could ill afford to take such a narrow view. It seemed myopic to ignore the political context when lending monies or engaging in project support in war-torn regions. Failure to promote good governance, in situations where the opportunity presented itself, seemed at odds with poverty alleviation. Accordingly, the Bank's December 2000 policy on Development Cooperation and Conflict stipulates: "The Bank recognizes that economic and social stability and human security are preconditions for sustainable development." The military security concerns of peacekeeping are now giving way to a broader definition of security, that is, "human security," which (more sympathetic to "nation-building") includes the protection of human rights and economic well-being as well as physical well-being. It also includes environmental security, justice under the rule of law, and development through its focus on poverty alleviation as an instrument of conflict prevention.

In 1992, the opportunity for readjustment of institutional inhibitions arose in two important areas—demilitarization in Africa, and peacemaking in Central America. The World Bank's entry into demilitarization, although outwardly responding to public expenditure concerns, particularly the imbalance in defense expenditure vis-à-vis social and productive investments, was based on a political calculation beyond its traditional reliance on purely macroeconomic factors. Understanding that idle standing forces in countries prone to war may serve to provide additional spurs for war, the World Bank—operating through its Africa Bureau, rather than any centralized initiative—undertook the difficult and novel task of devising incentives for demobilization in Uganda. Uganda's leadership had to be convinced to accept demobilization, fearing that it would be destabilizing to leave thousands of former soldiers restless and unemployed, ready to join anti-government militias. Demobilization required that the Bank promote the reintegration of ex-combatants through retraining and provision of land and employment opportunities. The initiative was successful, and a harbinger of others to come with full World Bank approval.[4]

Yet earlier the Bank did not innovate as well in its other "political" engagement of 1992, the implementation of the El Salvador Peace

---

[4]   See generally Nat J. Colletta, Markus Kostner & Ingo Wiederhofer, *The Transition from War to Peace in Sub-Saharan Africa* (World Bank 1996), *excerpts obtainable from* <http://www.worldbank.org/html/extpb/warpeace/ transit.htm>.

Accords. The Accords called for joint UN-World Bank efforts aimed at far-reaching political, social and economic reforms, including a rigorous economic stabilization and structural adjustment program, and demilitarization and reintegration of ex-combatants. Despite its formal collaboration with the United Nations, the World Bank in fact took no part in demilitarization efforts and restricted its efforts to purely macroeconomic matters. The results, as characterized by two distinguished commentators, "was as if a patient lay on the operating table with the left and right sides of his body separated by a curtain and unrelated surgery being performed on each side."[5] Still, it would plant the seeds for the Bank's more successful cooperation with the UN half a decade later in Bosnia, Kosovo and East Timor.

In 1995 James Wolfensohn ascended to the presidency of the World Bank, and with that came a strong new voice for engagement in the "political" arena. A small but significant outpost, the Post Conflict Unit, was established under the leadership of the former head of Africa War-to-Peace Transition Team, Nat J. Colletta and assigned to handle overall coordination of World Bank engagement in war-to-peace transitions. The search for "partnering" with various United Nations agencies began. Kofi Annan on behalf of the United Nations and James Wolfensohn on behalf of the World Bank realized they would be better positioned to deliver a stabilizing "peace dividend" to leaders opting for settlement of their armed conflicts if they worked together. As described by Secretary-General Kofi Annan in his Millennium Report, this new-found joint commitment means that "[c]onflict prevention, post conflict peace building, humanitarian assistance and development policies need to become more effectively integrated."[6] Provision of employment and economic opportunities thus came to be viewed as pivotal to peacemaking, and active participation by private enterprise as its indispensable component.[7]

---

5   Alvaro de Soto and Graciana del Castillo, "Obstacles to Peace Building," 94 *Foreign Policy* 69 (Spring 1994).

6   Kofi Annan, *We The Peoples: The Role of the United Nations in the 21st Century*, U.N. Doc. A/54/2000* (Mar. 27, 2000), para. 48, *also obtainable from* <http://www.un.org/millennium/sg/report/full.htm>. Integration of functions becomes critical "to transfer the momentum of crisis response to recovery, rehabilitation and development activities," United Nations Development Programme, *Bridging The Gap: A Report on Behalf of the Inter-Agency Standing Committee (IASC) Reference Group on Post-Conflict Integration*, August 1999, at 2, *obtainable from* <http://www.reliefweb.int/iasc/Documents/wg38_2.doc>.

7   *See* Secretary-General Proposes Global Compact On Human Rights, Labour,

Courting The Private Sector

Business community engagement in conflict-torn countries thus became a key focus for both institutions. At the Business-Humanitarian Forum in Geneva on January 27, 1999, Secretary-General Kofi Annan summarized a message delivered at various economic summits and business gatherings. "A fundamental shift has occurred in the UN-business relationship," he noted. "The United Nations has developed a profound appreciation of the role of the private sector, its expertise, its motivated spirit, its unparalleled ability to create jobs and wealth. . . . In a world of common challenges and common vulnerabilities, the United Nations and business are finding common ground."[8] The same theme was also articulated by World Bank President James Wolfensohn in his Comprehensive Development Plan of January 21, 1999. Referring in part to post conflict reconstruction, he reaffirmed that "it is absolutely clear that domestic and foreign private investment is the key to economic growth and employment."[9] Wolfensohn confirmed as Bank policy a trend that had been ongoing for the last five years or more, confirming the Bank's role in combating corruption, the absence of the rule of law, and inadequate public administration in grantee states. These

---

Environment, In Address To World Economic Forum In Davos, U.N. Press Release SG/SM/6881/Rev.1 (Feb. 1, 1999), *obtainable from* <http://www.un.org/News/Press/docs/1999/19990201.sgsm6881.r1.html>; *see also* Report of the Secretary-General on the Work of the Organization, U.N. Doc. A/54/1 (Aug. 31, 1999), paras. 136–139, *obtainable from* <http://www.un.org/Docs/SG/Report99/toc.htm>.

   8   Kofi Annan, Message to the Business Humanitarian Forum, Geneva, Jan. 27, 1999, *obtainable from* <http://www.bhforum.ch/report/mesage.htm>.

   9   J. Wolfensohn, A Proposal for a Comprehensive Development Framework (A Discussion Draft), Jan. 21, 1999, *obtainable from* <http://www.worldbank.org/cdf/cdf.pdf>. *See also* John Stremlau & Francisco Sagasti, *supra* note 25, calling for further examination of the World Bank's interactions with private-sector groups through two modalities: existing private-sector-oriented affiliates, such as the International Finance Corporation (IFC) and the Multilateral Investment Guarantee Agency (MIGA), and the Bank's encouragement of foreign investment by the business community. Stremlau and Sagasti note that "[O]ne of the most significant global developments in recent years has been a reversal in the ratio of public to private capital flows to developing countries. . . . [I]t is clear that the World Bank should intensify its relations with a range of other organizations—consulting groups and private firms from developing countries, the non-English-speaking academic community, the electronic mass media (especially international television), non-governmental organizations, and private foundations—in the interest of furthering its expanded role in post conflict reconstruction, good governance, and conflict prevention." *Ibid.*, ch. 4.5.

were seen as not only threats to economic prosperity, but, more omi-
nously, as precursors to state failure. Their neglect would lead to more
complex emergencies, threatening regional peace and setting back economic development for years to come.

In countries undergoing war-to-peace transitions, the failure of economic programs aimed at growth in a free market atmosphere can have
particularly damning consequences. In this environment, a quick influx
of capital and know-how is essential to serve as a counterweight to
recidivist violence. In countries where peace efforts are floundering, a
tangible promise of employment, trade, direct investment, and promotion of local enterprise can have a major stabilizing effect. Yet enlisting
the private sector at the stage where it matters most—shortly after a
peace treaty or accord is reached but where tensions remain inflamed
and violence can be sparked by the slightest provocation—is problematic. Although a growing number of private sector businesses and companies can be counted on to explore economic participation in post
conflict contexts, early engagement is generally shunned. Even assuming that issues of market size and demand can be satisfactorily resolved,
the absence of an established rule of law and good governance and the
lack of personal security bodes poorly for foreign investment, especially
where good opportunities abound elsewhere. Not surprisingly, therefore, engagement in areas of uncertain security and unpredictable future
is often deferred until conditions stabilize. Herein lies the predicament:
stabilization itself is dependent on private sector entry, and hence waiting for stabilization as a pre-condition for entry becomes a self-defeat-
ing proposition.

Today's challenge is, therefore, to find the means to make private
sector engagement attractive, especially at an early stage. Ideally, corporate participation would provide twin benefits: (1) investment, with
resulting jobs and opportunities, and (2) the provision of managerial
know-how and expertise to enable all the actors in the field—the World
Bank, the United Nations, NGOs and civil society—to operate in a more
streamlined and synergistic fashion.

War-Torn Krajina Needs Global "Connectivity":
The Shift from State Welfare to the Global Market

In Krajina, Croatia, there is a pressing need to shift from socialist welfare
and local household subsistence agriculture, to a new globally-oriented eco-

nomic development. The former mode of subsistence of wage employment in a State enterprise supplemented by household subsistence agriculture has been broken and is fundamentally irreparable. Many investments were politically driven and, therefore, made very little economic sense. Krajina's households are surviving on half of the old form of livelihood, that is, only on subsistence agriculture. It would make sense to develop this sector into an outward looking "agro-industry" that could produce natural food products such as olive oil, wine, nuts etc. and promote eco-tourism as well, consequently shifting from household consumption to regional and global markets.

To successfully make this market leap, "connectivity" has to happen: connectivity in the sense of "partnership" between the public and private sector, and the ability to obtain "information" to create and connect new health oriented food markets with households producing natural foods. Some key institutions (the Regional Technical Units with assistance from OSCE, the Local Area Development Associations with UNOPs assistance, and the Community Working Groups with assistance from numerous NGOs) have already successfully started to facilitate this shift through the provision to returning refugees of market information and new production and management technologies.

The strategy would be to build on that success through the value adding capacity of building inputs of technical assistance (expertise) and information technology (computers and internet connectivity). A local social and economic recovery fund could provide capacity building and production technology grants to NGOs, RTU, and LEDA to help small household based initiatives with the implementation of effective business development.

Reference: Colletta, Nat. Field visit to the Krajina, Croatia. September 1999.

Building on Business Interests in War-to-Peace Transitions

Surely, the private sector shares a vital interest in not allowing whole areas of the globe, including nearly half the African continent, to fall victim to entropy. Yet early entry has often proven most attractive to businesses whose engagement can often prolong rather than abate conflict. This has been particularly true with respect to extractive industries, such as the mining of natural resources, as well as firms engaged in the provision of security services.

Globalization has in this regard had a two-pronged effect. Facilitating privatization and trade liberalization, globalization has expanded the capacity for business to take advantage of rapid economic and technological transformations. It has also led to an increased focus on the human side of the ledger sheet: to the potential of the private sector for socioeconomic development and conflict abatement.[10] Multinational companies, whose revenues exceed the gross national product of many developing countries, can influence events on a global and micro scale,[11] supporting governments and others with whom they do business in seeking greater accountability. However, with competitive pressure to expand markets, international firms in emerging and developing economies often find it easier to continue the ways of old by working in tandem with corrupt leaders, rather than breaking with the past and joining forces toward building a more civil society.[12] This is far from inevitable. Business leaders in a great many different sectors are also finding themselves under increasing countervailing pressure, both from within their ranks and from outside sources like the NGO community, to serve as catalysts for positive change.[13]

A New Code of Conduct for Oil and Mining Companies Working in Conflict Areas

After more than a year of negotiations sponsored by the U.S. State Department and the British Foreign Office, five leading oil companies (Chevron, Texaco, Conoco, Royal Dutch Shell and BP Amoco) and two mining companies (Freeport McMoran and Rio Tinto) agreed on a new code of conduct. In this agreement, which was also signed by several human rights organizations including Amnesty International and Human Rights Watch, companies pledge to dis-

---

[10]   *See* Kofi Annan, *We The Peoples, supra* note 143, at 14 ("Greater consistency must be achieved among macroeconomic, trade, aid, financial and environmental policies, so that all support our common aim of expanding the benefits of globalization"). *See also* Jane Nelson, *The Business of Peace: The Private Sector as a Partner In Conflict Prevention and Resolution* (London: The Prince of Wales Business Leaders Forum, 2000), p. 20, *obtainable from* <http://www.international-alert.org/corporate/Pubs.htm> and <http://www.pwblf.org/csr/csrwebassist.nsf/content/f1d2a3a4b5.html>. Nelson details the involvement of multinationals like Microsoft, British Telecom, Dell, Oracle and IBM, among others, in mobilizing information and communications technology for humanitarian purposes in Kosovo and elsewhere. *Ibid.* at 108.

[11]   *Ibid.* at 20.

[12]   *Ibid.* at 44.

[13]   *See* J. Berman, "Boardrooms and Bombs: Strategies of Multinational Corporations in Conflict Areas," 3 *Harv. Int'l Rev.* 28 (Fall, 2000). *See also* Nelson, *supra* note 147, at 75–87 (discussing corporate decisions to maintain or withdraw investments when dealing with repressive regimes, and arguing, with a focus on Burma, Angola and the Sudan, that companies are now more likely to stay and improve a situation rather than to leave or work in concert with corrupt regimes).

courage private security companies and police from abusing people who live near their oil or mining fields. Oil-rich Nigeria is one of the developing countries where the military government used violent and repressive means against Chevron, Shell and other workers who were demonstrating for better benefits. By signing this human rights pact, these companies "cannot avoid their responsibility for human rights violations by maintaining that the abuses were inflicted by the local government, not the corporation." Harold Koh, the U.S. Assistant Secretary of State for Human Rights, believes that this code of conduct will soon become a global standard for all mining and oil companies and that it will also discourage these companies from trying to "maximize their profits by cutting corners on human rights." Even though this pact is voluntary, occurred violations that will be discovered by human rights organizations and posted on the Internet might produce a consumer backlash.

U.S. Secretary of State Madeleine Albright said that the new code of conduct "demonstrates that the best-run companies realize that they must pay attention ... to universal standards for human rights, and that in addressing these needs and standards, there is no necessary conflict between profit and principle."

Reference: Kempster, Norman. "Oil Companies Sign Human Rights Pledge," *Herald Tribune*, pp. 1A, 9A

Overall, the private sector record in positively influencing the course of peacemaking is a good one. In South Africa the business community was instrumental in enabling a smooth transition from an apartheid regime to a multiracial state, thus avoiding the prospect of a bloody civil war. Consolidated Goldfields, for example, arranged and paid for secret meetings between the ANC and top Afrikaners during the last few years of apartheid—sessions which are credited with building the groundwork for the negotiations to end apartheid.[14] The business community has also been active in supporting a peace agreement in Northern Ireland.

The experience of the private sector in Mozambique and in Gaza and the West Bank is also instructive, although the latter case illustrates the limits of what economic opportunity can accomplish in itself.

---

[14]   Robert Zoellick, "Strategic Philanthropy for Business," Keynote Address to the Business-Humanitarian Forum, Geneva, Jan. 27, 1999, *obtainable from* <http://www.csis.org/html/sp990127rbz.html>. *See also* Nelson, *supra* note 147, at 111–115 (discussion of individual and collective business efforts at peacemaking in South Africa, Zambia, the Philippines and Northern Ireland).

Mozambique's economic recovery, and the key role played by the private sector, is properly lauded. Since the end of its devastating civil war in 1992, Mozambique has changed from the second poorest nation in the world to a country with great economic promise. Growth rates have reached 10%, inflation has decreased substantially, and foreign investment is expanding. Mozambique continues to show signs of substantial post-war growth and development, only partially set back by the winter flood disasters of 1999.[15]

Several factors contributed to this success. The signing of a General Peace Agreement in Rome in 1992 brought an effective end to fighting, and cooperation of demobilized insurgents in establishing democratic political institutions.[16] Mozambique possesses an abundance of mineral resources, including natural gas and coal, which attract foreign investment. Perhaps most significant was the government's ability to work with the private sector at home and abroad, renouncing the remnants of its Marxist philosophy. Since 1992, President Chissano has privatized more than 900 of 1,250 government-controlled firms. In conjunction with UN agencies, the World Bank, and NGOs, international companies have spurred Mozambique's recovery[17] and the gov-

---

[15]   *See* "Mozambique: Insider View," *New York Times*, Dec. 4, 2000, at A6–A7 (advertising supplement noting "swiftly advancing liberal economic reforms" and "a government keen to cooperate with the private sector and woo foreign investment").

[16]   On the Mozambique peace process, see generally Aldo Ajello, "Mozambique: Implementation of the 1992 Peace Agreement," in *Herding Cats: Multiparty Mediation in a Complex World* (Chester A. Crocker, Fen Osler Hampson, and Pamela Aall, eds., 1999), p. 615; Cameron Hume, *Ending Mozambique's War: The Role of Mediation and Good Offices* (1994); and Richard Synge, *Mozambique: UN Peacekeepers in Action, 1992–1994* (1997).

[17]   See generally *Directory of American Firms Operating in Foreign Countries*, Vol. 3 (New York: Uni-World Business Publications, Inc., 1999); *World Investment Report 1998: Trends and Determinants* (New York: UN Conference on Trade and Development, 1998), *obtainable from* <http://www.unctad.org/en/docs/wir98ove.pdf>; Katherine Marshall, "From War and Resettlement to Peace Development: Some Lessons from Mozambique and UNHCR and World Bank Collaboration," Development Discussion Paper No. 633 (Harvard Institute for International Development, April 1998), *obtainable from* <http://www.hiid.harvard.edu/pub/pdfs/633.pdf>; "Benefits of Peace," 342 *The Economist* 44, March 12, 1997; "Better Times for a Battered Country," 349 *The Economist* 42, Dec. 5, 1998; Gary Younge, "City with a Poetic Edge: Mozambique Attempts to Put a Decade-Long Civil War Behind It," *The Guardian*, June 12, 1999; *see also* Joint Statement by Denmark, Finland, Sweden and the Netherlands, High Level Meeting on the Special Initiative for Africa and the Education Sector Strategy for Mozambique, UNESCO, Paris, July 7–8, 1997, *obtainable from* <http://www.unsia.org/cluster/educ/moza1.htm>; "War-To-Peace Transition in Mozambique:

ernment has continued to attract substantial foreign investment.[18] In Gaza and the West Bank, the private sector—spearheaded by the Palestinian diaspora and the support of the European Community—has created new banking systems, venture capital funds, and mechanisms for the privatization of telecommunications and other industries. American business has, however, been reluctant to invest in the area, and the recent breakdown of the peace process will undoubtedly retard matters. But the case of the Enron Corporation may be indicative of future possibilities for private sector entry. The U.S.-based energy and communications business has invested heavily in Gaza. Its entry was made possible through the extended range of the Overseas Private Investment Corporation's (OPIC) political risk insurance guarantees. The jobs created have given new impetus to a sluggish Palestinian economy.[19]

The Provincial Reintegration Support Program," *Findings Africa Region* No. 90, July 1997, *obtainable from* <http://www.worldbank.org/afr/findings/english/find90. htm>; Report of the Executive Board of the United Nations Development Programme and of the United Nations Population Fund, UN Doc. DP/CCF/MOZ/1 (Nov. 7, 1997), *obtainable from* <http://www.undp.org/rba/country/ccf/9730548e. htm>; War-Torn Societies Project in Mozambique (Geneva: UN Research Institute for Social Development, Sept. 1998), *obtainable from* <http://www.unrisd.org/ wsp/moza/ toc.htm>; "UNDP: Country Cooperation Frameworks and Related Matters; First Country Cooperation Framework for Mozambique (1998–2001)," and "Mozambique: Country Implementation Review," *The World Bank Participation Sourcebook* (World Bank Group, 1996), *obtainable from* <http://www.worldbank.org/ wbi/source-book/sb0211.htm>; "Mission of the Africa Region's Partnerships Group—Region: Sub-Saharan Africa" (World Bank Group), *obtainable from* <http://www.world-bank.org/afr/index/partnrs.htm>.

[18] According to the *Directory of American Firms Operating in Foreign Countries* (15th ed., New York: World Trade Academy Press, 1998), the following American companies have operated in Mozambique: Air Express International Corp.; Louis Berger International, Inc.; Deloitte Touche Tohmatsu International; DHL Worldwide Express; Enron Corp.; Ernst & Young, LLP; Johnson & Johnson; KPMG Peat Marwick, LLP; McCann-Erickson Worldwide; Pfizer Inc.; Wackenhut Corp.; and Xerox Corp. The following companies also have (or had) a presence in Mozambique, according to various business news sources: Coca-Cola (US), Flour Daniel GTI Inc. (US), Atlantic Richfield Co. (US), Cabot Corp. (US), Scimitar Hydrocarbons Corp. (Canada), Banco Mello (Portugal), Billiton PLC (UK), Commonwealth Development Corp. (UK), Marubeni Corp (Japan), Mitsubishi Corp. (Japan). See also "Mozambique: Insider View," *New York Times*, Dec. 4, 2000, *supra* note 152.

[19] *See generally* Rex Brynen, *A Very Political Economy: Peacebuilding and Foreign Aid in the West Bank and Gaza* (2000). *See also* John D. Clark and Barbara S. Balaj, *NGOs in the West Bank and Gaza* (World Bank, Feb. 1996). *See* for a comprehensive report on the Palestinian economy covering developments in the first half of 1999 as compared to the first half of 1998, including a special focus on donor disburse-

Yet clearly, as the events of the last year in the West Bank and Gaza and elsewhere have shown, peacebuilding investment does not guarantee progress. Investment can reinforce the power of repressive regimes.[20] It can lead to further graft and corruption. Nevertheless, in the critical phase of transition from war to peace, where former belligerents have laid down arms and allowed fledgling peace processes to proceed, foreign investment can play an indispensable role. It can help keep the peace through provision of regulated and accountable private security services and can thwart the provocations of those that stand to benefit from confrontation by offering an alternative to the message that the way to a life of minimal dignity lies open only through resumption of unbridled nationalist or tribal ambitions. By creating an aura of normalcy and confidence in a region's future, it can displace an atmosphere of despair and a mentality of "nothing left to lose" with broader horizons by new stakeholders in peace. Girded by jobs and economic opportunity as an antidote to alienation, the seemingly disinherited now have incentives to work to maintain stability and break the cycle of violence.

The nascent tendencies and ambitions within the business community for positive change can be mobilized to accomplish these ends. But

---

ments and public and private investment, Palestinian National Authority, Building the State of Palestine, UNESCO Report on Palestinian Economy. On U.S. efforts to promote economic growth and access to markets for Palestinian firms, *see especially* The U.S. Agency for International Development, West Bank and Gaza Mission, "The Gaza Industrial Estate," May 16, 2000. The report documents growth of the Gaza Industrial Estate (GIE) project aimed at promoting 20,000 jobs on-site and many more jobs in nearby feeder industries, as developed by a private sector investment company, Palestinian Industrial Estate Development and Management Corporation (PIEDCO), and the assistance provided by the U.S. Government in helping overcome political and bureaucratic obstacles to the development of the estate, especially the need for Palestinian-Israeli agreement on security and access procedures. Like other entrepreneurial projects in the Palestinian territories this has been stalled by the unrest in the region that began in late September 2000. In light of the economic setbacks sustained as a result of the recent unrest, the World Bank provided a $12 million grant to the Palestinian Authority to help alleviate the hardships. Although the amount was small, the move was groundbreaking. "This is a highly unusual move for the World Bank," said Joseph Saba, World Bank Director for the West Bank and Gaza, "since the Bank usually provides loans rather than grants." The Bank said it wanted the grant to serve as a catalyst for other donors. *See* "Palestinians Get $12 M World Bank Grant," Reuters, Dec. 6, 2000, http://www.washingtonpost.com/wp-dyn/articles/A28255-2000Dec5.html.

20   *See, e.g.*, the experience of Bosnia, where corruption and inefficiencies born of failed communist-era policies have contributed to the failure to sustain private

to do so will require conceptualization and implementation of a new structure capable of harnessing business capacity for service in the cause of peace. This new structure will provide businesses with additional incentives to enter into war-torn regions. It will provide the necessary training and guidelines for corporate social responsibility as benchmarks for future investors.

sector entry despite $1.5 billion in post-war public funds for reconstruction. See International Crisis Group, "Why Will No One Invest in Bosnia and Herzegovina?" April 21, 1999, *obtainable from* <http://www.crisisweb.org/projects/bosnia/reports/bh47main.htm>.

Chapter 12

THE NEW CORPORATE SOCIAL RESPONSIBILITY: PEACEBUILDING

Professor Rosabeth Moss Kanter of the Harvard Business School has shown that although "traditionally, business viewed the social sector as a dumping ground for spare cash, obsolete equipment, and tired executives," today the private sector tends "to approach the social sector not as an object of charity" but as an opportunity for "a partnership between private enterprise and public interest that produces profitable and sustainable change for both sides."[1] Although Kanter focuses largely on the private sector's role in the United States, the model of merged private/public interest is equally applicable to the activities of multinational corporations.

Moreover, the private sector can bring to bear, independently of its capacity to generate investment and trade, a catalytic role in assistance to peacebuilding activities. Its expertise in dealing with complicated problems involving a myriad of actors, and experience in complex negotiations, can provide a link between disparate and less flexible institutional approaches. Yet despite this confluence of interests, cooperative arrangements involving the private sector in the work of international institutions has just begun to extend beyond enhanced commercial relations and occasional advisory boards.

The World Bank's advocacy of a stronger role for the business com-

---

[1] Rosabeth Moss Kanter, "From Spare Change to Real Change: The Social Sector as Beta Site for Business Innovation," 77 *Harv. Bus. Rev.* 122 (May–June 1999), esp. pp. 122–123. Kanter cites IBM's Reinventing Education Program as a key example of business innovation, using the corporation's best talents to develop tools and solutions for systematic change at 21 sites in the United States and four other countries.

munity in post-conflict reconstruction has in practice devolved largely to inducing greater private investment through improved political risk insurance and loans administered by its affiliates, the Multilateral Guarantee Insurance Agency (MGIA) and International Finance Corporation (IFC). Too little has been done to meet the practical needs of the business community by shifting the Bank's attention from macroeconomics to microeconomics and the development of labor and capital markets.[2] However, the World Bank's more recent efforts in Bosnia, Kosovo, and most especially in East Timor, do show greater attention being paid to building the essential basis for private sector entry, including the rule of law that protects property rights and contractual commitments.[3]

Business and Legal Environment for Foreign Investment in War-Torn Society: Kosovo

As it seeks to mend the damage caused by war and years of neglect, Kosovo's economy must make the transition towards a modern, open, and market-based system.

Kosovo's economic future depends on:

- establishing the legal framework for private sector development;
- managing non-private enterprises effectively;
- putting in place the procedures for defining property rights; and
- helping people to understand the advantages of a new economy.

Because the state and socially-owned sector in Kosovo does not produce adequate revenue for the Kosovo Consolidated Budget, a vigorous private

---

2   The recent recommendations of the World Bank Operations Evaluation Department, for example, focus on renewed efforts at macroeconomic stabilization with practically no reference to other concerns of the business community. See Alcira Kreimer, John Eriksson, Margaret Arnold, and Colin Scott, *The World Bank's Experience in Post-Conflict Reconstruction* (1998).

3   East Timor presents the most concerted effort at UN-World Bank coordination, unhampered by the type of self-imposed legal restrictions hindering World Bank engagement in Bosnia and Kosovo (in the latter, Serbia nominally retains sovereignty, although it is not a member of the World Bank). The East Timor effort has been undertaken pursuant to the East Timor Joint Assessments Mission Draft Terms of Reference of November 3, 1999, as amended, which provide among other functions for the development of "accountable judicial institutions and processes." *See* Hansjoerg Strohmeyer, "Collapse and Reconstruction of a Judicial System: The Experiences of the United Nations Missions in Kosovo and East Timor," *Am. J. Int'l L.* (Jan. 2000).

sector must be created. To achieve this successfully, an adequate legal and institutional framework, currently lacking, must be constructed.

Three major areas are at the core for completion of a legal framework:

1) *Commercial Law:* Although the commercial laws of the Federal Republic of Yugoslavia were moving closer to Western European norms with reduced state involvement in the economy during the 1990s, these changes were not sufficient to encourage the market economy that Kosovo needs. The essential legal elements are:

   - company law;
   - bankruptcy law;
   - secured transactions law;
   - contracts (Sale of Goods) law;
   - foreign Investment law;
   - labor legislation; and
   - accounting standards.

2) *Commercial Dispute Resolution:* A market economy must have a fair and impartial system of resolving disputes among businesses, their customers, investors, and the authorities. These commercial courts would have jurisdiction over all disputes involving businesses, and would also maintain registers of all formally-established businesses.

3) *Taxation:* A sound tax system is necessary to provide revenue for public services such as education, public security, roads and public administration. Such a system must rest on the private sector, but must not be so burdensome that tax evasion is encouraged. Broad acceptance of the tax system will be critical in ensuring foreign investor confidence in Kosovo.

Once complete, Kosovo's commercial legal system will be similar to those of developed market economies in Europe and elsewhere.

Reference: UNMIK Enterprise Development Strategy in Kosovo, Pristina, August 2000

The United Nations' courtship of the business community has not extended to encouraging business involvement in the formulation and implementation of overall strategy. The UN Office for Project Services (UNOPS) has been lauded as exemplary for more positive UN-private sector relationships. To be sure, it provides a model of how a UN entity can operate in an efficient business-like manner, and thus overcome the reservations of the private sector in dealing with the United Nations. But UNOPS remains a contract procurement agency, dealing only with businesses seeking to sell goods or provide services directly to the United Nations.[4] It does not have a policy role with respect to foreign investment. And the larger goal of a meaningful role for the private sector in decision-making affecting post conflict reconstruction remains a cause without a champion or forum in the UN system, even within the Office of the UN Secretary-General.

In part, the UN and World Bank's reluctance to fully engage the private sector is due to a lingering lack of confidence in the private sector's willingness to sustain commitments in any one area, as witnessed by the capital flight and the 1998 downswings in Asia and other markets around the globe. Although only about 4% of world GNP is military-related, business contacts with developing countries remain popularly associated with images of businesses profiting from war. In fact, tourism is the world's fastest-growing industry, with more than 10% of total international GNP, and is a better representation of the posture of the business community. The tourism industry is particularly vulnerable to acts of terror, and like most multinational businesses employing millions of people worldwide, has a vested interest in containing political instability and turmoil, especially those with cross-border regional effects which can undermine successful investments and operations on a much wider scale.

Thus, despite lingering doubts about the sustainability of private sector commitment, there is general recognition that private capital, if properly channeled, is capable of enormous contributions to capacity-building and social reconstruction. Beyond stimulating labor markets that induce foreign investment, private capital can also create the necessary capital market institutions such as investment banks, development funds, venture capital funds, and—in former centrally-planned socialist economies— privatization mechanisms. It can augment public funding which often

---

4   On UN outreach to the private sector through the UN Office of Project Services (UNOPS), see Press Briefing by United Nations Office for Project Services, Apr. 6, 2000 (briefing by Reinhart Helmke, Executive Director, UNOPS), *obtainable from* <http://www.un.org/News/briefings/docs/2000/20000406.unops.doc.html>. Director Helmke argues that that new UN-business partnerships "recogni[ze] that the magnitude of moving into a conflict situation and relaunching a shattered economy [is] of such proportions that even with double or triple contributions from governments, the job could not be done by the United Nations alone." Since 1995, when UNOPS was established, it has created a project portfolio of $4 billion, an annual turnaround of about $800 million, and an income of $50 million which covers all costs.

suffers from false promises. Public promises of contributions, particularly those made in the immediate aftermath of events inducing widespread sympathy, often are not sustained over time.[5]

For these reasons, it would be useful to increase the proportion of private investment compared to public funding of projects in war-torn areas. Private investment controls a far greater fund of capital than governments ever can practically muster. But private capital flows will continue to bypass post conflict nations unless the UN and World Bank demonstrate that they are willing to share the risk of such investment to a far greater degree than in the past, and unless they can demonstrate that cooperation among all these sectors is mutually beneficial and welcome. Risk-sharing can include provision for political risk insurance at more favorable terms, and, generally, a receptivity to allowing the private sector to become more involved in strategy formulation and implementation affecting post conflict reconstruction.

Once the private sector does become engaged, it can be expected to encourage the development of a rule of law essential to secure investment, define property rights, form contracts, prevent reneging on debts, and otherwise aid in reducing the avoidable risks of investment. However, it cannot assume this task alone. The groundwork for judicial reform and the rule of law must be seen by international organizations and donor governments as a priority, not as something to be pursued after full stabilization of the security and political situation, but alongside it. Maria Livanos Cattaui, Secretary-General of the International Chamber of Commerce, opined: "Business cannot meet demands and expectations for which governments are primarily responsible—ensuring the rule of law, universal access to education, freedom of speech, fair distribution of wealth and an adequate safety net for the old, the sick and the jobless. What companies can do is to be good corporate citizens in their relations with the community in which they operate and in their treatment of employees, suppliers, sub-contractors, customers and business associates. They can conduct their business fairly, and resist corruption."[6] Quick-response legal teams aimed at setting up a rudimentary working court system, and backed by the leverage of donor states, are essential.[7] Otherwise one may fall into the trap

---

[5]   See *Good Intentions: Pledges for Postconflict Recovery* (Shepard Forman and Stewart Patrick, eds., 2000).

[6]   Cattaui, Maria Livanos, "Making Companies Good Citizens," Letter to the Editor in *Financial Times*, March 24, 1999, p. 18.

[7]   *See* Hansjoerg Strohmeyer, *supra* note 160.

of Bosnia, where rampant corruption has stilled the prospects of foreign investment.[8] In this way, the private sector will have a seat at the peace table, bringing with it proficiency in areas that complement traditional peacebuilding skills of international institutions, governments and NGOs.

Concomitantly with support for development of the rule of law, business can bring to bear its technical expertise. Competence in traditional business areas such as finance, product design, accounting, and marketing, as well as electronic commerce in all of its forms, are important for both emergency relief and longer-term prospects for economic growth. Corporations like Microsoft, IBM, and others in the computer and telecommunications industries have entered into partnering rela-

---

[8]   *See, e.g.*, Chris Hedges, "Leaders in Bosnia Are Said to Steal Up To $1 Billion," *New York Times*, Aug. 17, 1999, at p. A1. Corruption in Bosnia has thwarted business entry as well as international donor support. The problem is compounded by the fact that "even when laws are passed to contain fraud, politicians have blocked or ignored them." Judges fearing retribution are afraid to enforce the law. The Office of the High Representative in Bosnia has recommended an intensified effort against corruption while disputing the magnitude of loss from corruption claimed in the *New York Times*. See *Fighting Corruption in Bosnia and Herzegovina*, Press Release of August 18, 1999, Office of the High Representative, *obtainable from* <http://www. ohr.int/press/p990818a.htm>. But the rule of law has not been made operational in implementing the Dayton Peace Accords. *See* Harold Johnson, Associate Director of International Relations and Trade, U.S. General Accounting Office, "Bosnia: Crime and Corruption Threaten Successful Implementation of the Dayton Peace Agreement" (testimony before the Committee on International Relations, House of Representatives, July 19, 2000) (arguing for a broad-based anti-corruption strategy and calling on Congress to require that the State Department certify that the Bosnian national and entity governments have taken concrete steps to fight corruption as a condition of further assistance). The State Department has disagreed with the GAO recommendations, but Harold Johnson has noted that there is "no evidence that [the State Department's] reassessment of its current strategy addresses the underlying causes of corruption and the lack of reform." *Ibid. See also* B. Stein & S. Woodward, "A European 'New Deal' for the Balkans," 78 *Foreign Affairs* 95, 96 (Nov.–Dec. 1999) ("As in other war-torn parts of the world, the dangerous myth is being spread that much-needed private foreign investment will naturally follow major international aid . . . [but r]eports of financial corruption among Bosnian officials who manage public and donor funds, combined with delays in creating the cumbersome Dayton-prescribed economic institutions, have driven away Western corporate investors.") To remedy the situation, Stein and Woodward recommend that "[d]evelopment assistance should . . . be extended directly to private local institutions or be used to leverage private Western financing of Balkan projects. . . . [T]he West should make equity investments in Balkan business a priority." *Ibid.* at 103.

tionships with agencies such as the UN High Commissioner for Refugees (UNHCR), for example, introducing modern technology to keep pace with refugee registration and other critical needs in Kosovo and similar crisis areas.[9]

Humanitarianism and High Technology come to Kosovo: UNHCR and Microsoft

UNHCR cares for about 22.3 million refugees and displaced people in 120 countries. Until the 1999 crisis in Kosovo, the basic UNHCR refugee registration kit consisted of paper and pencils. In Kosovo, the information technology industry put its tools to work to assist UNHCR to help some of the most vulnerable people of the world. Sadako Ogata, UN High Commissioner for Refugees, praised this partnership of high technology and humanitarianism as a model for UNHCR's cooperation with the corporate world.

In Kosovo, Microsoft, together with six other companies (Compaq, Hewlett-Packard, Canon, Kingston Technology, Security World Ltd, and ScreenCheck B.V.) helped UNHCR to develop a portable computerized system for registration of thousands of refugees. This "Refugee Registration Kit," consisting of a digital camera, laptop computer and other accessories, speeds up the registration process of refugees, and therefore the reunification of families. The partnership of the information technology industry and humanitarianism is in this case not only beneficial for refugees but also for private business and its employees. As Mrs. Ogata said: ". . . it allows them to link their professional lives and their social concerns."

Further cooperation between high technology and UNHCR is highly desirable. Among possible future areas of cooperation are the provision of advanced information technology equipment for UNHCR field operations, skills training and jobs programs for refugees, and the creation of a volunteer "international technology corps" that would provide infor-

---

[9]   In contrast to Bosnia, where international civilian authorities have chosen to exercise little more than the power of persuasion, in Kosovo a UN administration—backed by more than 50,000 NATO-led troops—is authorized to take control of the territory's institutions with a view toward creating democratic self-government based on the rule of law. Perhaps as a result of this security gap, "the international investment needed for a successful transformation of Bosnia would be much greater than the already considerable investments in place there and in Kosovo." I. Daalder & M. Froman, "Dayton's Incomplete Peace," 78 *Foreign Affairs* 106, 112 (Nov.–Dec. 1999).

mation technology support in refugee emergencies around the world. Moreover, in addition to advancing development and provision of managerial and business expertise, the business community is positioned to contribute in a more systematic way to global stability. Businessmen tend to approach issues in a rational, realistic, pragmatic, and efficient manner. They deal with conflicts on a day-to-day basis. They are experienced in negotiations and they know *how and when to compromise*. These qualifications are very much needed and helpful in any conflict management process, and integration of business at the local level in conflict areas may help to persuade ground-level political actors to cooperate more effectively. Political, economic, ethnic, cultural and other differences—the underlying strata of international conflicts— are issues most multinational companies deal with, in one form or another, within their organizations. Moreover, as the global business community tends to be well placed politically—at both the upper and lower echelons of power—it often has the capacity to identify and assess growing tensions.

This potential can be tapped in a variety of ways beyond direct investment:

Assistance in Formulation of System-Wide Strategy. Senior-level meetings of business leaders with security, military and other government and non-government officials to express the viewpoint and ideas of business on conflict prevention and resolution, and on related issues that underpin a conflict, such as corruption, distribution of tax revenues and patronage, human rights issues, security, and judicial reform.[10]

Assistance in Overcoming Divisions Based on Divergent Institutional Cultures. In Kosovo and East Timor, the United Nations and the World Bank are undertaking ambitious efforts to help nations to learn to govern themselves effectively. Each institution is stretching the limits of its mandate and seeking to overcome differences in institutional approaches to socioeconomic problems. A neutral third party could help both actors to clarify or redefine their mandates in a way that provides a steadier compass for their work. Similarly, outreach by the World Bank and the United Nations to the NGO community may be more effective if an intermediary role can be played to overcome lingering suspicion and distrust.

Participation in Negotiation/Mediation Processes. Inclusion of disaffected groups in the economic life of a nation is an essential aspect of

---

[10]   *See* Nelson, *supra* note 147.

reconstruction, calling on private sector expertise in planning and coordination, including the support and development of local entrepreneurship and training programs in such areas as:

1) conceiving and implementing social justice policies among employees and contractors and within concession areas;
2) defining and maintaining the role of significant investors in the face of calls for autonomy and independence by sub-national groups; and
3) helping to manage socio-economic change stemming from significant investments in backward or underdeveloped regions within a country.

Yet modalities for interaction between the private sector and its counterparts in government, multilateral institutions and the NGO community have not progressed beyond advisory groups or *ad hoc* engagements in response to particular crises.[11] The framework that was established in the aftermath of the Second World War no longer seems capable of finding solutions to the problems that an increasingly connected and integrated world present. The growing power of corporate capital and the dwindling effectiveness of elected politicians are shaped within a world of "live coverage." Formerly, government capital controls ensured

---

[11]   The Business-Humanitarian Forum is one example, but it has dealt largely with emergency relief, rather than reconstruction. The Forum was first convened in Geneva on January 27, 1999 under the co-chairmanship of Sadako Ogata, the United Nations High Commissioner for Refugees, John C. Whitehead, Chairman of the International Rescue Committee, and John Imle, Vice-Chairman of the Unocal Corporation—stressing that "at present, only limited channels of communication exist between multinational corporations and humanitarian organizations." *See* The Business Humanitarian Forum, "Executive Summary" (Jan. 27, 1999), *obtainable from* <http://www.bhforum.ch/report/ index.htm>. Other business associations contributing to humanitarian and peace-related activities include Business for Social Responsibility, the Businessman's Forum, the Business Roundtable, the Stanley Foundation, and various national and local chambers of commerce, particularly the U.S. Chamber of Commerce in Washington, D.C. They are joined by smaller groups worldwide such as the Business for Global Stability Initiative, led by Israeli businessman Haim Roet. None claim any involvement with international organizations beyond the first stage of improving dialogue and opening channels of communication. In the United Kingdom, matters have progressed somewhat further than in the United States, with the Prince of Wales Business Council's coordination between business, government and the NGO community, but there are no active partnership arrangements with international organizations.

full employment, while controls on trade and subsidy policies allowed particularly vulnerable sectors and groups to be protected. The over-bearing shadow of all-pervasive state security, coupled with government controls, suppressed conflict. Today, big business and capital are in the ascent. The values multinational corporations espouse—minimal regulation, total liberalization of markets, maintenance of budgetary controls and low inflation, and the freedom of movement of goods, services, people, money and ideas—has found an echo in the multilateral institutions. This new confluence of forces has engendered a counter-response from those viewing this phenomenon as incarnating the perceived evils of globalization. Bet even those ardently mobilizing for change are increasingly recognizing that rejecting multilateralism is not the answer or as important as changing the impact of globalization. As Barry Coates, Director of the World Development Movement, said: "We are not anti-trade, but we are concerned with who makes the rules and who gets the benefits. We agree that there has to be a rules-based system for governing global trade. The alternative is a world of might is right protectionism." The IMF, the World Bank, the UN, the WTO, and other global bodies are also beginning to recognize that the call for a new global governance system cannot be ignored; and that more inclusive, transparent and accountable operations must be adopted for the sake of the very credibility of these institutions.[12]

Driving Corporate Social Responsibility: Inclusive Global Governance

Globalization's critics demand that corporations, governments and multilateral institutions alike be held accountable for what is deemed their legacies of exacerbating inequality and other global tensions. They insist corporate strategies for profit-making assist rather than conflict with peacebuilding.

The State of the World Forum, currently chaired by former Soviet Prime Minister Mikhail Gorbachev, has launched a Commission on Globalization to explore a more inclusive approach to global governance involving the private sector and civil society. In conjunction with the World Business Council for Sustainable Development, the Bellagio Forum on Sustainable Development, the World Bank, and a consortium of U.S. and European foundations, governmental agencies and corporations, the Business Environments Unit of Royal Dutch Shell will manage a "scenario planning" group to discuss the future of global-

---

[12]   Larry Elliott, "Multilateral Thinking," *The Guardian*, November 29, 2000, p. 22.

ization, human development, and global governance. The Commission will present its findings and recommendations in the fall of 2003.

In addition to the State of the World Forum's Commission and strategies for corporate conduct, discussed earlier, accountability and transparency are promoted in the business community through socially responsible investing and social auditing.

Socially responsible investing (SRI) means ensuring that companies that do well also do good. Investors can now purchase shares of stock and be guaranteed that those companies are meeting at least minimal standards of corporate social responsibility. The Domini 400 Social Index, the Dow Jones Sustainability Group Index, the Calvert Group Ltd., and the Broad Market Social Index, to name a few, track SRI performance. Thus, operational ethics affect shareholder value such that stock prices reflect how risk management is, or is not, conducted with environmental, social, *and* economic principles in mind.

Shareholder resolutions are increasingly popular tools used by partial owners (through holding a percentage of stock) of corporations to demand responsible behavior of corporations. Raising or voting for a particular resolution, be it divestment from a region of instability or promotion of an environmentally sustainable project in that region, potentially holds multinationals accountable for their performance. Several environmental NGOs have been particularly active in waging shareholder resolutions. Friends of the Earth, for example, supports Occidental Petroleum shareholders in voting for the termination of drilling of oil beneath U'wa indigenous territory in Colombia, where the tribe of 5,000 has threatened mass suicide should operations continue.

Social auditing is yet another tool used by third parties to verify accountability and transparency. What began as an internal process in which companies monitored and steered performance based on stakeholder input has shifted gears and, in alignment with changing social norms, has become a process increasingly conducted by independent third parties such as the consulting group KPMG. Social reports disclose attitudes about the company's values and principles, identify stakeholders and note their satisfaction with company policy, and assess performance levels against internal and industry-wide benchmarks. Social and ethical audits have become routine among corporations concerned with their reputation and image in terms of social responsibility. Corporations now offer third party confirmation that a company has attained set standards via social audit reports available to the public. For example, in June 2000, Nike posted information on its website collected through audits conducted by PriceWaterhouseCoopers. Nike is calling the initiative "Transparency 101."[13]

---

[13] *EMonitors Business and Human Rights Newsletter*, published by World Monitors, a New York-based consulting group that provides socially responsible business strategies to multinational corporations. Issue No. 55, June 7, 2000.

Global alliances that incorporate a more responsive and responsible private sector remain under close watch by third parties. All stakeholders, including shareholders, increasingly have avenues for influence to ensure that resources are used for appropriate peacebuilding activities. The goal is to accelerate the movement by businesses from simply offering *spare change* in the way of philanthropy toward assuming more active responsibility in global governance so that that *real change can take place* alongside profitable investment.

An example of this new awareness occurred recently in Chad. There, environmental NGOs raised concern over a proposed new oil pipeline, while human rights NGOs complained about the potential misappropriation of revenues by the government. The World Bank responded by conditioning a loan for the pipeline project based on environmental guidelines and set-up of a transparent, independently monitored escrow account for devoting profits to development purposes. The arrangement, which allowed oil companies to engage under the broader guidelines of the Bank, provides a model of multi-sectoral partnership that enables business to profit while meeting environmental and human rights concerns.

But genuine advances require more than piecemeal responses. They require a new architecture which provides the means for inclusiveness by fully engaging the potential of the multilateral institutions, the business community, and civil society in a unified approach to peacebuilding. This new structure could take the form of a Peace Transitions Council (PTC), as described in the next chapter, as a means for working at many levels to tie together multiple stakeholders in a new global governance.

Chapter 13

THE PEACE TRANSITIONS COUNCIL: STEPS TOWARD A NEW GLOBAL ARCHITECTURE OF PEACE

A Peace Transitions Council would work to close a number of gaps in the present system through meaningful partnering among key players in peacebuilding. It would aim at better coordination of functions and synergistic gains, taking advantage of what the private sector can contribute to central system-wide strategy, reconciliation of contending institutional principles and mandates, and coordination through integration of information systems to avoid redundancies in effort. Soliciting and recommending apportionment of public and private capital would be among its other useful functions.

It would build on efforts that have taken place within the UN system itself for better coordination of functions in post conflict scenarios. The UN Inter-Agency Steering Committee (IASC) on Post-Conflict Integration found a number of "planning mechanism failures" within the UN system, and between the UN system and the World Bank. Five critical planning elements were cited as missing:

- failure to bring in all relevant actors at the outset of the planning period;
- cumbersome nature of the planning instruments;
- disconnects between agreed strategies arising out of the instruments and individual agencies' programs and appeals;
- no mechanism for effective regional and sub regional (transborder) planning; and

- inadequate linkages between peace agreements and measures to ensure that "gaps" are closed.

Each of these missing elements could be filled through active private sector engagement in a PTC at global, national and local levels.[1]

Framework for Engagement: Legal and Operational Aspects of a Peace Transitions Council

Equality among PTC partners in sharing burdens and responsibilities along agreed divisions of labor is critical to its success. The private sector and NGO community would not be limited to an advisory function. The private sector could take the lead in encouraging foreign and local investment. It could, for example, plan training and the development of human capital in line with new technologies to create an attractive and disciplined workforce, retraining workers from inefficient enterprises to match entrepreneurial needs, and encouraging short-term worker training by use of new computerized, Internet-based distance learning technologies. The NGO community could focus on bridging relief, development, and good governance. In making recommendations pertinent to overall strategy, each partner would speak with an equal voice.

Although the actual modalities for PTC operations would necessarily evolve through negotiations and trial and error, the principles listed below are suggested as guidelines.

At the global level, the PTC would consist of 20 representatives, coming from and appointed by the respective entities of the United Nations, the World Bank, the NGO community, and the international business community, with 5 seats allocated to each. Terms of appointment should be for two years, subject to renewal. Representatives of the United Nations and World Bank would serve *ex officio*, concurrent with their existing positions. Private sector and NGO representatives would be expected to serve independently of their other affiliations. A President of the PTC would be elected by majority vote of the representatives. Such a representative mix of actors would be reflected in similar organizations at the regional, national and local levels.

---

[1]   See, generally, for earlier formulation of many of the ideas present in this chapter, A. Gerson, "The Private Sector's Role" in 95 *Am. J. Int'l L.* 102 (2001), special issue, "Symposium: State Reconstruction After Civil Conflict."

Global PTC headquarters could be located in Washington D.C., giving it proximity to the World Bank and to the ambassadorial and NGO communities. It would have a Secretariat and Executive Director. Operating expenses would be covered by joint assessments for all representative sectors. Private sector funding should come from as wide a base as possible, enlisting all segments of the business community. The focus should be on multinational corporate and global NGO engagement. The PTC would be convened on a regular basis to review peacebuilding efforts worldwide, and on an exceptional basis at the request of any of the parties or its President.

The PTC would establish links with regional organizations and development banks to share information and resources pertaining to common interests in peacebuilding missions and the avoidance of redundant efforts.

The PTC would seek to contribute to ongoing efforts at avoiding bureaucratic logjams and streamlining operations, including elimination of needless layers of bureaucracy in international organizations and crisis response architecture.[2]

The PTC would be directly answerable to no other authority, thus assuring its complete independence as an advisory body. It would encourage centralized decisionmaking with regard to overall strategy and planning, but not act as a decisionmaking entity with regard to functions normally assumed by the United Nations or the World Bank.

The PTC would initiate a data system, communications system, and control center that can integrate the pertinent data, on a real-time basis, of all of its constituent entities.

The PTC would be global in scope and focus on globalization as a potentially inclusive mechanism for rapid growth and development.

The PTC would aim to overcome differences between NGOs and private enterprise through demonstrating that joint participation advances common interest in peacebuilding. NGO autonomy would not be infringed upon insofar as all associations and implementation of recommendations would be voluntarily assumed.

In this way, the PTC would operate on two levels: (1) encouraging foreign investment and (2) providing advice and recommendations along

---

[2]   For example, the confusion of international agencies in the Bosnia reconstruction effort has been notorious, allowing opponents of the peace process to attempt to set one against the other, and permitting continued prosecution of ethnic war by other means.

a wide plane of issues affecting regional peace and stability. Composed of distinguished individuals noted for their objectivity and expertise, the PTC's recommendations would be hard to ignore. The private sector could contribute its expertise in the identification of realistic investment opportunities, management, provision of products and services, creation of new industries, and development of infrastructure. But by regularly interacting with multilateral institutions and civil society, the private sector would also become an integral part of international peace-building efforts.

It would thus enable coherence of approach through provision of multiple perspectives, better relate costs to means, and assess levels of commitment and commensurate goals. Country action plans could be developed that pay greater attention to labor market institutions, including necessary education and training, capital market institutions, including banking and development funds, and the development of legal institutions conducive to private sector entry. The PTC could bolster these efforts by promoting legislative and other measures aimed at further reducing the risk of foreign investment in troubled areas, such as enhanced political risk insurance to reward early entrants. Moreover, the PTC could serve as a model of cooperation for international organizations, NGOs and businesses in the field.

The PTC is, of course, only a working model. Issues to still be worked out include: Who will appoint representatives? Which industries, NGOs, and divisions of the World Bank and UN will be present? How will local governments and agencies be included? Will regional and national offices be created? Will specialized crisis management teams emerge? How will military forces factor into decision-making? Yet despite the necessary fine-tuning, the PTC model is ripe for implementation, enabling non-traditional actors to play an unprecedented role in conflict mitigation and resolution. Perhaps the best starting point is to pilot a PTC model in a few select post-conflict regions before moving on to the establishment of a global PTC.

Undertaking Projects

Applying the aforementioned guidelines, among the projects the PTC could undertake are the following:

1. Centralize targeted data collection. Even in the best of circumstances, private sector entry into war-to-peace transition countries will be realistic in only a relatively narrow class of cases. Those cases need to be identified, if only to persuade businesses that they should delve further. To date, there is no comprehensive data source available on such entry. A common data bank should be established, analyzing three different types of situations: (1) high-profile and politically prominent cases where resources are available—i.e., South Africa, West Bank/Gaza, Angola, Congo, Bosnia, and the Balkans; (2) low-profile conflicts, where resources are scant—i.e., Rwanda, Burundi and Somalia; and (3) partial-conflict nations—i.e., Colombia, Indonesia, and Sri Lanka. This data would also permit firmer conclusions about what conditions have induced economic entry, and what enhancements are necessary or desirable to induce further entry.

2. *Improve "atmospherics" of UN, IMF and World Bank relations with the business community and civil society.* The business community must be convinced that the World Bank and the United Nations are open to its concerns. One important measure is a demonstration of commitment to reducing the nature and amount of economic and personal risk presented in investment in transitional societies. Another is greater transparency in UN budgetary measures, to facilitate complementary planning. The PTC could also boost private sector confidence by allaying fears that certain UN efforts, such as aspects of Agenda 21 adopted at the 1992 Rio Conference on the Environment and Development (UNCED), are intended to lead to the mandatory transfer of corporate resources and know-how at less than market rates.[3] While the PTC certainly can not rewrite the Rio Agenda or any other international agreement, it can influence the way these documents are interpreted, and help assure that they are not misconstrued to create needless roadblocks to effective interaction.

---

[3] Agenda 21, the framework for action adopted at the Rio Conference, called for limitation of greenhouse gas emissions through the decreased use of fossil fuels and coal. *See* Agenda 21, United Nations Conference on Environment and Development, U.N. Doc. A/CONF. 151/26 (1992), *obtainable from* <http://www.un.org/esa/sustdev/agenda21text.htm> or <http://www.igc.org/habitat/agenda21/>. Toward this end, the United Nations Environment Program is authorized to facilitate "the transfer of environmentally sound technologies to the developing countries and assist" in their effective application. Agenda 21, *supra*, paras. 38.21–38.23; United Nations Framework Convention on Climate Change, May 9, 1992, adopted May 9, 1992, S. Treaty Doc. No. 102–38 (1992), 31 I.L.M. 849 (1992), Art. 4, para. 5. The transfer provision has been interpreted by some UN officials as including privately-owned technologies. Although the transfer is to be accomplished on a voluntary basis, the U.S. coal industry has raised concerns that the "transfer" provision will be used to demand the sale of technology at less than market rates. *See* R. Reinstein, "Understanding the Global Decisionmaker," 17(1) *Coal Voice* 23 (Winter 1994).

3. Place emphasis on early-stage entry. Without early-stage entrants in significant numbers, there is little springboard for subsequent entry. A critical mass of private business activity may have to be generated to invigorate the political/economic environment, and provide a counterweight against the continued influence of nationalist political parties or other conflict-prone actors. Building this "expeditionary" business community must begin with enhanced awareness in the corporate sector of profit opportunities in still anarchic stages—including the delivery of emergency humanitarian relief such as housing, food, medicine, and the provision of security—and in other areas such as the development of basic infrastructure.

In early entry where the security situation has stabilized, two questions are central to business: (1) Is there an opportunity to get enhanced returns because of market misapprehension of the degree of risk? (2) Is there an opportunity to establish a market position ahead of other future competitors?

By engaging in commercial activity in a region that others consider too risky, businesses can lay the groundwork for future long-term profits despite short-term risk. Early-entry businesses can establish a loyal consumer base, customize infrastructure for their own purposes, enact favorable deals and regulations with local government and already-existing businesses, and secure concessionary rights to land, water, and other resources that will sustain future profits.

The World Bank and the United Nations can create and advertise private opportunities for establishing a secure market position ahead of the competition, making use of their presence in the field and good working relations with the local government. They can open doors, in much the way that national governments do in developed markets. They can observe and facilitate the interaction between the private sector and the post conflict governments. Early private sector entrants interested in economic reform can then help to shape the economy to their liking, serving as benchmarkers in the region to ensure that forthcoming investors meet previously negotiated standards of operation. Thus, the business-government climate can be positively influenced for years to come, and the private sector can avoid being saddled with the corrupt or inefficient framework of a vestigial regime which a new government might otherwise be inclined to continue.

4. Court existing as well as potential business entrants. Much of the international private sector's awareness of opportunities in transitional countries is shaped by discussions with local private sector entities which have survived the years of conflict. The World Bank and the United Nations must pay greater attention to improved relations with these local companies. Often, local businesses will express resentment and uncertainty about the future, after dealing with the conflict-prone prior regime. World Bank discussion with new governments can help local business communities overcome these fears, which might otherwise deter international entrants. In a number of countries, including Liberia and Nicaragua, World Bank representatives have been working with the new governments to assure the honoring of contracts undertaken during prior regimes, so that the grievances of an earlier era would not be perpetuated.

5. *Make political risk insurance comprehensive and affordable.* Private sector entry is necessarily tied to a reduction of risk and assurance against the acute types of "political" risks inherent in transitional war-to-peace societies. Currently, some insurance is provided by the Multilateral Investment Guarantee Agency (MIGA). Private industry cannot compete with MIGA rates. However, MIGA provides only limited project insurance. For example, in Gaza, where the average proposed project is valued at $25 million, MIGA provided a maximum of $5 million insurance in 1999. In areas with ongoing armed conflicts or susceptible to renewed fighting, MIGA will not provide any insurance at all.

Post-conflict countries would benefit from the provision of privately-based primary political risk insurance, supported by MIGA reinsurance. American and international insurance companies may be willing to provide services under such an arrangement, which also has the advantage of employing private sector networks and capacities to launch effective advertising campaigns. Dialogue between the private sector and MIGA should be encouraged to assure the most effective allocation of resources—i.e., to balance the problem of too much risk (and therefore no investment) against too little risk (and resulting moral hazard). It would seem reasonable that the highest risk be allocated to MIGA, and that the private sector be permitted to take the next level of risks.

6. *Build bridges between the NGO, civil society and business communities.* Economic development by itself cannot rebuild a fractured society. Hence, the NGOs must be full PTC partners. NGOs are on the ground in conflict areas, know the local players, and are key in transitions from relief to development. NGOs have become a primary vehicle for the delivery of relief, and will continue to play a role in post conflict devel-

opment.[4] Care should be taken to build bridges and develop common aims between the private sector and the NGO community in post-conflict societies. If the business community represents economic development, the NGOs can help to represent the voice of the local community and the "public interest." Private sector engagement with NGOs and other civil society actors can be facilitated through a PTC framework, to visibly demonstrate the benefit that business brings to economic development, reconstruction and social stability. This in turn can serve as a model for interaction at the field level. Social responsibility and economic development have too often suffered as a result of the mutual suspicion and distrust that have too often, and unnecessarily, characterized relations between the business sector and NGO community.[5]

7. *Assist in popular advocacy and marketing and develop a strategy for an international response.* In an important policy paper, *Recovering From Conflict: Strategy for an International Response*, Shepard Forman, Stewart Patrick and Dirk Salomons have proposed a more coordinated approach to bilateral and multilateral aid for countries emerging from civil war.[6]

---

4   On the growing power and prominence of NGOs in advancing peace processes, see P. Aall, "Non-Governmental Organizations and Peacemaking," in *Managing Global Chaos: Sources and Responses to International Conflict* (C. Crocker, F. Hampson and P. Aall, eds., 1996); L. Gordenker and T. Weiss, "Devolving Responsibilities: A Framework for Analyzing NGOs and Services," in *Beyond Subcontracting: Task-Sharing with Regional Security Arrangements and Service-Providing NGOs* (T. Weiss, ed., 1998); and R. Wedgwood, "Legal Personality and the Role of Non-Governmental Organizations and Non-State Political Entities in the United Nations System," in Rainer Hofmann, ed., *Non-State Actors as New Subjects of International Law*, Kiel Walthur-Shucking Institute of International Law (Duncker & Humblot, Berlin, 1998).

5   *See* Nicanor Perlas, *Shaping Globalization: Civil Society, Cultural Power and Threefolding 1* (2000) (contending that: "[C]ivil society emerged from the Battle of Seattle as a third global force. It took its place beside business and government as one of the key global institutions that must now determine the quality and direction of globalization. The emergence of global civil society changes the world from a uni-polar to bi-polar world to one that is tri-polar."). Be that as it may, the scars between business and the NGO community from the "Battle of Seattle" during the 1999 World Trade Organization (WTO) summit have yet to be healed.

6   Shepard Forman, Stewart Patrick and Dirk Salomons, *Recovering From Conflict: Strategy for An International Response* (Center on International Cooperation, New York University 2000) *obtainable from* <http://www.nyu.edu/pages/cic/pubs/PayingEssentials02.11.html>. See also their companion volume, *Good Intentions: Pledges for Postconflict Recovery* (Shepard Forman and Stewart Patrick, eds.), *supra* note 162, especially, J. Boyce *Beyond Good Intentions: External Assistance and Peacebuilding.* On the urgent need for "far better coordination and discipline" among

They recommend the establishment of "a full-fledged Strategic Recovery Facility to facilitate timely and effective action."[7] Like a PTC, but without private sector participation, the Strategic Recovery Facility would encompass the United Nations, the World Bank and the IMF, regional organizations, governments and NGOs. As aid is the first step to recovery and provides the stage for private sector entry, the PTC should work closely with such a Facility toward a truly integrated approach. Indeed, functions of the proposed Facility might better be served by being merged or subsumed under the broader agenda and wider base of the PTC. This would, among other advantages, enhance opportunities for achieving common objectives through popular advocacy and marketing in support of post conflict initiatives by both donor governments and private sources. It would also recognize that, as in the case of Bosnia, even coordinated international aid is not enough to stimulate the foreign investment necessary to repair war-torn countries.[8] Rather, what is needed is a broad-based strategy where the strength of market economies, operating under the aegis of the rule of law, helps to guide postwar reconstruction.

8. Assist in combating corruption. The business community has an enormous stake in combating corruption. While individual firms may prosper in a corrupt atmosphere, private foreign investment on a larger scale is stifled by the absence of open market economies. In Bosnia, for example, McDonald's refused to set up operations after demands by officials for bribes, and large Italian and German construction companies pulled out after heavy losses.[9] Self-policing through industry-wide standards, however, can provide an effective mode of regulation even where others have failed. A PTC would have the authority and reach to implement such codes of conduct, making a pariah of any business entity that engages in corrupt practices beyond the reach of the Foreign Corrupt Practices Act and other international standards.[10]

---

aid agencies, see also C. Lancaster, "Redesigning Foreign Aid," 79 *Foreign Affairs* 74, 80 (Sept.–Oct. 2000).

[7] S. Forman, S. Patrick and D. Salomons, *ibid.*, p. 11.

[8] *See* B. Stein & S. Woodward, *supra* note 165.

[9] *See* Chris Hedges, "Leaders in Bosnia Are Said to Steal Up To $1 Billion," *supra* note 165.

[10] Current international initiatives against corruption include the OECD standards denying the tax deductibility of bribes and calling on member countries to criminalize international bribes, and the Inter-American Convention on Illicit Payments.

9. Assist in privatization of "governmental" functions. Partnership with the private sector should facilitate the privatization of functions that are not efficiently handled by governments or international institutions. Such activities may span the gamut from provision of humanitarian relief to infrastructure reconstruction as part of peacebuilding. It could even include the provision of security services.[11] Control is not wrested from governments or institutions, but structured and regulated, so that operational responsibility is allocated to the sector most capable of efficiently providing needed services. Establishing the right mix of private-public responsibility is a task ideally suited for PTC engagement, and indeed probably could not be established in the absence of such an arrangement.

10. Support exchange of research and knowledge of best practices. Research would be based on expressed needs from the bottom up and endeavor to help shape legislation and policies of governments. It would fill critical information and knowledge gaps among the many actors, ensuring a level playing field and full public accountability. Such free flows and access would help dispel rumors, give voice to those typically marginalized, provide a source of inclusion and preemptive action, and generally build the institutions for democratic dialogue and the mediation of differences before they become sources of grievance and violence. Meaningful partnering arrangements—between the United Nations, the World Bank, and the private sector, along with the NGO community—are a necessary and welcome development. Regional disorder and civil conflicts have replaced aggression as the world's number one security concern. No longer impeded by superpower rivalries, and empowered by the advent of globalization and innovative leadership at the United Nations and the World Bank, effective partnering

---

11   The problem of local security has been addressed only through the advisory functions of the UN Civil Police Administration. But CivPol has limited effect when local police agencies are corrupt or are committed to nationalist conflict. The High Commissioner for Refugees has faced the dilemma of the intermingling of armed nationalist militias with civilians in refugee camps, in conflict areas such as East ad West Timor, and the African Great Lakes, without any Security Council mandate for UN peacekeepers to provide an alternative source of order in the camps. The privatization of security services in the pursuit of civil peace need not, however, be limited to developed economies. Nor should the experience of well-known private security firms like Executive Outcomes and Sandline operating in Africa be considered indicative of the prospects for successful deployment of privatized guard and security services operating under UN auspices in a regulated framework.

among all the major stakeholders in building and sustaining peace is an idea whose time has come.

Today, private sector flows have begun to outpace public sector flows to developing countries. The challenge lies in encouraging capital to enter countries and regions torn by war, and in using partnership arrangements to support the evolution of civil societies based on market-driven economies and girded by the protection of human and property rights. To accomplish this, the private sector must be given a greater stake in shaping the outcomes of war-to-peace transitions.

Formation of a Peace Transitions Council would allow a unified approach in formulating and implementing strategy for recovery. Of course, the success of a PTC in meeting the demands of peacebuilding are not assured. As always in partnerships, questions of costs and benefits will arise. Adding another layer of bureaucracy often appears to be an invariable consequence of creating new fora for shared decision-making. Similarly, additional delay sometimes results when consultation with a broader group of stakeholders is encouraged. Yet, with active private sector and NGO engagement in strategic planning and management, these costs can be minimized and easily outweighed by the benefits. Fortunately, the boldness of new ideas, coupled with a greater readiness for shared responsibility by the United Nations, the World Bank, the private sector, and the NGO community, bodes well for transforming peace through partnering, from concept to reality, through a new institutional framework for collaboration.

CONCLUSION

Privatizing peace is an idea whose time has come. Its mainstay is commitment to a unified field approach to peacebuilding, and in particular to recognition of the fact that the private sector, for all its flaws, is the engine of economic growth and that peace and economic progress are often, if not always, inextricably linked.

Globalization provides opportunity as well as danger. It can be tapped to sustain fragile peace processes and to harness the energy of the private sector through privatization of functions no longer within the exclusive competence of multilateral institutions or governments, or, it can be ignored, setting forth no new benchmarks of accountability and transparency, and thus dooming fledgling peace processes to failure. As Mark Malloch-Brown, Director of the UN Development Programme, has observed: "The steamroller of economic globalism is not matched by the development of a global politics that can respond to it."[1]

Privatizing peace, ideally under the aegis of a new global coalition envisioned by the concept of a Peace Transitions Council, would halt the negative impacts of economic globalism while harnessing its energy, so that the fruits of a nascent partnership between the public and private sectors can reach fruition in a new, more stable, world order. That idea is no longer a dream. Multilateral institutions have realized their limitations. Enlightened leadership has emboldened real, if still not sustained, change. The business and NGO community have begun to take seriously the business of bridging their differences. What remains is a question of will and adequate structures. Peace hangs in the balance. It is our hope that the ideas herein presented will have contributed to making the right choices.

---

[1]   Perlstein, Steven, "A New Politics Born of Globalization: Leaders Coming to a Consensus on the Need for Rules to End the Excesses of Free Trade," *Washington Post*, October 10, 2000.

ANNEXES

Annex I

LEGAL ASPECTS AND DRAFT ARTICLES OF INCORPORATION FOR A MODEL PEACE TRANSITIONS COUNCIL*

1. Overview of Peace Transitions Council

The Peace Transitions Council ("Council") will be an organization consisting of business leaders and non-governmental organizations ("NGOs"), focusing on the economic development of post-war countries through private investment, and provision of advice and counsel in coordination with officials from the World Bank and United Nations relative to such transitions. The Council will study barriers to private investment that exist in post-war countries as well as measures that may reduce the risk of entry and which would reward early entrants. The Council will also work with various governments, including the United States government, and may also promote specific legislation advancing these interests.

2. Creating the Council

There are three options for creating the Council:

- AIBL:incorporate and seek recognition as a 501(c)(4) organization; or
- incorporate and seek recognition for separate but related Section 501(c)(3) and 501(c)(4) organizations.

A. Incorporation

Under all three options, the organization must first incorporate. Incorporation of a nonprofit corporation in the District of Columbia is

---

* Prepared by John Scheib of the Bar of District of Columbia.

governed by the District of Columbia Code (the "D.C. Code"). The D.C. Code provides for the incorporation of nonprofit corporations for charitable, educational, research, and political purposes. D.C. Code § 29–504.

The D.C. Code requires that every corporation maintain a registered office and a registered agent. D.C. Code § 29–509. The registered agent must be authorized to do business in the District of Columbia. Id.

The D.C. Code requires the filing of articles of incorporation and bylaws. The articles of incorporation specify factual information about the company, including the name of the corporation and the number of original directors. D.C. Code § 29–530. The articles of incorporation must be signed by three incorporators and filed with the Mayor. D.C. Code § 29–529. The articles of incorporation will establish the initial members of the Board of Directors. D.C. Code § 29–530. Draft articles of incorporation for the Council are at Tab A.

Upon the filing of the articles of incorporation, the District of Columbia will issue a certificate of incorporation. After the certificate is issued, the Directors shall hold an organizational meeting; five days notice for the meeting is required. D.C. Code § 29–534. At the organizational meeting the Directors should approve the bylaws, elect the officers and transact certain other business. Id. Alternatively, the Directors may act by unanimous written consent in lieu of a meeting.

The bylaws set forth the entity's organizational rules. They address many issues, including annual meetings, voting rights, quorums, directors' qualifications, number of directors (must be at least three), designation and appointment of committees, and appointment and election of officers. D.C. Code §§ 29–514 to 29–524. Draft bylaws for the Council are at Tab B.

B. 501(c)(3) Organizations

The Internal Revenue Code provides for charitable, educational, and research organizations in Section 501(c)(3). To qualify under Section 501(c)(3), an organization must file an exemption application (Form 1023) with the Internal Revenue Service, and the application must be approved. A Section 501(c)(3) organization receives preferential tax treatment, but the scope of its permissible activities is limited. Specifically, such an organization has the following advantages:

- It can promote a position on issues if done in an academic manner after a full and fair exploration of the issues (i.e., absent melodramatic, one-sided arguments);

- contributions to the organization are tax deductible for the donor; and
- it is exempt from paying federal taxes.

The deductibility of contributions may significantly enhance the Council's ability to raise funds and attract resources from both corporations and individuals.

However, a Section 501(c)(3) organization also has several disadvantages:

- It is prohibited from engaging in political activities, including endorsing or opposing particular candidates for public office; and
- it may not engage in significant lobbying (domestic or foreign) activity.

Thus, the decision whether to incorporation this kind of organization under Section 501(c)(3) generally turns on the amount of lobbying the organization intends to engage in.

If lobbying is intended to be a small component of the Council's purpose, Section 501(c)(4) status is generally preferred. In our case, an insignificant amount of lobbying may be sufficient to meet the Council's objectives if member companies lobby on the same issues. If the Council members' companies engage in lobbying on an issue advanced by the Council, however, the Council must not coordinate or provide materials or assistance to the companies to advance the lobbying effort. On the other hand, if lobbying is intended to be a major part of the Council's mission, the Council will not qualify for Section 5901(c)(3) status.

C. 501(c)(4) Organizations

The Internal Revenue Code provides for lobbying organizations in Section 501(c)(4). A section 501(c)(4) organization may have lobbying activities as its primary purpose. A 501(c)(4) organization has the following advantages:

It may engage in unlimited lobbying;

- the organization may engage in partisan political activities, subject to federal and state law, but such activities may not be the primary purpose of the organization; and
- contributions may be deductible, at least in part, as business expenses.

A 501(c)(4) organization, however, has several disadvantages:

- Contributions to 501(c)(4) organizations are not tax-deductible charitable contributions;
- political expenditures are taxed;
- all solicitations must disclose the non-deductibility of contributions (subject to limited exceptions); and
- it must disclose the percentage of funds used for lobbying and political activities so that members can calculate business expense deductions.

Notwithstanding the usual preference for Section 501(c)(3) status, the Council may be better off with Section 501(c)(4) status if the bulk of its financing comes from member companies. Although contributions to a Section 501(c)(3) organization are tax-deductible as charitable contributions, charitable contributions are often hard to explain to shareholders. Thus, corporate members of the Council may not be able to give as freely to the 501(c)(3) organization. To the extent that contributions to a 501(c)(4) are deductible, they are deductible as a business expense. These deductions are much easier for corporations to "hide" in a balance sheet and justify to shareholders. They may be justifiable if they are made with an eye toward opening new markets for the corporation's products and services.

The Council will need to be a Section 501(c)(4) organization only if lobbying will be a substantial component of its efforts. Even if the Council initially opts for Section 501(c)(3) status, the Council would have to create a separate 501(c)(4) organization if lobbying becomes a substantial component of the Council's activities. The Council may proceed for many years without needing to devote substantial resources to lobbying. Nevertheless, the Council may choose to seek 501(c)(4) recognition if potential member companies prefer a business expense deduction over a charitable deduction.

D. Issues Arising From Creating Both a 501(c)(3) and a 501(c)(4)

Several issues would arise if the Council is established as a 501(c)(3) organization and later establishes a sister 501(c)(4) organization. In general, a 501(c)(3) organization's resources may never be used to subsidize activities that the 501(c)(3) organization could not itself conduct. Each organization must have a separate corporate structure, including separate names, articles of incorporation, bylaws, employer identification numbers and boards of directors. In addition, the 501(c)(3) organization must maintain adequate records to demonstrate that its funds are not being used for lobbying activities beyond those permissible under Section 501(c)(3) organization. The organizations may share resources, such as staff, facilities and equipment, but the 501(c)(4) organization must pay for its full share of these costs. In addition, the organizations must act independently of each another. For example, the 501(c)(3) organization must not permit the 501(c)(4) organization to use educational materials prepared by the 501(c)(3) organization for political purposes. There are additional rules that would be important should the Council decide to establish separate 501(c)(3) and 501(c)(4) organizations, including rules pertaining to joint fundraising and the making of grants or loans by one organization to the other.

E. Recommendation

The best alternative for creating the Council is to incorporate it in the District of Columbia as a nonprofit corporation. The organization should then apply for 501(c)(3) status. As a 501(c)(3) organization, the Council will be able to raise funds through tax-deductible contribution. Although the Council would be limited in the amount of lobbying it could do, a sister (c)(4) organization could later be formed if lobbying becomes a part of the organization's mission.

Before concluding that the Council should become a 501(c)(3) organization, however, the corporate leaders should be asked whether the charitable contribution deduction or the possible business deduction makes it easier for them to make financial contributions to the Council. If there is a strong consensus that the business deduction is preferable we will have to weigh the relative merits of (c)(3) versus (c)(4) status in greater depth.

3. Financing the Council

The Council may receive financing from several sources. Contributions from member corporations, which are tax-deductible as charitable contributions to a 501(c)(3) corporation, and possibly tax-deductible as a business expense to a 501(c)(4) corporation is one source. The District of Columbia Code provides that nonprofit corporations may have more than one class of members. The only requirement is that the designation of such classes, the manner of election or appointment, and the qualifications and rights of the members of each class must be set forth in the articles of incorporation or in the bylaws. D.C. Code § 29–512. One option is to make a financial contribution a prerequisite to a particular class of membership. This class might be designated the "Inner Council." Requiring that members of the Board of Directors be affiliated with an "Inner Council" member may provide an additional fundraising incentive. Another option is to create multiple classes of membership based on varying levels of financial contribution.

Finally, the Council should attempt to solicit grants from both the government and other institutions.

Draft Articles of Incorporation
of Peace Transitions Council

ARTICLES OF INCORPORATION
OF PEACE TRANSITIONS COUNCIL

We, the undersigned natural persons of the age of eighteen years or more, acting as incorporators of a corporation under the provisions of the District of Columbia Nonprofit Corporation Act, adopt the following Articles of Incorporation:

Section 1. Name. The name of the Corporation shall be Peace Transitions Council (the "Corporation").

Section 2. Duration. The period of duration of the Corporation shall be perpetual.

Section 3. Purposes. The Corporation shall be organized exclusively for charitable and educational purposes within the meaning of section 501(c)(3) of the Internal Revenue Code of 1986, as amended, or the corresponding provision of any subsequent tax law (the "Code"), and such purposes shall include the following:

monitoring and promoting, from a private industry perspective and that of NGOs (non-governmental organizations), economic development initiatives in post-war countries;

synthesizing information from a wide variety of sources, including governmental and inter-governmental early warning networks, the world press, networks of scholars, activists, journalists, and worldwide non-governmental organizations relative to peace transitions;

conducting public education on policy issues by various means including the use of state-of-the-art electronic and Internet communication sites;

carrying on any activities in connection with the foregoing purposes, including regular meetings with World Bank and United Nations officials, or doing any other thing that is necessary or appropriate to further or facilitate the foregoing purposes; and engaging in any lawful act or activity for which a nonprofit corporation may be organized under the District of Columbia Nonprofit Corporation Act.

Section 4. Membership. The Corporation may, but is not required to, have members. The conditions of membership in the Corporation, the rights, obligations and role in the affairs of the Corporation of its members, and the classification of members, if any, shall be as provided in the Bylaws of the Corporation. Such members shall be nonvoting.

Section 5. Board of Directors. The Board of Directors of the Corporation shall be the governing body of the Corporation, and the affairs of the Corporation shall be managed by the Board of Directors. The Board of Directors' voting power shall include, without limitation, the power to adopt, alter, amend, or repeal these Articles of Incorporation and the Bylaws of the Corporation, provided that any such amendment shall be consistent with the requirements of section 501(c)(3) of the Code. The manner by which Directors shall be elected or appointed shall be as provided in the Bylaws of the Corporation. The number of Directors shall be fixed by the Corporation's Bylaws, except that there shall not be less than three (3) in number.

Section 6. Powers. In order to facilitate the fulfillment of its purposes, the Corporation shall have and may exercise all powers available to corporations under the District of Columbia Nonprofit Corporation Act, as the same now exists or may hereafter be amended. Nothing herein contained shall be deemed to authorize or permit the Corporation to carry on any activity, exercise any power, or perform any act that a corporation formed under the District of Columbia Nonprofit Corporation Act, as the same now exists or may hereafter be amended, may not at the time lawfully carry on or do.

Without limiting the powers that the Corporation may lawfully exercise, the Corporation shall have the power to take and receive funds from the Government of the United States, state and local governments, charitable, educational or other nonprofit organizations (including foundations), profit-making corporations, and individuals.

Notwithstanding any other provision of these Articles of Incorporation:

No part of the Corporation's net earnings shall inure to the benefit of, or be distributed to, any Director or officer of the Corporation, or to any individual, except that the Corporation shall be authorized and empowered to pay reasonable compensation for services rendered and to make payments and distributions in furtherance of the purposes described in section 3 of these Articles of Incorporation, provided such purposes are consistent with the purposes allowed under section 501(c)(3) of the Code.

No substantial part of the activities of the Corporation shall consist of carrying on propaganda, or otherwise attempting to influence legislation, and the Corporation shall not in any manner participate in or intervene in (including the publication or distribution of statements) any political campaign on behalf of or in opposition to any candidate for public office.

The Corporation shall exercise only such powers and shall conduct or carry on only such activities as are consistent with the exempt status of organizations described in section 501(c)(3) of the Code and the regulations thereunder (as they now exist or as they may hereafter be amended), contributions to which are deductible under section 170(a) of the Code.

Section 7. Liquidation. In the event of the dissolution or termination of the Corporation or the winding up of its affairs, the remaining assets of the Corporation, after all liabilities and obligations of the Corporation shall have been paid, satisfied, and discharged, or after provision has been made therefor, shall be distributed exclusively for one or more of the purposes described in section 3 of these Articles of Incorporation in such manner, or to one or more organizations described in section 501(c)(3) of the Code, as the Board of Directors shall determine; and none of such remaining assets shall be distributed to or divided among any of the Directors or officers of the Corporation or any other private individual.

Section 8. Registered Office and Agent. The registered office of the Corporation in the District of Columbia shall be located at 1025 Vermont Avenue, N.W., Washington, D.C. 20005. The registered agent of the Corporation at such address shall be CT Corporation System.

Section 9. Initial Board of Directors. The number of Directors constituting the initial Board of Directors shall be [number (*)]. The names of the persons who are to serve as Directors until the first annual meeting or until their successors are elected and qualify shall be as follows:

Name   Address
[Insert names and addresses]

Section 10. Incorporators. The names and addresses of the incorporators shall be as follows:

Name   Address
[Insert names and addresses]

The powers of the incorporators shall terminate upon the filing of these Articles of Incorporation.

Section 11. Indemnification of Officers and Directors. To the fullest extent permitted by section 29–505(14) of the District of Columbia Nonprofit Corporation Act or the corresponding provision of any such subsequent law, the Corporation shall indemnify its officers and Directors.

[End of text; signature pages follow]

Bylaws of Peace Transitions Council

A District of Columbia Nonprofit Corporation

ARTICLE I
NAME AND OFFICES

Section 1.01. Name. This corporation shall be known as Peace Transitions Council (hereinafter the "Corporation").

Section 1.02. Registered Office. The registered office of the Corporation in the District of Columbia shall be located at 1025 Vermont Avenue, N.W., Washington, D.C. 20005. The registered agent of the Corporation at such address shall be CT Corporation System.

Section 1.03. Other Offices. The Corporation may also have offices at such other places both within and without the District of Columbia as the Board may from time to time determine or the business of the Corporation may require.

ARTICLE II
MEMBERSHIP

Section 2.01. Members. Membership shall be based on payment of an annual contribution, with one class of membership. Members shall have no voting rights but shall receive information from the Corporation. [This is in preference to multiple classes of membership with different rights.]

ARTICLE III
DIRECTORS

Section 3.01. General Authority. The business and affairs of the Corporation shall be managed by or under the direction of a governing body of persons (designated individually as "Directors" and collectively as the "Board of Directors" or "Board"), which may exercise all powers of the Corporation.

Section 3.02. Composition of Board. The Corporation shall be governed by a self-perpetuating Board of Directors consisting of not less than three (3) Directors, as may be fixed from time to time by resolution of the Board of Directors. [Resolutions could expand or contract the size of the Board.]

At the first meeting of the Board of Directors held after the filing of the Corporation's Articles of Incorporation, the three Directors named therein shall elect such Directors as they deem necessary for the proper management of the Corporation. Alternatively, the Directors named in the Articles of Incorporation may elect new Directors by unanimous written consent.

Section 3.03. Term of Office. The term of office of each Director ordinarily shall be three (3) years. To provide for staggered expiration of Directors' terms, the three Directors elected initially shall have the following terms: one shall serve a one-year term, one shall serve a two-year term, and one shall serve a three-year term. The term length applicable to each Director shall be specified in the resolution electing the initial Directors. Each Director shall hold office for the term for which he or she is elected and until his or her successor shall have been elected and qualified. A Director whose term of office is expiring may vote with the other Directors in the election of his or her successor. A Director whose term is expiring shall be eligible to be reelected.

Section 3.04. Chairperson/Co-Chairpersons. The Board may appoint a Chairperson and/or Co-Chairpersons of the Board as it may deem appropriate to hold such office for such period, to have such powers, and to perform such duties as the Board may from time to time establish by resolution.

Section 3.05. Removal of Directors. Any Director may be removed at any time, with or without cause, by the unanimous affirmative vote of all other members of the Board of Directors.

Section 3.06. Resignation. Any Director may resign at any time by giving written notice to the Chairperson, the President, the Secretary or the

Board. Such notice shall take effect at the time specified therein, and the acceptance of such resignation shall not be necessary to make it effective. If any Director should tender his or her resignation to take effect at a future time, then the Board of Directors shall have the power to elect a successor to take office at such time as the resignation shall become effective.

Section 3.07. Vacancies. Any vacancy occurring on the Board of Directors may be filled by the affirmative vote of a majority of the remaining Directors present at a meeting at which a quorum is present. A Director elected to fill a vacancy shall be elected for the unexpired term of his or her predecessor in office.

Section 3.08. Meetings of the Board of Directors. The Board may hold meetings, including annual, regular and special meetings, either within or without the District of Columbia.

Section 3.09. Annual Meeting. The annual meeting of the Board for the election of Directors and for the transaction of such other business as may properly come before the meeting generally shall be held in August of each year at the time and place designated by the President. Notice of the annual meeting, stating the place, date and time of the meeting, shall conform to the requirements for notice and waiver of notice set forth in Article IV of these Bylaws. The notice of the annual meeting need not specifically state the business to be transacted thereat.

Section 3.10. Regular Meetings. Regular meetings of the Board or any committee thereof may be held without notice at such times and at such places as shall from time to time be determined by the Board or committee, as the case may be. The notice of regular meetings, if any, need not specifically state the business to be transacted thereat.

Section 3.11. Special Meetings. Special meetings of the Board or any committee thereof may be called by the President, by the Secretary at the request of one or more Directors, or by a majority of Directors. Notice of such special meeting, stating the place, date and time of the meeting, shall conform to the requirements for notice and waiver of notice set forth in Article IV of these Bylaws.

Section 3.12. Quorum and Voting. A quorum of the Board shall be a majority of the number of Directors. The affirmative vote of a majority of the Directors present at a meeting at which a quorum is present shall be the act of the Board, except where the act of a greater number is required by these Bylaws, the Corporation's Articles of Incorporation or statutory provision. If a meeting cannot be organized because a quorum has not attended, the Directors present thereat may adjourn the meeting from time to time, without notice other than announcement at the meeting, until a quorum shall be present.

Section 3.13. Majority. In the event that the Board or any committee thereof or its members present at any meeting consists of an even number of persons, a majority means one-half of the number of such persons plus one.

Section 3.14. Action Without Meetings; Telephone Meeting. Any action required or permitted to be taken at any meeting of the Board of Directors or of any committee thereof may be taken without a meeting if all members of the Board or committee, as the case may be, consent thereto in writing and the writing or writings are filed with the minutes of proceedings of the Board or committee. Members of the Board of Directors, or any committee designated by such Board, may participate in a meeting of such Board or committee by means of conference telephone or similar communications equipment by which all persons participating in the meeting can hear each other, and participation in a meeting pursuant to this Section 3.14 shall constitute presence in person at such meeting.

Section 3.15. Committees. The Board may, by resolution passed by a majority of the Directors in office, designate one or more committees, each committee to consist of two (2) or more Directors, which committees, to the extent provided in said resolution, shall have and exercise the authority of the Board in the management of the Corporation. Other committees not having and exercising the authority of the Board in the management of the Corporation may be designated and appointed by a resolution adopted by a majority of the Directors present at a meeting at which a quorum is present. The designation of any such committee and the delegation thereto of authority shall not operate to relieve the Board, or any individual Director, of any responsibility imposed upon the Corporation or the Director by law.

Unless otherwise specified in a resolution of the Board, at all meetings of each committee a majority of the total number of members of the committee shall constitute a quorum for the transaction of business, each member of the committee shall have one vote, and the affirmative vote of a majority of the members of the committee present at any meeting at which there is a quorum shall be an act of the committee. Each committee shall keep regular minutes of its meetings and report the same to the Board when requested to do so by the Board.

Section 3.16. Compensation of Directors. The Directors of the Corporation shall serve in their capacity as Directors or committee members without compensation but may be reimbursed for reasonable expenses, if any, incurred in carrying out the purposes of the Corporation.

ARTICLE IV
NOTICES

Section 4.01. Notices. Whenever the Articles of Incorporation, Bylaws, Board resolutions or provisions of statute require that notice of a meeting be given, such notice shall state the place, date and time of the meeting, and shall be served on each Director by mail addressed to the person to be notified at his or her address as it appears on the records of the Corporation, with postage thereon prepaid, at least seven (7) days prior to such meeting. Such notice shall be deemed to have been given at the time when the same shall have been deposited in the United States mail. Notice may also be given by personal delivery, telephone, telefax, facsimile, overnight delivery service, telegram or other form of transmission, generally available to the public and reasonably designed to timely convey such information, at least two (2) days prior to such meeting. Notice shall be deemed to have been given when sent.

Section 4.02. Waiver of Notice. Whenever any notice is required to be given under the Articles of Incorporation, the Bylaws, Board resolutions or provisions of statute, a waiver of notice in writing that is signed by the person(s) entitled to such notice before or after the time of the event for which notice is required shall be deemed equivalent to notice. Attendance of a person at a meeting shall constitute a waiver of notice of such meeting, except when the person attends a meeting for the express purpose of objecting, at the beginning of the meeting, to the transaction of any business because the meeting is not lawfully called or convened. Neither the business to be transacted at, nor the purpose of, any regular or special meeting of the Directors or members of a committee of Directors need be specified in any written waiver of notice unless so required by the Articles of Incorporation or these Bylaws.

ARTICLE V
OFFICERS

Section 5.01. Positions. The Board shall appoint the officers of the Corporation. The officers of the Corporation shall be a President, a Vice-President, a Secretary, a Treasurer and such other officers as the Board from time to time may appoint. Any two or more offices may be held simultaneously by the same person, except that no one shall at the same time occupy the offices of President and Secretary. No officer shall execute, acknowledge or verify any instrument in more than one capacity.

Section 5.02. Term of Office. The officers of the Corporation shall hold office for a term of one (1) year (or, if shorter, until the annual meeting that falls within one (1) year of the commencement of such term) or until their successors are chosen and qualified or until their earlier resignation or death. No officer may serve for a term exceeding three (3) years without receiving formal reappointment by the Board.

Section 5.03. Removal. Any officer may be removed, with or without cause, at any time by an affirmative vote of two-thirds (2/3) of the Board.

Section 5.04. President. The President is expected to attend all meetings of the Board and any committee meeting thereof as needed, ensure that all orders and resolutions of the Board are carried into effect, and in general perform all duties normally incident to the office of President and such other duties as may be prescribed by the Board from time to time. In furtherance, but not in limitation, of the duties and responsibilities hereinbefore described, the President, any Vice-President and such officer or officers as may be authorized by the Board may sign and execute any deeds, mortgages, bonds, contracts or other instruments that the Directors have authorized to be executed or have delegated to an authorized person the discretion to execute on behalf of the Corporation, except in cases where the signing and execution thereof shall be expressly delegated by the Directors or by these Bylaws to some other officer or agent of the Corporation or shall be required by law to be otherwise signed or executed.

Section 5.05. Vice-President. In the absence of the President or in the event of the President's inability to act, the Vice-President shall perform the duties of the President and when so acting shall have all the powers of, and be subject to all the restrictions upon, the President. The Vice-President shall perform such other duties and have such other powers as the Board or, if authorized by the Board to do so, the President may from time to time prescribe.

Section 5.06. Secretary. The Secretary is expected to attend all meetings of the Board, shall record all the proceedings of the meetings of the Board in a book to be kept for that purpose, and shall perform like duties for the committees of the Board, when so requested. When unable to perform such duties, the Secretary may delegate the taking of minutes to another Board member. The Secretary shall ensure that all notices are duly provided in accordance with the provisions of these Bylaws, as required by law or as directed by the Board or the President. The

Secretary shall ensure that the books, reports, statements, certificates and all other documents and records required by law are properly kept and filed and shall perform such other duties as may be prescribed by the Board or by the President, under whose supervision the Secretary shall function. The Secretary shall have custody of the corporate seal, and the Secretary shall have authority to affix the same to any instrument requiring it. When so affixed, it may be attested by the signature of the Secretary. The Board may give general authority or specific authority to any other officer to affix the corporate seal and to attest the affixing by such officer's signature. The Secretary may also attest all instruments signed on behalf of the Corporation by the President or the Vice-President. The Secretary shall in general perform all duties incident to the office of Secretary.

Section 5.07. Treasurer. The Treasurer shall be responsible for all corporate funds of the Corporation, shall keep full and accurate accounts of receipts and disbursements in books belonging to the Corporation, and shall be expected to deposit all moneys and other valuable effects in the name and to the credit of the Corporation in such depositories as may be designated by the Board. The Treasurer or his or her designee(s) shall disburse funds of the Corporation as ordered by the Board, taking proper vouchers for such disbursements. The Treasurer shall render to the Board, at its regular meetings or when the Board so requires, an account of all financial transactions of the Corporation and of the financial condition of the Corporation. The Treasurer shall perform all other duties incident to the office of Treasurer and such other duties as from time to time may be assigned by the Board.

Section 5.08. Vacancies. A vacancy in any office of the Corporation because of death, resignation, removal, disqualification or other reason may be filled for the unexpired portion of the term of that office by the Board.

Section 5.09. Fidelity Bonds. The Corporation may secure the fidelity of any or all of its officers or agents by bond or otherwise.

ARTICLE VI
INDEMNIFICATION AND RELATED MATTERS

Section 6.01. Indemnification. To the fullest extent permitted by the laws of the District of Columbia as those laws presently exist or hereafter may be amended, the Corporation shall (a) indemnify any person (including the estate of any person) who was or is a party or is threatened to be made a party to any threatened, pending or completed action, suit or proceeding, whether civil, criminal, administrative or investigative, by reason of the fact that such person is or was a Director, officer, employee or agent of the Corporation or is or was serving at the request of the Corporation as a Director, officer, employee or agent of another corporation, partnership, joint venture, trust or other enterprise against expenses, including attorneys' fees, judgments, fines and amounts paid in settlement (except judgments, fines and amounts paid in settlement in connection with an action or suit by or in the right of the Corporation) actually and reasonably incurred by such person in connection with such action, suit or proceeding and (b) pay expenses incurred by any Director, officer, employee or agent in defending a civil or criminal action, suit or proceeding in advance of the final disposition of such action, suit or proceeding.

The indemnification provided herein shall not be deemed to be exclusive of any other rights to which persons seeking indemnification may be entitled under any agreement or vote of disinterested Directors, including rights under any insurance policy that may be purchased by the Corporation to the extent permitted by the laws of the District of Columbia as they presently exist or hereafter may be amended.

Section 6.02. Liability to the Corporation. No Director shall be personally liable to the Corporation for monetary damages for breach of fiduciary duty as a Director, except (a) for any breach of the Director's duty of loyalty to the Corporation, (b) for acts or omissions not in good faith or that involve intentional misconduct or knowing violation of law, or (c) for any transaction from which the Director derived an improper personal benefit.

Section 6.03. Insurance. The Corporation may purchase and maintain, to the full extent permitted by the laws of the District of Columbia as they presently exist or hereafter may be amended, insurance on behalf of any officer, Director, employee, trustee or agent of the Corporation and any person who is or was serving at the request of the Corporation as an officer, Director, employee, partner (general or limited), trustee or agent of another enterprise against any liability asserted against him or her or incurred by him or her in any such capacity or status.

ARTICLE VII
GENERAL PROVISIONS

Section 7.01. Calendar Year. The Corporation shall operate on a calendar year unless otherwise determined by the Board.

Section 7.02. Contracts, Checks, Notes, Etc. All contracts and agreements authorized by the Board and all notes, drafts, checks, acceptances, orders for the payment of money and negotiable instruments obligating the Corporation for the payment of money shall be signed by at least one officer of the Corporation or by such other number of officers or employees as the Board may from time to time direct.

Section 7.03. Corporate Seal. The corporate seal, if any, shall have inscribed thereon the name of the Corporation, the year of its organization and the state of incorporation. The corporate seal may be used by causing it or a facsimile thereof to be impressed, affixed or otherwise reproduced.

Section 7.04. Deposits. All funds of the Corporation not otherwise employed shall be deposited promptly to the credit of the Corporation in such banks, trust companies or other depositories as the Board or, if authorized by the Board to do so, the President or Treasurer may direct. For the purpose of making such deposits, any checks, drafts and other orders for the payment of money that are payable to the Corporation may be endorsed, assigned and delivered by any officer of the Corporation or in such manner as may from time to time be determined by resolution of the Board.

Section 7.05. Compensation. The Board shall determine the compensation of counsel, officers, employees and agents of the Corporation. No compensation or reimbursement of expenses will be made that in any way would adversely affect the Corporation's qualification under section 501(c)(3) of the Internal Revenue Code of 1986, as amended (or the corresponding provision of any subsequent tax law).

Section 7.06. Loans. No loans shall be contracted for or on behalf of the Corporation and no evidence of indebtedness shall be issued in the name of the Corporation unless authorized by a resolution of the Board. Such authority may be general or may be confined to specific instances. No loans shall be made by the Corporation to its Directors or officers.

Section 7.07. Voting Securities of Other Corporations. The President shall have the authority to vote on behalf of the Corporation those securities of any other corporation that are owned or held by the Corporation and may attend meetings of stockholders or execute and deliver proxies for such purpose.

Section 7.08. Form of Records. Any records maintained by the Corporation in the regular course of its business, including its books of account and minutes books, may be kept on, or be in the form of, punch cards, magnetic tape, photographs, microphotographs or any other information storage device, provided that the records so kept can be converted into clearly legible written form within a reasonable time. The Corporation shall so convert any records so kept upon the request of any person entitled to inspect the same.

Section 7.09. Amendments. The Articles of Incorporation and the Bylaws may be altered, amended or repealed and new Bylaws may be adopted by the affirmative vote of two-thirds (2/3) of the entire Board, provided that prior notice has been given to all members of the Board in accordance with the notice provisions set out in Article IV herein.

ARTICLE VIII
PROHIBITION AND LIMITATIONS

Section 8.01. Prohibition Against Sharing in Corporate Earnings.

(a) No part of the earnings of the Corporation shall inure to the benefit of or be distributable to its incorporators, Directors, officers or other private persons, except that the Corporation shall be authorized and empowered to pay reasonable compensation for services rendered and to make payments and distributions in furtherance of the purposes set forth in the Articles of Incorporation.

(b) All Directors and officers of the Corporation shall be deemed to have expressly consented and agreed that, upon the dissolution or winding up of the affairs of the Corporation, the Board shall, after paying or making provision for the payment of all the liabilities of the Corporation, dispose of the remaining assets of the Corporation exclusively for the purposes and in the manner set out in the Articles of Incorporation.

Section 8.02. Exempt Activities. In all events and under all circumstances, and notwithstanding merger, consolidation, reorganization, termination, dissolution or winding up of the Corporation, whether voluntary or involuntary or by operation of law:

(a) The Corporation shall not have or exercise any power or authority either expressly or by interpretation or operation of law, nor shall it directly or indirectly engage in any activity, that would prevent it from qualifying (and continuing to qualify) as a corporation described in section 501(c)(3) of the Internal Revenue Code of 1986, as amended (or the corresponding provision of any subsequent tax law).

(b) No substantial part of the activities of the Corporation shall consist of carrying on propaganda or otherwise attempting to influence legislation; nor shall it in any manner or to any extent participate in, or intervene in (including by publishing or distributing statements), any political campaign on behalf of or in opposition to any candidate for public office.

(c) Neither the whole, nor any part or portion, of the assets or net earnings of the Corporation shall be used, nor shall the Corporation ever be organized or operated, for objects or purposes other than those set out in the Articles of Incorporation.

MEMORANDUM OF LAW ON LEGAL STATUS OF UN OPERATIONS IN KOSOVO AND EAST TIMOR*

Rebuilding Kosovo: UNMIK as a "Trustee Occupant"

Introduction

Stable peace in the wake of intra-national ethnic conflict requires economic progress, and private capital is the *sine qua non* of successful sustained economic development. Investment and private sector engagement cannot simply wait for a comprehensive rule of law and market-oriented political institutions to be established. Nothing will ever be fixed if the private sector waits for everything to be fixed before economic development begins. Instead, economic development must be integrated with building a rule of law, and both must proceed in tandem.

Establishment of a War-to-Peace Transitions Business Council, greater use of trust funds to permit World Bank support of private enterprises, emphasis on local ownership, and—where necessary—use of private security services and political risk insurance create minimum conditions within which private investment is possible. Kosovo provides an important opportunity—a kind of laboratory—for testing these innovations. The international community, especially the UN, has an enormous stake in a successful outcome in Kosovo. Progress in Kosovo requires that the UN administration of the area be tied to an appropriate governing theory of international law that is sufficiently flexible to provide for economic development supported by private capital, and that the UN quickly devolve power to local institutions.

In Kosovo, the UN has a broad and strong mandate under Security

---

*   Prepared by Henry H. Perritt, Jr.,*Dean and Professor of Law, Chicago-Kent College of Law* and John M. Scheib of the Bar of the District of Columbia

Council Resolution 1244 ("SCR 1244") to do whatever is appropriate in its civil administration role, not only to preserve peace and protect human rights, but also to support economic development. To the extent that legal change or institutional reconfiguration is necessary in pursuit of these goals, the UN Mission in Kosovo ("UNMIK") has sufficient law-making and executive authority to effect the changes. Additionally, the "Interim Government of Kosovo," linking competing political factions under the December, 1999 agreement to establish a Joint Administrative Structure, is proving its effectiveness in restoring order and delivering basic services in many parts of Kosovo, even before clarification of its legal or political mandate.

Acceptance of the trustee occupant theory—explained below—to validate UN authority, and faster movement by the UN to work through the Interim Government of Kosovo to mobilize private capital, are essential prerequisites for success in Kosovo.

The Sovereignty Problem and the Trustee Occupant Concept

SCR 1244, while recognizing Yugoslav sovereignty, vests UNMIK with "basic civilian administrative functions where and as long as required." This authority is to be transferred to "local provisional institutions," and eventually from them to institutions emerging from the final political agreement, under UNMIK oversight. UNMIK expressly is directed to support the reconstruction of key infrastructure and other economic reconstruction. Section 6 of UNMIK Regulation No. 1 expressly provides for UNMIK's administration of movable and immovable property registered in the name of FRY. UNMIK thus possesses the necessary legal authority to adopt legislation and to take executive steps to create and to transfer property rights necessary to economic development and the attraction of foreign capital.

UNMIK should be understood as a trustee occupant of Kosovo, exercising most of the important attributes of sovereignty on behalf of the people of Kosovo, and empowered to transfer these attributes to interim governmental entities, to private investors, and to institutions defined by the ultimate political settlement. Yugoslavia can be understood to have a reversionary interest which might be altered in an ultimate political settlement.

In 1973, Allan Gerson developed the idea of "trustee occupant" to explain the status of the West Bank. Israel's occupation of the West Bank after the "Six-Day War" of 1967 challenged traditional notions of international law: "Sovereignty is retained by the beneficiary people although in a state of suspension . . . if and when the inhabitants of the territory obtain recognition as an independent state, as has already happened in some mandates, sovereignty will revive and vest in the new state."

The distinction between trustee occupant and belligerent occupant is important. "Unlike a belligerent occupant, [the trustee occupant] would not be barred from implementing any changes in the existing laws or institutions providing such amendments were in the best interest of the inhabitants, since the *raison d'être* for requiring adherence to the status quo ante—preservation of the ousted legitimate sovereigns or reversionary interest—would no longer be relevant."

The UN entered upon its duties in Kosovo, not as a belligerent, but with the consent of Yugoslavia. UNMIK is a trustee, with explicit authority to administer Kosovo for the benefit of its peoples, including authority to make changes in legal institutions. Thus, adopting a belligerent occupant characterization would impose limitations on UN civil administration power that would be inconsistent with the express terms of UN SCR 1244.

The UN Security Council resolution in Kosovo recognizes the independent interests of the people of Kosovo. UN SCR 1244 negates usual customary international law duties to the reversioner by the terms of paragraph 11. The rights and duties associated with the reversionary interest, if any, will be decided in the political settlement contemplated by U.N. SCR 1244. In the meantime, it is not necessary to know the nature of the reversionary interest in order to understand the powers and duties of the trustee.

The basic concept of trustee occupant in international law dovetails nicely with the powers of a trustee under the common law and under civil law analogies. Within this analytical framework, Kosovo itself—or the property comprising Kosovo—is the res that the United Nations holds in trust. The Federal Republic of Yugoslavia's agreement to UN Security Resolution 1244 is akin to placing Kosovo in trust voluntarily. A trustee has the power to transfer trust property, even when a transfer cuts off reversionary interests, as long as the trustee exercises the power consistently with the terms of the trust and its purpose.

The United Nations, as trustee, has fiduciary duties to the beneficiary —the peoples of Kosovo. Under trust law, it is not necessary that the beneficiary be known at the creation of the trust. The beneficiary must be ascertainable when the trust is created, but that includes a beneficiary who is not yet ascertained or in existence at the time the trust is created. The identity of the beneficiary/reversioner is an open question accompanied by a duty in the trustee to resolve the question, much like when a court holds property in trust until it can determine the property's rightful owner.

How Shall the UN's Duties as a Trustee-Occupant Duties Be Exercised?

The trustee occupant concept, combined with language in the Security Council Resolution encouraging devolution of governmental powers to autonomous authorities within Kosovo, supports aggressive UN action to modify law, establish new legal institutions, and to encourage the investment of private capital, moving as rapidly as practicable to give autonomy to local institutions. The October, 1999 report of the International Crisis Group ("ICG") recommends a similar pragmatic approach, urging UNMIK to work through de facto Kosovar Albanian institutions at the local and municipal levels rather than focusing on controversies over who has political and administrative authority.

Legitimacy of Interim Local Entities

Under the trustee occupant concept, the U.N. Mission in Kosovo ("UNMIK") has the legal authority to be the governor of Kosovo, but cannot govern without associating itself with local provisional institutions, as Security Council Resolution 1244 recognizes, by authorizing UNMIK to delegate its authority to provisional local institutions.

Part of the problem relates to the uncertain legitimacy of interim local entities. None of the candidates has won an election that would be considered free and fair by international standards. Until elections are held, UNMIK should embrace the pragmatic solution recently suggested by the International Crisis Group, maintaining formal political authority in UNMIK, while granting full administrative responsibility to local authorities actually in control. Agreement among competing centers of political power within Kosovo, in December, 1999, to establish an "Administrative Council" removed perceived barriers to UNMIK grant of operational authority to local institutions, while reserving policy oversight to itself.

Legitimacy comes from action, as well as elections, and action is what Kosovo needs. Support for the action-oriented political centers in Kosovo can be accompanied by tutelage in democracy and rule of law, filling the void of inexperience. UNMIK must encourage those within the Kosovar communities who favor action. The risk of deferring devolution until an exact balance among competing groups can be achieved is stalemate. One of the banes of progress in the Balkans is the propensity of political actors to debate the past endlessly, seeking to find justification for actions in the recent past from historical events hundreds of years ago. UNMIK should not reward those who want to sit on the sidelines and criticize, waiting for their opponents to fail, rather than developing initiatives of their own.

Clarifying Property Ownership

Despite the utility of the trustee occupant concept, ownership of relevant property is likely to remain murky for an indefinite period. Some sort of property law regime is necessary in Kosovo in order to attract private (and public) capital. Investors must be able to own something that they receive in exchange for their investment. "UNMIK shall administer movable or immovable property, including monies, bank accounts, and other property of, or registered in the name of the Federal Republic of Yugoslavia or the Republic of Serbia or any of its organs, which is in the territory of Kosovo."

Beginning in 1989, Milosevic accelerated his efforts to displace Kosovar Albanian control over state and social property (two distinct categories) in Kosovo, with control being shifted to Serbian and foreign ownership, often by integrating Kosovar enterprises with Serbian enterprises. The Kosovars simply are unwilling to pay rent to people they view as occupiers without color of legal authority. The UN, by recognizing Yugoslav law as of March, 1999, in its initial issuance of Regulation No. 1, ratified these ownership interests. In early December, UNMIK promulgated Regulations No. 24 and 25, repealing its initial determination to apply Yugoslav law in effect in June, 1999, instead substituting UNMIK regulations as primary law, with Yugoslav law in effect as of 1989 as a fallback. This represents significant progress in resolving the stalemate, while still leaving to be resolved competing claims over specific property.

The problem is not unlike that which confronted the Czech Republic after the "Velvet Revolution," when much controversy surrounded the sorting out of property interests of those who were displaced by the Communists after the Second World War, and by the Nazis before that. The problem also is not unlike that confronting Cuba, in which economic development must confront competing claims to property that was seized by the Communists when Castro came to power.

Now UNMIK and the Interim Government of Kosovo must develop answers to the following questions and appropriate doctrinal and institutional approaches to implement the answers:

- Whose property interests should be recognized as legitimate, • and whose should be nullified?
- How can competing claims to the same piece of property be made known so they can be resolved?
- What kind of compensation should be provided to those whose property interests are qualified but were rejected, and by whom should the compensation be paid?
- How can alienation and use of property be facilitated now, while competing claims are being worked out? In other words, how can clouds on title be removed?

Resources and Mechanisms for Economic Development

Conceptually, three questions present themselves:

1) From where will investment capital and expertise come for economic development?
2) How shall projects be selected?
3) What capital market mechanisms are necessary to aggregate capital and channel it to project development?

Sources of Capital

Three possible sources of capital exist: (1) private investors with no particular past connection to Kosovo; (2) public sector sources organized through the Stability Pact for South Eastern Europe by the European Bank for Reconstruction and Development ("EBRD") or the World Bank; and (3) the Albanian Diaspora. The willingness of the first category of investors to invest in Kosovo depends upon the existence of projects and associated business plans that promise a payback within a reasonable time frame and political risk insurance. The other two sources may be less insistent on clear assurances of a return or protection against political risk.

Any viable program of economic development for Kosovo must include mechanisms for harnessing technical expertise, including entrepreneurship training, assistance in establishing business plans, marketing and distribution systems, legal frameworks for investment and supply contracts, and design of provisions to secure investment through political risk insurance, collateral, letters of credit, and reorganization of failed enterprises. The necessary expertise is available from technical assistance organized through the international community, from private sector investors and from the Diaspora.

Picking Projects

Viable economic development requires good projects for investment. Understanding the economic development and reconstruction challenge in post-war Kosovo requires considering four distinct sectors of the economy. The four sectors involve:

1) State-owned activities performing public functions. Developing this sector primarily involves questions of public finance and political legitimacy.

2) State-owned infrastructure facilities. Developing this sector involves a mixture of public finance, privatization, and commercial law questions, and also almost certainly depends upon mobilizing sources of investment capital from international sources such as the World Bank.

3) Large socially-owned enterprises. Developing this sector primarily involves questions of privatization, property law, and commercial and company law. Because of controversies over property ownership, development of this sector will involve negotiations and agreements among the UN, the World Bank, the Interim Government of Kosovo, and foreign owners of property.

4) Small and medium enterprise ("SME") development and purely private ownership. Developing this sector involves making a reality of the ideas for mobilizing Diaspora capital, and offers the best prospect for proceeding independently of UN action, and creating productive jobs quickly.

Both UNMIK and the Interim Government of Kosovo initially expressed the view that the first reconstruction and development priority should be agriculture and the reopening of heavy industry in order to create the maximum number of jobs. The main problem with this strategy is that both agriculture and heavy industry in Kosovo are inefficient and cannot compete effectively in world markets. There may, however, be arguments for developing certain agricultural and certain heavy industry facilities, so that Kosovo can become self-sufficient in certain food stocks and building materials, which are in heavy demand as war damage is repaired.

A sounder strategy would make sure that other sectors of the economy develop in order to absorb excess employment from the heavy industry sector. In that way, development can proceed without the political difficulty of restarting inefficient heavy industry facilities and then subsequently having to shut them down or to lay off substantial parts of the work force who cannot find other jobs, in order to make the enterprises efficient and privatizable. This means a strong emphasis, from the beginning, on small and medium enterprise ("SME") development.

Small and medium enterprise ("SME") development is an attractive priority because it takes advantage of the entrepreneurial energy of the Kosovars, legal problems of state and social ownership are few, or absent altogether, in the case of start-up enterprises; many bureaucratic barriers associated with UN and World Bank involvement are minimized; and the legal reform requirements are more modest.

Capital Market Mechanisms

A comprehensive banking law need not be in place before necessary capital market functions can be performed. Even before such new development intermediaries are developed by the international community, through the World Bank's International Finance Corporation or otherwise, immediate action is possible to finance SME development. By one estimate, the Albanian Diaspora contributed between one-half to one billion dollars annually for ten years through the "three-percent fund" during the period of Serb dominance and a war. If the same amount can be mobilized as investment capital for SMEs now, that represents a substantial source of capital. The problem is effective intermediation. How do entrepreneurs apply for capital—or to put the idea in more private sector terms, how to they make an initial public offering? How do investors know about particular enterprises they might want to invest in? And how do they evaluate the quality of the opportunity and then enter into suitable legal arrangements protecting security of the capital?

Technical assistance is needed to develop model contracts, and mechanisms to provide investor security, such as accounts receivable financing agreements.

Conclusion and Recommendations

Kosovo is a laboratory for nation-building. In particular, it provides an opportunity for a highly-motivated indigenous population, an extensive Diaspora accustomed to supporting the indigenous population financially, NGOs, and IGOs to develop new techniques for promoting economic development in a market context in a country in transition. UN Security Council Resolution 1244 ("SCR 1244") vests the United

Nations Mission in Kosovo ("UNMIK") with most of the attributes of sovereignty, while reserving formal sovereignty in the state of Yugoslavia. The trustee occupant concept provides a benchmark for interpreting how UNMIK should exercise this authority. That concept, combined with language in the Security Council Resolution encouraging devolution of governmental powers to autonomous authorities within Kosovo, supports aggressive UN action to modify law, establish new legal institutions, and to encourage the investment of private capital, moving as rapidly as practicable to give autonomy to local institutions. Agreement among competing centers of political power within Kosovo, in December, 1999, to establish an "Administrative Council," removed perceived barriers to UNMIK grant of operational authority to local institutions, while reserving policy oversight to itself.

INDEX

Breaking the cycle of poverty, war, and greed, 24–26
Cold War and, 7–8
Fragmentation issue, 5–7
Globalization, 8–9
Multiple perspectives, 13–15
UN and World Bank efforts, 9–10
Response to post conflict situations, 15–28
Unified field approach, 11–13
PEACE
PRI as an incentive for peace, 57–64
PEACE ENFORCEMENT, 86–87
Multinational troops and, 87
Privatizing and, 87–88
PEACE TRANSITION COUNCIL (PTC) XII, 155–165
Framework for engagement, 156–158
Legal and operational aspects of, 158–165
Legal aspects and draft articles of incorporation
Articles of incorporation, 176–179
Bylaws, 179–189
Creating the Council, 171–178
Financing the Council, 175–176
Model, 171–189
Privatizing peace, 167
Undertaking projects, 158–165
Combat corruption, 163
Data collection, 158–159
Early-stage entry, 160
Exchange of research and knowledge, 164
NGO involvement, 161–162
Political risk insurance, 161
PEACEBUILDING
See PUBLIC-PRIVATE-CIVIL SOCIETY PARTNERSHIPS
PEACEKEEPING
Role of private sector in, 85–86
PEACEMAKING, 83–85

Targeting sanctions and incentives for peace, 84–85
PEOPLE'S REPUBLIC OF CHINA, 72
PERU, 61
PHILIPPINES
Corruption and, 45
POLAND, 30
POLITICAL RISK, 49–67
Business and conflict
Corporate analysis and decision-making, 64–67
Business strategies for managing risk, 53–55
Risk mitigation strategies, 53–54
Definition, 50–51
Overseas Private Investment Corporation, 61–64
Political risk insurance (PRI), 54, 55–57
Incentive for peace, 57–61
Types of, 56
Private political risk insurance, 64
PRIVATE SECTOR
Addressing the legacy of war, 122–123
Benefits of partnering, 32–34
Codes of conduct, 136–137
Corporate social responsibility, 143–154
Downside and upside of privatization, 29–30
Gradualism versus shock therapy, 30–31
Obstacles to investment, 49
Privatization is not replacement, 31
Privatizing peacekeeping, 83
Privatizing security, 83–97
Problem or panacea, 29–34
Public funding vs private investment, 147–148
Public sector distinguished, 34
Rethinking privatization, 31–32
Self-interest means a humanitarian perspective, 124–125